THE IRISH CHURCH, ITS REFORM AND THE ENGLISH INVASION

This book radically reassesses the reform of the Irish church in the twelfth century, on its own terms and in the context of the English Invasion that it helped precipitate. Professor Ó Corráin sets these profound changes in the context of the pre-Reform Irish church. He re-examines how Canterbury's political machinations drew its archbishops into Irish affairs, offering Irish kings and bishops unsought advice, as if they had some responsibility for the Irish church: the author exposes their knowledge as limited and their concerns not disinterested.

The Irish Church, its Reform and the English Invasion considers the success of the major reforming synods in giving Ireland a new diocesan structure, but equally how they failed to impose marriage reform and clerical celibacy, a failure mirrored elsewhere. And when St Malachy of Armagh took the revolutionary step of replacing indigenous Irish monasticism with Cistercian abbeys and Augustinian priories, the consequences were enormous. They involved the transfer to the bishops and foreign orders of vast properties from the great traditional houses (such as Clonmacnoise and Monasterboice) which, the author argues, is better labelled asset-stripping, if not vandalism.

Laudabiliter satis (1155/6), Pope Adrian IV's letter to Henry II, gave legitimacy to English royal intervention in Ireland on the specious grounds that the Irish were Christians in name, pagan in fact. Henry came to Ireland in 1171, most Irish kings submitting to him without a blow, and, at the Council of Cashel (1171/2), the Irish episcopate granted the kingship of Ireland to him and his successors forever – a revolution in church and state. These momentous events are re-evaluated here, the author delivering a damning verdict on the motivations of popes, bishops and kings.

DONNACHADH Ó CORRÁIN was emeritus professor of medieval history at University College Cork. He published widely on early medieval Irish institutions, culture, law, literature, historical sources and the Viking wars.

Diarmait mac Dondchada Meic Murchada .xlui. & ba rí Lethi
Moga uili eside & Midi eside. A éc i Ferna iar ṁbúaid oṅgtha &
athirgi in .lxᵒi. anno aetatis suae. Saxain. iarsin miserabiliter reg-
nant. Amen.

Diarmait son of Donnchadh Mac Murchada ruled for 46 years
and he was king of all the Southern Half of Ireland and of Meath.
He died at Ferns after the victory of unction and penance in the
sixty-first year of his age. The English miserably rule after that.
Amen.

Book of Leinster, p. 39d (*c.*AD 1151xc.1187)

The Irish Church, its Reform and the English Invasion

DONNCHADH Ó CORRÁIN

Trinity Medieval Ireland Series: 2

FOUR COURTS PRESS

Set in 10.5 pt on 14 pt Minion for
FOUR COURTS PRESS LTD
7 Malpas Street, Dublin 8, Ireland
www.fourcourtspress.ie
and in North America for
FOUR COURTS PRESS
c/o IPG, 814 N. Franklin Street, Chicago, IL 60610

First edition 2017
First paperback edition 2022

A catalogue record for this title
is available from the British Library.

ISBN 978-1-80151-053-0

Printed in Ireland
by SprintPrint, Dublin.

Contents

Abbreviations

AASS   *Acta Sanctorum ... a Sociis Bollandianis* (Antwerp, Paris, & Brussels, 1643–1931; repr. Brussels, 1965–70)

AB   Annals of Boyle = *The annals in Cotton MS Titus A. XXV* (ed. A. Martin Freeman, Paris, 1929)

AC   *Annals of Clonmacnoise* (ed. Denis Murphy, Dublin, 1896)

AFM   *Annala Rioghachta Eireann: Annals of the kingdom of Ireland by the Four Masters* (ed. John O'Donovan, 7 vols, Dublin, 1848–51)

AI   *Annals of Inisfallen* (ed. Seán Mac Airt, Dublin, 1951)

ALC   *Annals of Loch Cé* (ed. W.M. Hennessy, 2 vols, RS 54, London, 1871)

ALI   *Ancient Laws of Ireland* (transcribed & translated by Eugene O'Curry and John O'Donovan; prepared for press by W.N. Hancock, Thaddeus O'Mahony, Alexander Richey & Robert Atkinson, 6 vols, Dublin & London, 1865–1901)

ASMD   John T. Gilbert (ed.), *Chartularies of St Mary's Abbey Dublin with the register of its house at Dunbrody and Annals of Ireland*, RS 80 (2 vols, London, 1884–6), ii 241–86 (Annals of St Mary's Dublin)

ATig   'Annals of Tigernach' (ed. Whitley Stokes in *Revue Celtique* 16 (1895), 374–419; 17 (1896), 6–33, 119–263, 337–420; 18 (1897), 9–59, 150–97, 267–303; repr. Felinfach 1993, 2 vols)

AU   *Annals of Ulster* (ed. W.M. Hennessy & B. Mac Carthy, 4 vols, Dublin, 1887–1901); *Annals of Ulster* i (ed. Seán Mac Airt & Gearóid Mac Niocaill, Dublin, 1983) [all published]

BCLL   Michael Lapidge & Richard Sharpe, *Bibliography of Celtic-Latin literature* (Dublin, 1985)

BL   *Book of Leinster* (ed. R.I. Best, Osborn J. Bergin, M.A. O'Brien & Anne O'Sullivan, 6 vols, Dublin, 1954–83)

BL Cat   Standish H. O'Grady, Robin Flower & Myles Dillon, *Catalogue of Irish manuscripts in the British Museum*, 3 vols (London, 1925–53; repr. [vols. i–ii only] as *Catalogue of Irish manuscripts in the British Library* (Dublin, 1992)

CCH   *Collectio canonum hibernenis* = Herrmann Wasserschleben (ed.), *Die irische Kanonensammlung*, 2nd ed. (Leipzig, 1885; repr. Aalen, 1966)

CGH   *Corpus genealogiarum Hiberniae* i (ed. M.A. O'Brien, Dublin, 1962)

CIH   *Corpus iuris hibernici* (ed. D.A. Binchy, 6 vols, Dublin, 1978)

CLA   *Codices latini antiquiores* (ed. E.A. Lowe, 13 parts & supplement, Oxford, 1934–72)

CLH   *Clavis litterarum Hiberniae* (D. Ó Corráin, Turnhout, 2017) [reference to numbered sections]

CS   *Chronicon Scottorum* (ed. W.M. Hennessy, RS 46, London, 1866)
DACL   *Dictionnaire d'archéologie chrétienne et de la liturgie* (ed. Fernand Cabrol
              & Henri Leclerq, 15 vols, Paris, 1907–53)
DTC   *Dictionnaire de théologie catholique* (ed. E. Vacant, E. Mangenot & E.
              Amann, Paris, 1903–50)
EILS   Early Irish Law Series (Dublin, 1983–)
FA   *Fragmentary Annals of Ireland* (ed. J.N. Radner, Dublin, 1978)
HBS   Henry Bradshaw Society for editing rare liturgical texts (London, 1891–)
HE   Venerable Bede, *Historia ecclesiastica gentis anglorum*
Hib   Collectio canonum hibernensis (see also CCH for edition)
ITS   Irish Texts Society (London, 1899–)
Kenney,   James F. Kenney, *Sources for the early history of Ireland: ecclesiastical*
  Sources   (Columbia NY, 1929)
Lec facs.   *Book of Lecan* (facsimile, ed. Kathleen Mulchrone, Dublin, 1937)
LL   *Book of Leinster* (facsimile, ed. Robert Atkinson, Dublin, 1880)
LU   *Lebor na hUidre: Book of the Dun Cow* (ed. R.I. Best & Osborn J. Bergin,
              Dublin, 1929)
MacCarthy's
  Book   *Miscellaneous Irish annals* (ed. S. Ó hInnse, Dublin, 1947), 2–115
MartO   *Martyrology of Oengus the Culdee* (ed. Whitley Stokes, HBS 29, London,
              1905; repr. Dublin 1984)
MGH   Monumenta Germaniae Historica
MGH PLAC   MGH Poetae Latini Medii Aevi
MGH SRG ns   MGH Scriptores Rerum Germanicarum nova series
MGH SRG us   MGH Scriptores Rerum Germanicarum in usum scholarum
MGH SRM   MGH Scriptores Rerum Merovingicarum
MGH SS   MGH Scriptores (in folio)
MIA   *Miscellaneous Irish annals* (ed. S. Ó hInnse, Dublin, 1947)
NHI   *A new history of Ireland*, ed. T.W. Moody, F.X. Martin, F.J. Byrne, Art
              Cosgrove, Dáibhí Ó Cróinín et al. (Oxford, 1976–2005)
PL   Patrologia Latina (ed. J.P. Migne, 221 vols, Paris, 1844–64)
PLS   Patrologiae Latinae supplementum (ed. A. Hamman & L. Guillaumin, 5
              vols, Paris, 1958–74)
RS   Rolls Series (Chronicles & Memorials of Great Britain & Ireland during
              the Middle Ages, 1–99, London, 1858–97)
SLH   Scriptores Latini Hiberniae (Dublin 1955 –)
TP   John Strachan & Whitley Stokes (ed.), *Thesaurus palaeohibernicus* (2 vols
              & supp. Cambridge & Halle a. S., 1901–10, repr. in 2 vols, Dublin, 1975)

Journal titles (if abbreviated) are usually abbreviated in accordance with the 'International list of periodical title word abbreviations', International Organization for Standardization (ISO) 1077: 1990 and 4: 1997.

Introduction

T HE TERM 'REFORM' is here used without any implication that what the reformers of the eleventh and twelfth centuries wished to bring about was morally, spiritually, socially, or administratively superior to what they wished to change. They themselves acted in the full conviction that such was their proceeding, but convictions do not equal achievements, nor even goals. They saw their mission as one to purge the Irish church and society at large of abuses, abolish evil customs and purify the clergy. Whether from piety or thoughtlessness (I think the second) modern historians have usually felt that the reformers were on the side of the angels, that what they sought were all genuine and highly desirable moral and organisational improvements in church and society. This is an assumption. If it is so, it must be demonstrated; if not, it must be abandoned. Besides, Irish historians insist on treating Irish society as if it were unique. It was not. Nor were the problems of its church.

No value judgements attach to the term 'reform' here. It is simply descriptive of the attitude and programme of those who undertook it.

Reform meant quite different things to different reformers. Some wanted an organisational change – one might call it a managerial revolution – a restructuring of church administration, arranged in pyramid shape, under the rule of diocesan bishops, with the pope at the apex – one that was hardly thought out carefully and minutely planned. It is very unlikely that all reformers wanted a papal monarchy. Why should a papal monarchy work well, or even work at all? What some wanted was to make the Irish church just like the one in France and England, but one doubts whether they had thought their plan through. If they had, they might have thought otherwise.

There were to be varying degrees of independence of the interventions of secular rulers, especially in the case of the church's vast properties. But the relationship with kings and lords was exceedingly difficult; it varied widely from country to country, from province to province; there was constant conflict, as one must anticipate; and the problem was never solved. If the business of souls was a business (and it was), then others than clerics wanted part of the action – and the profits.

Still others undertook what they chose to see as a renewal of monasticism and especially the introduction to Ireland of the leading continental orders (principally Cistercians and Canons Regular of St Augustine) in place of the indigenous monastic structures, which they spurned. To judge from St Bernard's wilder statements (his sources were the Irish reformers, especially Malachy and his coterie), they felt that Irish monasticism could not at all be put to rights. Why exotic monasticism should succeed is neither discussed nor explained: it was accepted as better because it was said to be, and that much proved to be false. There is hardly any evidence that promoters of foreign orders weighed the severe cultural consequences of their decisions, or even thought seriously and deeply about what they wanted. They appear over-impressed by foreigners, and as fatuous as their historians.

Yet others sought to change some social structures of lay society (but not others), especially marriage where practices were plainly at variance with contemporary church prescriptions. One must stress prescriptions, not practices. One scarcely learns from reformers of all colours (and their naive historians) that their prescriptions were nowhere observed in Christian Europe, least of all by kings such as Henry II, who falsely proposed himself as a reformer, and was accepted by such a devious pope as Alexander III.

Another novelty was pursued evidently without any deep consideration of the consequences for wider society, as well as for the church itself: reformers ignored the married clergy of the primitive church. Instead, despite the well-founded warnings of prudent thinkers, they planned to impose clerical celibacy in a rigorous way on the whole body of the clergy, regular and secular, making it a separate clerical caste. But what if the clergy remained incontinent? And they did: high and low, in the papacy, in the parish, in the habits of a dozen religious orders.

These differing programmes conflicted to a degree and not all reformers agreed, or found one another agreeable.

Here I propose to look at the Irish church before the reform, and the plans and acts of the reformers. I bear in mind that priests, bishops and popes – and reformers among them – have all the vices of humanity. Reliable sources, mostly transmitted by churchmen, tell us that popes make war, bishops go to battle, priests kill and venerably holy abbots demand the hanging of offenders against them and their churches. But the commandment, 'Thou shalt not kill', stands without qualification. Desire and ambition, greed for property and appetite for the pleasures of life, are as embedded in the church's clergy as in the members of all other institutions, and ever will be.

One cannot, as a historian, take the assertions of clerics, the holy, even unc-
tuous words of those eloquent in the deceptive language of piety and well-
endowed with the goods of the world, as simple statements of self-evident truth
and devotion. Let us take a few examples. Clerical writers, in their laborious and
abundant hagiographies, consciously composed fictions of cures and saintly
miracles to extract the offerings of the faithful. Many of these faithful were
poor, fearful of being beggared by the loss of their breadwinners, bewildered by
their troubles, trustful of their clergy. But hagiographers borrowed miraculous
fictions from one text to another, presenting them as historical facts that proved
the virtues and intercessory powers of their founder, to whom the ignorant
faithful prayed and gave gifts. Is this, in any sense, an honest practice? However
valuable hagiography may be for historical purposes (and it is invaluable), even
a superficial reading should disabuse the inattentive historian of any assump-
tions that the texts of the clerics tell the truth.

Is one to assume that St Bernard's outpourings about St Malachy and his
miracles are veracious accounts of what actually happened? Witnesses? His
lamentable remarks about the Irish church and Irish culture are demonstrably
false. What was his purpose? To make a European saint closely associated with
his order and for its benefit – and he succeeded. For him that was truth: for us
successful self-serving lies. He knew his report would be very widely read in the
Western church. He must have had some idea of its consequences. His sanctifi-
cation of Malachy – like much else in his narrative – is historically worthless,
and he knew it. So Adrian IV's account of the Irish church in his letter
Laudabiliter satis. So, too, the self-serving and untruthful letters of pope
Alexander III that reveal his humiliation and deception.

The label *caveat emptor* attaches to the works of popes, bishops, abbots and to
those of many apparently worthy authors. The historian's mind must ever be ruled
by constant questioning, constant doubt, without respect of persons or office.

This brief work was written as part of a larger unfinished work, and put
aside for other tasks about eight years ago. It has been updated a little. I regret
that I am not now in a position to rewrite it to take recent developments into
account, as I ought. I am profoundly grateful to Professor Marie Therese
Flanagan and Professor Seán Duffy who read this essay and saved me from my
many errors and infelicities. Fidelma Maguire has greatly improved the style
and presentation.

Cork
In festo S. Cianani Doim Líacc
24 November 2016

NOTE ON SOURCES USED

It is very difficult to sketch any satisfactory outline of the institutions of the Irish church of the ninth, tenth and eleventh centuries. The rich sources of the seventh and eighth centuries – synods, canon law collections, penitentials and contemporary hagiography – are no more.[1] One can still draw on the remarkable *Hibernensis* or *Collectio canonum hibernensis* of the eighth century on the reasonable understanding that many of its provisions still stood.[2] Some texts of the vernacular laws are relevant but their firm dating is a problem. In general, much the same applies to the hagiography. I have leant heavily on the contemporary annals, but their evidence on contemporary institutions is meagre and information on institutions and change is wrested from them with difficulty.

1 Ludwig Bieler (ed. & tr.), *The Irish penitentials*, SLH 5 (Dublin, 1963).   2 Hermann Wasserschleben (ed.), *Die irische Kanonensammlung* (Leipzig, 1885; repr. Aalen, 1966).

CHAPTER I

The Irish church: episcopal organisation

IN THE EYES OF THOSE who would reform it the Irish church lacked a proper
episcopal hierarchy in the canonical sense, though there were many bishops,
of many kinds – far too many according to reformers.[1] Some may appear purely
monastic: for example, Dub Innse, 'sage (*saoi*) and bishop of the community of
Bangor (*espucc muintire Bennchair*)', that is, bishop of Bangor and its depend-
encies as distinct from the bishop of a region, but another collection of annals
calls him 'venerable bishop (*suí-epscop*) of Ireland' – probably high-sounding
encomium.[2] Annalistic obituaries are somewhat ambiguous: often, they appear
to give not a synchronic notice of the offices held, at the same time (or subsequent times) by a leading cleric, but a brief *cursus honorum*, an outline of his
career in the church. It appears, however, that some combine the office of bishop
in one house with superior in another, sometimes in more than one. Mael
Finnén mac Uchtáin, bishop of Kells and coarb of Ultán (i.e., superior of
Ardbraccan) and Cairnech (i.e., superior of Dulane),[3] both in Co. Meath, is an
example. With these one must contrast bishops who hold monastic office but
who are represented as ruling over large areas, co-terminous with lordships or
petty kingdoms. A few examples from the tenth century: Coscrach mac Maíl
Mochérge, *epscop Tige Mo Chua & na cCommand*,[4] 'bishop of the church of
Timahoe and of Comainn' (portion of the territory of the king of Loígis); Dub
Dá Bairenn, 'venerable bishop (*suí-epscop*) of Mag Breg (i.e., the plain of Meath)
and coarb of Búite (i.e., superior of Monasterboice), master of Latin learning of
Leinster' (966);[5] Mael Finnia ua hAenaig, lector or head of school (*fer léigind*) of
the church of Fore and bishop of Tuatha Luigne, a territory in the north of Co.
Meath (993);[6] Cairpre Ó Ceithernaig, 'noble bishop of Uí Chennselaig', the south
Leinster over-kingdom (1095).[7] Others are described as bishops of whole over-
kingdoms or provinces: for example, Máel Brigte mac Brolaig, abbot of Scattery
and 'archbishop of Munster' (900/1);[8] Máel M'Aedóc mac Diarmata of Uí

---

1 C. Etchingham, 'Bishops in the early Irish church: a reassessment', *Studia Hibernica*, 28 (1994), 35–62:
26–31; idem, *Church organisation in Ireland AD 650 to 1000* (Maynooth, 1999), 177–94; idem, 'Episcopal
hierarchy in Connacht and Tairdelbach Ua Conchobair', *J Galway Archaeol Hist Soc*, 52 (2000), 13–29.
2 AFM 953 (951); AI 954; cf. 'Fingin epscop muintire Iae' (CS 966 (964)). 3 AU 969.1. 4 AFM 933 (931).
5 AFM 966 (964). 6 AFM 966 (964); AU 993.5 = AFM 993 (992). 7 AU 1095.10. 8 AI 901; CS 900; AFM

5

Chonandla, the abbatial lineage of Glenn Uissen, i.e., Killeshin, Queen's Co., 'sage and bishop of Leinster', slain by the Vikings in 917 in the battle of Cenn Fúait (near St Mullins, Co. Carlow),[9] also called 'archbishop, abbot of Killeshin, choice scribe, anchorite and master scholar in Latin learning and Irish law';[10] Mochta, 'bishop of Uí Néill and priest of Armagh' (924);[11] Tuathal mac Aenacáin 'bishop of Leth Cuinn' (northern half of Ireland) but he was also 'scribe, bishop of Duleek and Lusk and steward of the community of Patrick (Armagh) southwards of the mountain', a grand pluralist, if he held all these offices together;[12] Eogan mac Cléirig 'bishop of Connacht', almost certainly a member of the Uí Fiachrach Aidne dynasty in the south of Connacht (969);[13] Anmchad 'bishop of Leinster', also called 'bishop of Kildare' (981);[14] Cormac ua Finn 'venerable bishop (*suí-epscop*) of Munster' (1020);[15] Céle mac Donnacáin, 'chief senior of the Irish i.e., bishop of Leinster', who died in Glendalough in 1076;[16] Mael Caemgin 'noble bishop of Ulaid' (1086);[17] Erchad Ó Mael Fogamair 'archbishop (*airdespucc*) of Connacht' (1086);[18] Connmach Ó Cairill 'noble bishop of Connacht' (1092);[19] Mael Brigte (mac in tSaír) Ó Brolcháin 'noble bishop of Kildare and of the province of Leinster' (*cóicid Laigen*), who died in 1097.[20]

There were also *chorepiscopi* who served local districts.[21] The origin of *chorepiscopi*, 'country bishops' – and they go back to the earliest period of church history – lay in the need of the bishop to oversee the secondary churches of his diocese founded in communities that were more-or-less or wholly distinct from that of the episcopal seat. Thus they were subordinate bishops of limited jurisdiction who administered sub-divisions or regions of dioceses. They were ordained by a single bishop, and they themselves were not allowed to ordain priests or deacons. Scarce in the West generally, the title becomes common there in the eighth century and soon *chorepiscopus* and *coepiscopus* 'assistant bishop' became confused.[22] Using the term *conepiscopus* the *Hibernensis* gives a clear definition for Irish practice: '*Conepiscopi*, that is, the vicars of the bishop or [bishops] of one *plebs*; they are ordained by one bishop; these, however, are ordained by the bishop of the adjacent *civitas* acting on his own'.[23] The *plebs* is identical with the *túath* (or the larger *olltúath, mórthúath*),

---

900 (895). **9** AU 917.3; C. Etchingham, 'The battle of Cenn Fúait, in 917: location and military significance', *Peritia*, 21 (2010), 208–32. **10** AFM 917 (915). **11** AU, AFM 924. **12** AU AI 929; AFM 929 (927). **13** AU 969.1. **14** AI, ATig 981; AFM 981 (980). **15** AFM 1020. **16** AFM 1076. **17** AU 1086. **18** AU AFM 1086. **19** AU 1092.9. **20** AU 1097.5. **21** D. Ó Corráin, 'Irish vernacular law and the Old Testament', in Próinséas Ní Chatháin & Michael Richter (ed.), *Ireland and christendom: the bible and the missions* (Stuttgart, 1987), 284–310: 306. **22** C.J. Hefele & J. Hergenröther, *Histoire des conciles*, tr. & corr. Henri Leclercq & Charles de Clercq (11 vols, Paris, 1907–52), ii/2 1198–237; DTC v 1706–7; William Smith & Samuel Cheetham, *Dictionary of christian antiquities* (2 vols, London, 1875–80), i 353–5. **23** Hib 1:6: 'Conepiscopi [*leg*. chorepiscopi, coepiscopi?] i.e., vicarii episcoporum vel unius plebis ab uno episcopo

in effect the smallest political community, and in Irish usage the term *civitas* can be understood in at least two ways: firstly, as an episcopal seat, and by extension, diocese; and secondly, as a major church, and the Irish canonist probably accommodated both meanings. *Riagail Phátraic* speaks of *primepscop cecha tuaithe accu fri huirdned a n-oessa graid* 'a principal bishop of every *túath* to ordain their clergy'.[24] This is best understood as meaning that there is a principal or presiding bishop whose diocese consists of several *túatha* (or *mórthúatha*) and who confers holy orders; and a *chorepiscopus* with a lesser local ministry (though still a bishop for all purposes except conferring major orders) whose area of jurisdiction corresponds to the *túath*, perhaps *mórthúath* (a somewhat larger kingdom comprising several *túatha*). This arrangement continued into the twelfth century (as did a like one in a few other places in France and Germany) and helps account for the large number of bishops who attended the great twelfth-century synods.

Bishops who were monks, whether monks by choice, deposed bishops, penitent ones, or retirees, are common enough in the eighth century and later, in Ireland and elsewhere. Some continental monasteries had the papally approved right to have their own bishops, for example, St Martin of Tours: 'it is to have its own bishop as in the earliest times by whose preaching the people ... may obtain remedy'.[25] There were bishops of great churches, such as Clonmacnoise or Trim – there was a 'bishop of Clonmacnoise' and others of the community, though bishops, who did not bear that exalted title. Some bishops exercised episcopal jurisdiction over the lands and churches of a mother church, whether as a bloc or as widely distributed parcels. Bishops had high status, and celibate bishops the highest honour of all clergy,[26] and houses that had any bishop as superior – whether a member of the community, or hireling – had a correspondingly higher status.[27] It appears, too, that episcopal orders were conferred on eminent clergy as a mark of personal distinction, titular bishops, so to speak – an ancient practice of the church.[28] The complaints, made in two letters to Muirchertach Ó Briain, king of Ireland, by archbishop Anselm of

ordinentur, hi autem a solo episcopo civitatis, cui adjacent ordinentur'; cp. CIH iv 1432.3–10 which has reference to a bishop *for lár achaidh* 'in the middle of the countryside'. **24** CLH 623; CIH vi 2129.6–7 = J.G. O'Keeffe (ed. & tr.), 'The rule of Patrick', *Ériu*, 1 (1904), 216–24: 218 §1; 'prim-epscop cecha primtuathi i nEirinn' in the corresponding text in E.J. Gwynn (ed. & tr.), 'The rule of Tallaght', *Hermathena*, 44 (1927), second supplemental volume, 80 §60; CLH 628; Etchingham, *Church organisation*, 134–46, 154–68. **25** H. Zimmerman (ed.), *Papsturkunden, 896–1046* (2nd ed. Vienna, 1988–9), §332 (29 September 996). **26** ALI iv 362.19–23 = CIH ii 581.11–14 (*Miadshlechta*, tract on status, dated to the first half of the eighth century, by D.A. Binchy, *Studia Hibernica*, 2 (1962), 63); Liam Breatnach, *Companion to the Corpus iuris hibernici*, EILS 5 (Dublin, 2005), 27, 264–5 (§5.46). **27** CIH vi 2270.6–24, vi 2101.41–2102.5; D. Ó Corráin, 'Irish vernacular law and the Old Testament', 301–5. **28** J.H. Todd, *St Patrick, apostle of Ireland: a memoir of his life and mission* (Dublin, 1864), 45–8.

Canterbury (*sed.* 1093–1109) about the consecration of Irish bishops (which repeat some of those of his predecessor Lanfranc, †1089), if overdone, make sense in this context:

> We hear also that bishops, who should be to others a form and example of canonical religion, as we have heard, are irregularly consecrated either by single bishops or for places for which they should not be ordained.[29] Likewise, it is said that bishops are indiscriminately chosen without any definite diocese; and a bishop, just like any priest, is ordained by a single bishop. This is completely contrary to the holy canons which prescribe that those who are thus instituted or ordained, together with those who ordain them, should be deposed from the episcopal office. It is not possible, according to God's law, to constitute a bishop without a definite diocese and people which he oversees, for even in ordinary life a man who has no flock to tend cannot have the name or duty of shepherd … A bishop must not be ordained by less than three bishops.[30]

Rhetoric apart, Anselm's complaints (if, in fact, well grounded) are two: bishops must be consecrated by three bishops and only for a definite diocese, and neither rule is observed. The Irish knew very well that a bishop should be consecrated by at least three bishops,[31] but they (like the early British church) did not always obey the rules. However, the consecration of a *chorepiscopus* by a single bishop was perfectly canonical, but *chorepiscopi* were now on the way out in the West generally, while still present in Ireland. A decree of the bishop Simon Rochford's synod of the diocese of Meath, held near Trim in 1216, citing an earlier decree of the synod of Kells (1152), provides evidence for their continuing presence and for the remedy proposed to ease the transition to regular dioceses: 'as *chorepiscopi* and the bishops of the smaller sees in Ireland died off, archpriests … should be elected in their place and should succeed them'.[32] It is probably true that Anselm has, to a degree at least, confused the ordination of bishops and that of *chorepiscopi*.[33] Besides, Anselm was thinking of dioceses

29 C.R. Elrington & J.H. Todd (ed.), *The whole works of the Most Rev. James Ussher, D.D.* (17 vols, Dublin, 1847–64), iv 521 (Epistola 35), 524 (hereafter Ussher, *Whole works*). **30** Ibid., 524 (Epistola 36). **31** Hib 1:4–5. **32** David Wilkins (ed.), *Concilia Magnae Britanniae et Hiberniae* (4 vols, 1737, repr. Brussels, 1964), i 547a ('Cum dominus Johannes Paparo … legatus in Hibernia, in synodo generali tenta apud Kenanas in Midia, anno gratiae MCLII, inter alias salubres constitutiones, tunc et ibidem factas, ordinaverit, ut decedentibus chorepiscopis, et exiliorum sedium episcopis in Hibernia, in eorum locum eligerentur et succederent archipresbyteri a diocesanis constitutendi, qui cleri et plebis solicitudinem gerant infra suos limites, et ut eorum sedes in totidem capita decanatuum ruralium erigerentur'). **33** Alphons Bellesheim, *Geschichte der katholischen Kirche in Irland* (3 vols, Mainz, 1890), i 321–3.

quite different from the complex, often discontinuous, interlocking but clearly delimited areas of jurisdiction that were dioceses for the Irish.

The appearance of bishops of large kingdoms and of whole provinces in the Irish annals in the tenth and eleventh centuries must point to significant changes and developments: large-scale territorialisation and the emergence of a higher grade of bishop, corresponding to the provincial king. However, the lack of legal materials and especially of synodal decrees leaves us in the dark about details. The term 'archbishop' (*airdespucc*) as used in pre-reform Irish sources is generally taken to mean 'eminent bishop' or the like. In the early church it is used for the bishops of the principal sees, and the Irish, who were well-read in patristics, no doubt used it generally in that sense rather than meaning the bishop who presided over an ecclesiastical province, the only sense it had for the reformers. However, one should not rule out the idea that its use in Ireland in the eleventh century and the very early twelfth had begun to take on the colour of the contemporary canonical archbishop, and that as more than just an aspiration, especially amongst bishops closely associated with greater kings such as Muirchertach Ó Briain (r. 1086–1114, 1115, 1118) and Tairdelbach Ó Conchobair (r. 1106–56).

Bishops were powerful, and their power may have grown in the eleventh century. Had they not been powerful, the reform bishops could scarcely have been so successful in radically re-organising the church and forcing a new structure upon it in the teeth of vested interests of venerable antiquity. But they had their limits, and one is clear: whatever their nature, monastic or non-monastic, the traditional bishops did not, in their own right, control the property necessary to maintain reform-style bishoprics. Remarkably, the reformers were able to strip the assets of the older churches to make good that deficit.

Irish ideas about bishops and dioceses, then, were conservative, tolerant of diversity, and did not take into account significant recent changes in canon law. Some think the Irish church knew little or nothing of the False Decretals of Ps-Isidore, compiled in Francia, in the second quarter of the ninth century,[34] but this is unlikely. This influential text expounded a monarchical theory of church structure and a clear chain of command that emphasised the pope's authority and the subjection of the bishops to the direct power of the papacy. Its author defined the role of the bishop in his diocese and pointedly rejected *chorepiscopi* (whom he saw as parasites) and bishops without dioceses. At the base of this

---

34 Note, however, that Modena, Bib, Capitolare, O. I, 4, s. ix², a copy of the Decretals written at Modena, has clear traces of Insular hand (L. Schiaparelli, *Influenze straniere nella scrittura italiana dei secoli VIII e IX*, Studi e Testi 47 (Rome, 1927), 20).

tight structure was the priest in his parish who had a life-long cure of souls. By the second half of the eleventh century, when the Gregorian reform was in full swing, Ps-Isidore was universally accepted as genuine (indeed many decretals recur in Gratian's authoritative *Concordia discordantium canonum*, also called the *Decretum, c.*1140) and provided canonical support for some of the central ideas of the reformers.[35] The *Dictatus papae* (1074–5), a list of the reformist canons representing papal powers as Gregory VII saw them, drew heavily on Ps-Isidore. In the light of these canonical developments and the teaching of contemporary canon lawyers, Irish reformers were soon to see the organisation of their own church as decadent and eccentric, and in the early twelfth century they proposed an orthodox diocesan structure with metropolitan archbishops and a primate.

MONASTERIES

No Irish monastic rule is extant, despite constant statements to the contrary, mostly by clerical historians. Columbanus's *Regula monachorum* is a sermon on monasticism and a detailed treatment of the divine office; the eccentric *Regula coenobialis* attributed to him is neither his work nor a monastic rule.[36] Other texts, for example the Old-Irish *Rule of Ailbe,* deal with monastic matters, but are not rules.[37]

Remarkably, the *Hibernensis* has little to say of monks. It gives the etymology of the term (*monachus*) and offers a peculiar history of monasticism. The idea is attributed to Elias, the origin to John the Baptist; and John the Baptist, Paul and Anthony, the Desert Fathers, hermits and cenobites are accounted monks. From these derive 'the sacred institution of monks throughout the whole world'. It speaks of the morals and practices of monks: the good, the bad and the wicked; the hermit with no ties to the world, who refuses gifts, who feeds himself by his own labour or receives his food as charity, and who devotes his life to prayer; the cenobite who lives a communal life, always busy with study, prayer or service to others; the vagabond monk, who wants the name but not the discipline, who runs about with girls, retails monastic gossip, lives by no

---

35 Paul Fournier in A. d'Alès (ed.), *Dictionnaire apologétique de la foi catholique* (4th ed., 5 vols, Paris, 1925–31), i 903–10; idem, 'Études sur les fausses décrétales', in Paul Fournier, *Mélanges de droit canonique,* ed. Theo Kölzer (2 vols, Aalen, 1983), i 23–201; Horst Fuhrmann, *Einfluss und Verbreitung der pseudoisidorischen Fälschungen*, MGH Schriften 24 (3 vols, Stuttgart, 1972–4). **36** CLH 330–1; G.S.M. Walker (ed. & tr.), *Sancti Columbani Opera*, SLH 2 (Dublin, 1957), 122–69. **37** CLH 632; Joseph O'Neill (ed. & tr.), 'The rule of Ailbe of Emly', *Ériu,* 3 (1907), 92–115.

rule, obeys nobody and occupies himself with worldly matters. There was a continuous problem with wandering monks, sent by no authority, who went about the churches and provinces and abandoned monastic tonsure and dress. They engaged in tale-telling, selling relics of the martyrs, extolling the virtues of their portable reliquaries, claiming to be what they were not, and winning a reputation for holiness amongst the laity.[38] Such vagabond monks wandering amongst the laity (*gyrovagi*) should be excommunicated.[39]

The fugitive monk posed a more difficult problem. Could he be accepted by another abbot? Some held that the fugitive and the abbot who received him should both be excommunicated, but circumstances altered cases. A monk who wished to live under a more severe rule should not be detained against his will. One who deserts a degenerate monastery is to be received as 'one fleeing the flame of hell', without any consultation with his abbot: 'the wolf is to be avoided … the den of thieves to be abandoned'.[40] A monk cannot be a member of two monasteries at once; he is to return to the church of his first profession and serve only there. The monk is to possess no private property, only necessities, and he is to hand over anything he acquires to his abbot. Monks may not withdraw from communal life, 'out of ambition and vanity' says one canon, and live in solitary cells, but the abbot may permit monks who have proved themselves by good works to have separate cells within the monastic enclosure.[41] Adomnán's *Life of Columba* offers the clearest, if idealist and retrospective, description of the early Irish monastery.[42]

Apart from four or five other mentions of monks in the strict sense of the word, all other examples of *monachus* in the *Hibernensis* refer to the type of monastic servitor known as *manach* (pl. *manaig*).[43]

MONACHI, MANAIG

Some monks ceased to be monks and became owners and farmers of church lands. To a degree, they shared their position with the founder's kindred (*fine érlama*) and the kindred of those who donated the land for the monastery (*fine griain*).[44] Lands granted to the church by kings and nobles came with their

38 Hib 39:1–3. 39 Hib 39:10. 40 Hib 39:7, 12. 41 Hib 39:13, 15, 16. 42 CLH 230; William Reeves (ed.), *The Life of St Columba, founder of Hy, written by Adamnan* (Dublin, 1857); A.O. Anderson & M.O. Anderson (ed. & tr.), *Adomnán's Life of Columba* (Edinburgh, 1961, 2nd ed. Oxford, 1991); Richard Sharpe (tr.), *Adomnán of Iona: Life of St Columba* (London, 1995). 43 Hib 29:7, 30:3, 40:15, 42:15 (monks); Hib 2:15, 17:9, 18:3, 18:7, 34:3 (*manaig*). 44 Thomas Charles-Edwards, 'Érlam: the patron saint of an Irish church', in Alan Thacker & Richard Sharpe (ed.), *Local saints and local churches in the early medieval West*

landowners and tenants, who now served the church. The important change from monk to *manach* happened at a very early period of Irish monasticism and, in effect, these persons became both the economic underpinning of the church and a community of the church with important rights. The derived terms *mainche* 'service' (from *manach* or Latin *monachia*), *manchaine*, came to mean service far outside a church context, for example, in the sense of the personal service owed by a dependant to his lord.[45] Evidence for this development is found in *Aipgitir chrábaid* 'Primer of piety', written c.AD 600 by Colmán mac Béognai, in the earliest phase of Irish monasticism. According to this stylish monastic tract on spirituality, the true monk should avoid *fáitbe mbráithre, bríathra inglana, acairbe taithisc, toísam fri secnapaid, síthugud fri cúrsachad, comairb do manchaib* 'derision of fellow-monks, impure words, asperity of reply, resistance to the prior, unruliness at reproof, strife with the monastic tenants (*manaig*)'.[46] There is a pointed opposition between *bráithre*, literally 'brethren', and *manaig*. The *manaig* are one of the most stable groups in Irish church life: they are there by the late sixth century, they survived the twelfth-century reform in one form or another, they are called *nativi* in later medieval documents, and persons very like them, called 'termoners' (*termonnaig* from *termonn* 'sanctuary, church land') can be traced in the church extents and visitations of the sixteenth and early seventeenth centuries.[47] For this reason, and because of the great stability of Irish church property, it is probably permissible to use the legal commentaries of the eleventh and twelfth centuries as evidence. They sustained the church by their labours and payments – its higher and lower clergy, its buildings, its schools, its scholars, its scriptoria, its workshops. Their personnel, their organisation and various classes fall below the radar in the literature of the reformers (as do their likes elsewhere) though their payments are assumed, for example, when tithes are mentioned. In certain circumstances, they could succeed to high ecclesiastical office.

(Oxford, 2002), 267–90. **45** CIH v 1770.16–27 = ALI ii 194; R. Thurneysen (ed. & tr.), 'Aus dem irischen Recht II', *Z Celt Philol*, 15 (1925), 238–76: 240 §2 (*Cáin soerraith*). **46** CLH 846; Vernam E. Hull (ed. & tr.), 'Apgitir chrábaid: the alphabet of piety', *Celtica*, 8 (1968), 44–89: 62 §10; idem, 'The date of *Aipgitir crábaid*', *Z Celt Philol*, 25 (1956), 88–90; Pádraig P. Ó Néill, 'The date and authorship of *Apgitir chrábaid*: some internal evidence', in Próinséas Ní Chatháin & Michael Richter (ed.), *Ireland and christendom: the bible and the missions* (Stuttgart, 1987), 203–15; Thomas Owen Clancy & Gilbert Márkus (tr.), 'The alphabet of devotion', in idem (ed.), *Iona: the earliest poetry of a Celtic monastery* (Edinburgh, 1995); John Carey (tr.), *King of mysteries: early Irish religious writings* (Dublin, 1998), 231–45. I depart from Hull's translation. **47** James Ussher, 'Of the original and first institution of corbes, herenaches and termon lands', in C.R. Elrington (ed.), *The whole works of James Ussher* xi (Dublin, 1864), 421–5; St John D. Seymour, 'The coarb in the medieval Irish church', *Proc Roy Ir Acad (C)*, 41 (1932–4), 219–31; Henry A. Jefferies, 'Erenaghs in pre-plantation Ulster: an early seventeenth-century account', *Archivium Hibernicum*, 53 (1999), 16–19; idem, 'Erenaghs and termonlands: another early seventeenth-century account', *Seanchas Ardmhacha*, 19 (2002), 55–8.

Manaig lived a disciplined life in close contact with the church and its clergy, or at least purported to do so. They are 'the people of the church'; they are described in the *Liber Angeli* of Armagh (mid seventh century) as 'serving the church in legitimate matrimony'.[48] They occur in *Cáin Adomnán* (*c*.AD 700) as 'the lawful laymen with their proper wives who are under the rule of Adomnán and of a proper, wise and holy confessor'.[49] They are in the law text *Críth gablach* (*c*.AD 700): 'This is the vassal of baptism (*aithech baitside*) if he is guiltless, innocent of theft, of plunder, of homicide except in the day of battle or in self-defence; and he lives in lawful wedlock; and observes continence on fast days, on Sundays and in Lents'.[50]

There is a detailed contract between the *manaig* and their church in regard to pastoral care. The church provides sacred ministry, they support the church by their payments.

There are two types of *manaig*: *sóer-manaig* and *dóer-manaig*, literally 'free' and 'unfree' *manaig*. Some *dóer-manaig* are those the church has saved, as an act of charity – from the gibbet, from execution for violent killing, from prison – by paying off their liabilities.[51] Others are '*manaig* of famine', *manaig* who abandoned their church in time of famine because it could not support them, or perhaps free farmers, ruined by famine, who offered themselves and their lands to the church in return for maintenance. Others are serfs (*fuidir, senchléithe*), acquired with the land, as were slaves. *Sóer-manaig* are of diverse origin. Some, for example, descend from the free landowners of estates granted by great lords to the church. Here the church simply takes over the regalian rights of the previous owner. Some are oblates (*alumni*), children donated to the church, with their assets, educated by the church and obliged to remain in its service for life.

Manaig and their superior formed a corporate body with mutual rights and obligations. The superior may not alienate church estates without their consent because they have a common interest in the overall property-holding

---

48 'in matrimonio ligitimo' means living in canonical marriage (*Liber angeli*, §§15–16= Bieler, *Patrician texts in the Book of Armagh*, 186–7); cf. CIH vi 2231.1–8 (*Bretha nemed*): '… ar us [=is] e triar nad scara comudh co bas: ceile fri tigerna iar ndigbail tsed do dernuind, manach fria airchindech, cetmuinter dligthech fria ceile iar n-urnaidm … ni forscarud manach fria airchindeach co suige n-ega'. **49** CLH 622; Kuno Meyer (ed. & tr.), *Cáin Adamnáin: an Old-Irish treatise on the Law of Adamnan*, Anecdota Oxoniensia, Mediaeval & Modern Series, 12 (Oxford, 1905), 24 §34. **50** 'Is é aithech baitside inso dia mbé in<n>a enncai cen gait, cen brait, cen guin doíne acht láa catha no nech toshaig a chenn fair. Os hé cona lánamnas choir & denmai i n-aínib & domnachaib & chorgasaib': CIH iii 779, lines 18–20 = Binchy, *Críth gablach*, 6, lines 142–6; Eoin MacNeill (tr.), 'Ancient Irish law: the law of status or franchise', *Proc Roy Ir Acad (C)*, 36 (1923), 265–316: 289; a later reference to the *aithech baitside* states *ina fuil gnimiu laích lais* 'since he does not have the functions of a warrior and he is not *sui iuris*, he may not undertake suretyship *ar is gae greine dogairter* 'for he is called a man of straw' (CIH ii 585, line 17). **51** R. Thurneysen, 'Irisches Recht', *Abh Preuss Akad Wiss*, phil-hist Kl, Jhrg 1931, Nr. 2 (Berlin, 1931), 65 §7; Binchy, *Críth gablach*, 23, lines 578–9.

of their church. Likewise, a *manach* may not alienate goods without the superior's consent.[52]

Manaig had well-established rights against their church: 'every *manach* who is dutiful towards his church shall not be expelled from her' and the superior was required to treat them with respect.[53] The *manach* may not abandon his superior or his church.[54] Whoever deserts is a fugitive, but he may go for good reason: decay, crime, famine, or if he abandons his land for God's sake.[55]

The *manach* retained personal ownership of his property, whether real estate or mobilia (wealth in herds, artifacts and treasure). Side by side, there was property owned as allod by the church as an institution that was administered by the superior: demised, leased to tenants, and repossessed at will. However, the vernacular laws show that the church tended to extend its property at the expense of the *manaig*. They needed protection, and that was offered by the vernacular laws.

Superiors of great churches often behaved as did great secular lords: they engaged in conflicts over property with other churches and sometimes with the kings and secular lords. The *manaig* supplied the manpower, the clergy the leadership: 'Service for hosting, for a military encampment, for redeeming a pledge, for an assembly, for exacting vengeance, for attack and defence within the territory, for the service of God, for aiding the work of the Lord; the service of everyone is due to his lord, his kindred, his abbot (*ab*)'. The rights of the church and its senior personnel are levied to the full: 'Every entitlement of venerable persons is bound in law, exacted, sued out, and paid over'.[56] The 'venerable persons' (*nemed*) are the ecclesiarchs, the superiors and senior office-holders of the church: bishop, abbot, deputy abbot, canon lawyer, scholar, head of schools and the like.

EARLY AND LATER MIDDLE AGES

In time the early Irish monastery changed in membership, structure and function. So, too, did the *manaig* but in their case the essentials survived. There is no detailed contemporary account of the later houses. The great houses of the eleventh and twelfth centuries have had a poor press from historians who are

---

52 Hib 17:9: 'De oblatione monachi nihil proficiente sine abbatis permissu'. 53 CIH ii 433.26–27, iv 1289.32–38; Hib 37:36. 54 CIH vi 2231.1–8 (*Bretha nemed*): '... ar us [=is] e triar nad scara comudh co bas: ceile fri tigerna iar ndigbail tsed do dernuind, manach fria airchindech, cetmuinter dligthech fria ceile iar n-urnaidm ... ni forscarud manach fria airchindeach co suige n-ega'. 55 CIH v 1818.13–16 = ALI iii 64.20–6. 56 CIH ii 525.21–28 = ALI iii 4–13 (*Córus bésgnai*).

so impressed with the ravages of the Vikings that they conclude, in the face of the evidence, that clerical life and religious practice had sadly degenerated.[57] What appeared to be corroborative evidence for this decay is found in the naive complaints of the Irish reformers, the writings of St Bernard, and the letters of pope Gregory VII, archbishops Lanfranc and Anselm of Canterbury, and especially pope Alexander III. The nature of these religious houses has caused historians many difficulties. They were not Benedictine houses (whatever meaning we may attach to that wide term), and their senior members are more likely to resemble well-endowed secular canons, whose communal and individual wealth maintained within them different kinds of coenobitic communities of varying severity, houses of mendicants (as in Clonmacnoise), houses of Céli Dé,[58] and cultural institutions – scriptoria, libraries and schools of Latin and Irish learning. One cannot reconcile the Armagh of St Bernard with the great house that produced the fine twelfth-century manuscript of Gregory the Great's *Moralia in Job* in a delicate minuscule (Oxford, Bodleian Library, Laud Misc. 460; s. xii) or the Harley Gospels (London, British Library, Harley 1023; s. xii) in Irish minuscule with glosses in Latin and Irish, or the Gospels of Mael Brigte (s. xii[1]; AD 1138), illuminated, and with Jerome's prologues and copious commentary and glosses. Like arguments may be made for the high culture of other houses, for example Clonmacnoise, Glendalough and Monasterboice

In addition, their clergy supplied pastoral care to extensive areas in units that were, in role and organisation, parishes. For example, Clonmacnoise claimed extensive rights in the large kingdom of Tethbae, to the east of Lough Ree.[59] One reads this as pastoral care in parishes with its corresponding remuneration.

Many were very large and rich foundations with very extensive resources in land and they had been wealthy since the seventh century and before. Bishop Tírechán, writing on behalf of Armagh about 670, provides evidence for an impressively extensive affiliation of churches. He lists nearly eighty individual churches said to be founded by St Patrick and thus, in the conventions of history of this kind, claimed as dependants of Armagh as their mother-church. They owed her services and payments.[60] One can add more churches and estates to

57 D. Ó Corráin, 'Vikings in Ireland: the catastrophe', in Howard B. Clarke & Ruth Johnson (ed.), *The Vikings in Ireland and beyond: before and after the battle of Clontarf* (Dublin, 2015), 485–98, esp. 493–7. 58 William Reeves, *The Culdees of the British Isles as they appear in history with an appendix of evidences* (Dublin, 1864; repr. Feilinfach, 1994).   59 D. Ó Corráin, 'Mael Muire the scribe: family and background', in Ruairí Ó hUiginn (ed.), *Lebor na hUidre*, Codices Hibernenses Eximii, 1 (Dublin, 2015), 1–28: 9–10. 60 Ludwig Bieler (ed. & tr.), *Patrician texts in the Book of Armagh*, SLH 10 (Dublin, 1979), 122–66; Richard Sharpe, 'Churches and communities in early medieval Ireland', in John Blair & Richard Sharpe (ed.), *Pastoral care before the parish* (Leicester, 1992), 81–109: 87–9.

this list from the mid-ninth-century *Vita Tripartita*,[61] and it is likely that Armagh's affiliation was indeed very much larger. A hagiologist, of the eighth century or so, under the heading 'All these holy virgins whose places and names we will enumerate were subject to St Brigit', lists nearly eighty female foundations and, in addition, about twenty male ones subject to St Brigit's church at Kildare.[62] This list draws on very early records: very many churches and estates are early in form and unidentified. Kildare's affiliation was widely spread. Cogitosus' *Vita Brigitae* (written *c.*AD 670–80) grandiloquently describes Kildare as 'the head of almost all the churches of the Irish ... whose *paruchia* is spread throughout the whole land of Ireland and extends from sea to sea'; and 'it, together with all its church lands throughout the whole of Ireland, is the most secure city of refuge'.[63] A remarkable document, the Irish Life of St Finnbarr, preserves an early medieval list of fifty-one churches claimed as dependants of Cork – some near, some far away – and probably extracted from the early archives of Cork to meet the property crisis of the Hildebrandine or Gregorian reform.[64] Clearly these are by no means all Cork's properties.

These churches, the heirs of the age of the saints, the real proprietors of ecclesiastical lands and the rulers of many dependent churches, were themselves usually ruled by hereditary ecclesiastical lineages, some long established, some more recent recruits, all members of aristocratic families. These prominent clerics, often only in minor orders, belong to the managerial cadre of the traditional churches, an élite of rulers, power-brokers and property-holders. They are not, in general, representative of the ordinary clergy.[65]

The terms used for superiors of churches in the tenth, eleventh and twelfth centuries are essentially those of the pre-Viking period though what they sig-

61 CLH 246; W. Stokes (ed. & tr.), *The Tripartite Life of Patrick* (2 vols, London 1887), i 1–267; K. Mulchrone (ed.), *Bethu Phátraic: the Tripartite Life of Patrick* (Dublin, 1939). 62 CLH 799; P. Ó Riain (ed.), *Corpus genealogiarum sanctorum Hiberniae* (Dublin, 1985), 112–18, §670.1–88. 63 CLH 228; *Acta Sanctorum ... a Sociis Bollandianis* (Antwerp &c., 1643–1931), 1 Feb., 135 (prol. §2), 141 (viii 39); S.J. Connolly & J.-M. Picard (tr.), 'Cogitosus's Life of St Brigit: content and value', *J Roy Soc Antiq Ire*, 117 (1987), 5–27. 64 CLH 250 ii; C. Plummer (ed. & tr.), *Bethada náem nÉrenn: Lives of Irish Saints* (2 vols, Oxford, 1922), i 11–22 = P. Ó Riain (ed. & tr.), *Beatha Bharra: St Finbarr of Cork: the complete Life* (London, 1993), 54–91. Only nine of these can be found in the decretal letter of Innocent III (1199), setting out and confirming the possessions of the diocese, again based on the archives of Cork, and again a response to a property crisis (M.P. Sheehy, *Pontificia Hibernica* (2 vols, Dublin, 1962–5), i 105–9 (§39); Diarmuid Ó Murchadha, 'The Cork decretal letter of 1199 AD', *J Cork Hist Archaeol Soc*, 106 (2001) 79–100. On Hildebrand see H.E.J. Cowdrey, *Pope Gregory VII 1073–1085* (Oxford, 1998) Karl Leyser, *Communications and power in medieval Europe: the Gregorian revolution and beyond* (London, 1994). 65 D. Ó Corráin, 'Dál Cais – church and dynasty', *Ériu*, 24 (1973), 51–63; idem, 'The early Irish churches: some aspects of organisation', in idem (ed.), *Irish antiquity: essays and studies presented to Professor M.J. O'Kelly* (Cork, 1981), 327–41; 328–31; idem, 'Island of saints and scholars: myth or reality?', in Oliver P. Rafferty (ed.), *Irish Catholic identities* (Manchester, 2013), 32–61: 36–9.

nify will have changed. They are monastic in origin but we must be careful not to give these terms a classical Benedictine sense. The Benedictine rule (sometimes rigorous, sometimes lax) was the virtually universal monastic observance of the Continent from the ninth century,[66] and what was not Benedictine appeared alien to many. *Abbas*, Irish *abb* 'abbot', is very widely used as a synonym for 'superior': those who are called *abb* in one set of annals are called *princeps* or *airchinnech* in another. Here *princeps* means not 'prince' but 'church superior'; it is first attested in the annals in 683, but is found in the earliest canonical texts;[67] and *principatus* is the term used for the office of *princeps*.[68] The *Hibernensis* devotes a whole book to the office and there are other references to it elsewhere in the text.[69] Its exact Irish equivalent is *airchinnech*, anglicised 'erenagh'; the office is called *airchinnecht*. The term *airchinnech* is old: it occurs in the vernacular laws; it first appears in the *Annals of Ulster* in 814 and from the middle of the tenth century it replaces *princeps*. This is translation, not institutional change. According to the same annals, many *principes* were also bishops in the ninth century and in the first half of the tenth,[70] but this declines sharply after the mid-tenth century, and may point not to laicisation but to a tendency among superiors to remain in minor orders. In the last analysis, *airchinnech* means 'superior of a church', great or small. *Comarba* (in Latin *heres*), anglicised as 'coarb', is the successor of the saintly founder, usually at his principal foundation – an erenagh from another perspective. Well attested in Old-Irish legal and religious texts, it first appears in the *Annals of Ulster* in 851, though it is found earlier in other annals, and occurs some 209 times in the *Annals of Ulster* between 851 and 1200. After 936 'coarb of Patrick' becomes the unchanging title of the superior of Armagh. The same person sometimes held office as bishop and coarb: there are nine examples in the *Annals of Ulster* between 850 and 1115, and many more in the other annals. But the coarb did not need to be a priest or bishop: Slógedach ua Raithnén was coarb of Mo Laise of Leighlin when a deacon; later he became a bishop and coarb of St Ciarán of Seir.[71] Others were coarbs and scribes or coarbs and heads of the monastic school. Their roles and learning were varied: Fínnechta mac Cellaig, 'coarb of Derry, bishop and sage jurist of Irish law';[72] Muiredach mac Crícháin, coarb of

---

66 Adalbert de Vogüé, *Adalbert de Vogüé, La règle de saint Benoît*, 7 vols, SC 182–6 (Paris, 1971–2); idem, *La règle de saint Benoît* (Paris, 1972). 67 For example, in 'Canones Hibernenses IV' (CLH 618; in Ludwig Bieler (ed. & tr.), *The Irish penitentials*, SLH 5 (Dublin, 1963), 170). 68 There are 79 examples of *princeps* in AU between 682 and 1010 (the last), and eight examples of *principatus*; J.-M. Picard, 'Princeps and principatus in the early Irish church: a reassessment', in Alfred P. Smyth (ed.), *Seanchas: studies in early and medieval Irish archaeology, history and literature in honour of Francis J. Byrne* (Dublin, 2000), 146–60. 69 Hib 37; Hib 39:2, 41:1–5, 43:6, 56:2. 70 For example, AU 814, 858, 872 (bis), 874, 875 (bis), 879 (bis), 883, 885, 895, 903, 904, 925, 918, 927, 936. 71 FA §365 [=868?]; AFM 888/89 (885). 72 AU 939; AFM 939 (937).

Colum Cille and Adomnán, 'sage, bishop, virgin, and lector of Armagh, worthy to be coarb of Patrick, who died in his seventy-fourth year … and was buried with honour and reverence in front of the altar in the stone church of Armagh';[73] Flaithbertach ua Ceithinán, coarb of St Tigernach of Clones, 'elder, sage, and eminent bishop', who was wounded by Uí Briúin and died of his wounds in his *civitas*;[74] or bishop Maicnia, coarb of St Búite of Monasterboice, who died 'full of days' in 1039.[75]

The terms coarb and erenagh may apply to the head of any church, from great churches, like Clonmacnoise, Rahan or Lismore, to the most modest local church that delivered pastoral services, baptism and burial rites to the local community. The coarb or erenagh of the tenth and eleventh centuries was not usually a bishop, nor an abbot in the conventional sense. Often not in major orders (sub-deacon, deacon and priest) but almost invariably in minor orders because otherwise his church was not in good standing,[76] he was often superior of a large lay and clerical community with many churches, and his church is often called *civitas*. In some ways the greater among them resembled the ruler of an imperial German episcopal city. He was usually but not always a once-married member of a high-status lineage of professional churchmen that included amongst its members scholars, writers, administrators and ordained clergy; a governor of a large church with an extensive campus and its dependent churches elsewhere who had his law officers, tax gatherers (in Armagh's case, officials grand enough to be recorded in the annals), and treasury officials; the manager of the far-flung properties of a large corporation; the patron of schools and scholarship, of secular and ecclesiastical studies and creative literature; and an eminent religious leader under whom were many churches, within the extensive original foundation and outside it, and sometimes far distant. And there were many of his kind in the Irish church, but none as influential as the coarb of St Patrick at Armagh. In the eyes of the reformers, this office, however venerable its history, was an aberrance, an odd inheritance from the past, a deviant institution, and they wished to replace the coarb with a purely ecclesiastical episcopal potentate like, but hardly spiritually superior to, the feudal bishops of contemporary Europe.

CLERICAL CELIBACY AND HEREDITARY SUCCESSION

For the reformers, Irish and foreign, ideologues of clerical celibacy, the coarbs of Patrick and their like were a scandal because they tended to be non-celibate

---

73 AU 1011; AFM 1011 (1010). **74** AU 1011. **75** AU 1039. **76** CIH i 1–2 = ALI v 118–24.

and hereditary. But non-observance of clerical celibacy and its inevitable con-
sequence, hereditary succession, were found everywhere within the church to
a greater or lesser degree. In the West, clerical celibacy was little observed by
the eighth century and, in the tenth, priests, bishops and archbishops lived
publicly with their wives (and some with concubines as well), promoted their
children to offices in church including that of bishop, and endowed them with
its property (daughters got churches or church property as dowry and a like
practice is also known in Ireland).[77] The practice was condemned at the council of London in 1174.[78] And when reformers demanded the observance of clerical celibacy in the eleventh century, they were met by organised, well-reasoned
and voluble clerical opposition, and in places by violent resistance, even
killings.[79] The saintly and scholarly Abbo of Fleury (†1002) was murdered by
the monks of La Reolé in Gascony because he insisted on celibacy; the reforming bishops of Passau and Mainz feared for their lives in 1074; and the Norman
clergy drove their reform-minded archbishop out of a provincial council in a
hail of stones in 1072.[80] Though clerical marriage was the norm in the Irish
church and hereditary succession long established, there is no suggestion that
the reformers ever met with clerical violence when they insisted on celibacy;
there are no accounts of civil disorder or political conflict arising from the
reform movement as such, as happened elsewhere in Europe. The Irish kings
appear to be the compliant supporters of the reform, anxious to profit from it
if possible, but generally benevolent.

There are two kinds of hereditary succession: collateral succession by which
the relatives of office-holders succeed their kinsmen in office; and lineal succession by which the descendants of office-holders – sons and grandsons – were
heirs to offices in church and to the endowments that went with them. The first,
unexceptionable in Irish eyes, occurs in the very earliest period, for example, in
Iona shortly after the days of Columba himself. There are very many examples
of the second – regarded as acceptable but not the ideal – from the ninth and
tenth centuries,[81] and it can be traced in the pre-Viking period, and even to the
seventh century. A poem of advice, probably eleventh century, puts it succinctly: 'Let the abbot's son enter the church … let the cleric's son go on circuit,
to sing psalms joyfully'.[82]

---

77 CIH i 4.1–4 = ALI v 128, v 1882.34; cf. Hib 32:20. 78 Hefele-Leclerq, *Conciles*, v/2 1060; for a Breton
example see PL 148, 674 (Juthaël bishop of Dol, deposed 1076). 79 DACL ii/2 2802–32; DTC ii/2 2068–
87; Henry C. Lea, *A history of sacerdotal celibacy in the christian church* (2 vols, 3rd ed. rev. London, 1907),
i 164–359. 80 Lea, op. cit., 177, 270–4, 282, 308. 81 Ó Corráin, 'Dál Cais – church and dynasty', 51–63. 82
Tadhg Ó Donnchadha (ed. & tr.), 'Advice to a prince', *Ériu* 9 (1921–3), 43–54: 48 §27, 49 §29.

PLURALISM AND FEDERATIONS

The churches were the owners of vast properties, towns had grown up about them, and they were ruled by lordly lineages, often closely related to royal dynasties and sometimes directly by members of the royal dynasty itself. Pluralism, that is, clerical double-jobbing in the sense of holding high office in two or more monasteries concurrently, was well-established in pre-Viking Ireland[83] and it continued into the ninth, tenth and eleventh centuries. It reflects two separate kinds of activity: the first, the successful clerical careers of ambitious individuals, the second the expansionism of large monastic institutions. The second is far more important. Some are described as abbot, erenagh, or coarb of a major monastery and 'of other monasteries' (*et aliarum civitatum, & ala n-aile cell*). The classic case is Colmán mac Ailella 'abbot of Slane and of other monasteries in Francia and Ireland' who died in 825. There are other examples, but this kind of description does not occur in the annals much after the end of the ninth century.[84] Some bishops ruled in two or more churches: for example, Tuathal mac Aenacáin, 'scribe and bishop of Duleek and Lusk and steward of St Patrick south of the Fews' (a third occupation) who died in 929; Cináed ua Con Mind, bishop of Lismore and Scattery, poet and scholar (†958); and Ailill mac Maenaig, bishop of Swords and Lusk (†967).[85] Others combined the office of bishop and monastic superior: for example, Mael Póil (†1001), bishop of Clonmacnoise and coarb of St Féichín of Fore; Cuindén of Connor (†1038), bishop, abbot, lector and coarb of St Mac Nisse of Connor and St Colmán Ela of Lynally; and Gilla Críst (†1104), bishop of Clonmacnoise and erenagh of Ardagh.[86]

Clearly, political influence played a role: Marcán (†1010), brother of Brian Bóroime, was abbot of Killaloe, Iniscaltra and Terryglass. Flaithbertach (†1014) mac Domnaill, brother of the high-king Mael Sechnaill, was a grand pluralist: superior of Clonmacnoise, Clonard, Fore and Tomgraney. His nephew Domnall, son of his brother Mael Sechnaill, succeeded him as superior of Clonard in 1014 and Domnall's son Flann married Caíntigern, daughter of ua Lachtnáin, lector of Clonmacnoise, and two of their children were kings of Meath in the eleventh century.[87]

Some instances of pluralism indicate close alliances over long periods between churches, some geographically close, some widely separated: for

---

83 ATig 742; AU 748, 773, 778, 781, 782, 784, 785, 787, 788, 789, 796. **84** AU 825; AU 835, 838, 840, 864, 882, 888, 901. **85** AU 929; AI 958; AFM 967 (965). **86** AFM 1001 (1000), AC 1001 (994), CS 1001 (999); AU, AFM 1038; ATig, FM 1104, CS 1104 (1100). **87** AU 1010; AU, AI 1014; Annette Kehnel, *Clonmacnois – the church and lands of St Ciarán: change and continuity in an Irish monastic foundation* (Münster, 1999), 262; Paul Byrne, 'The community of Clonard, sixth to twelfth centuries', *Peritia*, 4 (1985), 157–73: 165–6.

example, Movilla and Dromore (both in Co. Down) belong in the first category,[88] Connor (Co. Antrim) and Lynally (King's Co.) in the second.[89] Still others represent the relationship between the mother church of a federation and its dependants. Here the superior of a dependent church holds office as vice-abbot, lector, priest, or bishop in the mother church. Sometimes, one person is the superior of many churches: bishop Ailill Ó Nialláin (†1093) was superior of Clonmacnoise, Tomgraney and Kilmacduagh;[90] Conaing Ó Fairchellaig (†1059) was erenagh of Drumlane and coarb of the churches of St M'Aedóc in Connacht and Leinster – a series of offices that made him head of the paruchia of M'Aedóc and the ruler of vast properties.[91] Others were even more powerful: Mugrón (†980), religious poet and superior of all the Columban houses in Ireland, controlled far greater resources.[92] From the mid-ninth to the early twelfth centuries, we find Clonmacnoise linked by pluralist ties with Ardagh, Clonard, Cloondara (Co. Longford), Devenish, Emlagh (Co. Meath), Fennor (Co. Meath), Fore (Co. Westmeath), Kells, Kilmacduagh, Roscommon, Roscrea and Tomgraney.[93] These connections represent the institutional nexus of power, influence and income of Clonmacnoise and the ambitions of the ecclesiastical families connected with it, but the detailed constitutional and fiscal structure escapes us because the rentals and archival records have perished. Some flavour of such relationships is found in the obit of bishop Cormac ua Cillín (†966), who belonged to an ecclesiastical lineage of the ruling lineage of Uí Fiachrach Aidne. He was a *sapiens* (distinguished scholar)[94] and senior, and superior of Clonmacnoise, Roscommon and Tomgraney (Co. Clare). He built 'the great church of Tomgraney and its round

---

88 AU 953, 993, 1043. 89 AU 867, 901, 954; AFM 965 (963); AU 976, 1038. For details of the relationship between these churches see T.M. Charles-Edwards, '*Érlam*: the patron saint of an Irish church', in Alan Thacker & Richard Sharpe (ed.), *Local saints and local churches in the early medieval West* (Oxford, 2002), 267–90: 282–4. 90 AU, AI, CS, AFM 1093. 91 AU, ATig, AFM 1059. 92 AU, AFM 980; AU 1062; Máire Herbert, *Iona, Kells and Derry: the history and hagiography of the monastic* familia *of Columba* (Oxford, 1988, repr. Dublin, 1996), 82–3; TP ii 305–6; Kuno Meyer (ed.), 'Mitteilungen aus irischen Handschriften', *Z Celt Philol*, 10 (1915), 338–48: 340; Charles Plummer (ed. & tr.), *Irish litanies*, HBS 62 (London, 1925), 78–85; Gerard Murphy, *Early Irish lyrics* (Oxford, 1956), 32–5 §14. 93 Ardagh (AFM 1104); Clonard (CS 838, AU 926, AU AI 954, AU 1014–15); Cloondara (CS 979 (977)); Devenish (AU CS 869 = AFM 869 (867); AU 896); Emlagh (AFM 950 (948)); Fennor (AFM 1024); Fore (AU 891; CS 922; AU 1001, 1014–15); Kells (AU, AFM, AI 1070); Kilmacduagh (AU 1093); Roscommon (CS 966 (964); AFM 980 (979); AFM 1025; AU 1052; AFM 1088); Roscrea (AU 839, AFM 839 (838); AU 920); Tomgraney (CS 966 (964); AU, AI 1042; AU 1093; AFM 1100); Kehnel, *Clonmacnois*, 51–89, 340–1. 94 Colin A. Ireland, 'Aldfrith of Northumbria and the learning of a *sapiens*', in Kathryn A. Klar, Eve E. Sweetser & Claire Thomas (ed.), *A Celtic florilegium: studies in memory of Brendan O Hehir*, Celtic Studies Publications, 11 (Lawrence MA, 1996), 63–77; Michael Richter, 'The personnel of learning in early medieval Ireland', in Próinséas Ní Chatháin & Michael Richter (ed.), *Ireland and Europe in the early middle ages* (Stuttgart, 1996), 275–308.

tower'. In a marginal note in *Chronicon Scottorum* he is called *liath na ttri lemenn* 'the grey one of the three leaps' – a sardonic comment on the vaulting ambition of a man whose family, a cadet branch of a declining lordly lineage, began their rise to power as clerics in Tomgraney.[95]

KINGS AND CLERICS

Relations between kings and clerics were troublesome and complicated, not least because very many clerical lineages were closely related to royal dynasties. Though churchmen and jealous guardians of the church's rights and properties, they were still deeply involved in dynastic matters. We find senior members of dynasties holding high church office, for example Donnchad mac Domnaill was deputy abbot of Clonard while in the running for the kingship of Tara, when he was slain in 924.[96] Clerics from major churches rule as kings, especially in times of dynastic conflict, presumably as compromises. For example, Rebachán (†934) mac Mothlai, abbot of Tomgraney, was king of Dál Cais at a time of dynastic lineage change from the line of Dímma Superbus to Uí Thairdelbaig (with whom the kingship remained).[97] Ólchobur (†796/7) mac Flainn meic Eirc was scribe, bishop, anchorite and abbot of the island church of Scattery in the Shannon estuary, but he appears also as king of Munster at a time of dynastic disarray amongst the ruling Eóganacht. His father, Flann (†762), was king of the powerful regional kingdom of Uí Fidgeinte, as was his brother Scandlán (†786).[98] More remarkable still are the cleric-kings of Munster – Feidlimid mac Crimthainn (†847), and his successors, Ólchobur mac Cinaeda, abbot of Emly (a major church of the Eóganacht) and king of Cashel (r. 847–51), and Cormac mac Cuilennáin, bishop and scholar (r. 901–8). Kings took offices within churches: Muiredach (†863) mac Maele Dúin was deputy abbot of Armagh and king of Ind Airthir, the petty kingdom in which Armagh lay;[99] Cathal (†829) mac Dunlaing was king of Uí Chennselaig and deputy abbot of Ferns.[100] More striking still, Muiredach mac Brain was king of Leinster (r. 884–5) and abbot of the great church of Kildare. A metrically elegant praise poem laments his death but makes no reference to his clerical role:[101]

95 CS 966 (964). 96 CS 924 (923) Donnchadh mac Domnaill tanaisi <abbad> Cluana Iraird, ridamna Temrach iugulatus est a fratre suo. 97 AI 934: Quies Rebacháin meic Mothlai abb Tomma Grene & rí Dail Chais; Lec. facs. 229raa43–rb7 (Dál Cais king list). 98 AU, AI, 762, 786; AU 796; AI 797. 99 AU 863.2. 100 AU 829.5. 101 Kuno Meyer (ed. & tr.), 'Bruchstücke der älteren Lyrik Irlands', *Abh Preuss Akad Wiss*, phil-hist Kl. Jhrg 1919, Nr 7 (Berlin, 1919), 31 §113.

> Great sorrow for Muiredach of Mag Lifi,
> a warrior of many bands;
> king of Leinster to the sea-shore,
> son of Bran, pride of Ireland.

The bare record in the annals does not allow us to reconstruct any details of the relationship between king and church in these cases. It is likely that kings laid hands on church estates and used their role in church to enhance their standing and authority. The problem ridden relationship of lay and clerical power remained a live issue and is subtly discussed in the twelfth-century narratives, *Aided Diarmata meic Fergusa Cerrbeoil* and *Bórama*.[102]

VIOLENCE AND WAR

Inevitably, the churches, as great landowners ruled by aristocrats, were drawn into the chronic warfare of early medieval Ireland. The large houses (with their surrounding towns) were so important that they were strategically significant in war, local and provincial, and were regularly subject to attack.[103] Kings sacked the great churches of their enemies, and robbed them. A good example of tit-for-tat plundering (and this must do duty for many) occurs in 1031: Sitric, king of Dublin, plundered the church of Ardbraccan in the kingdom of Meath; two hundred people were burned to death in the stone church; two hundred more were taken prisoner; and herds of cattle were driven off. Conchobar ua Maelechlainn, king of Meath (r. 1030–73), replied: he plundered and burned Swords, within the kingdom of Dublin, and took large numbers of prisoners and many cows.[104] Sometimes churches defended themselves. When Étrú Ó Conaing, called *rígdamna* of Munster, a discard and dissatified Dál Cais royal, attacked Emly in 1032 as a means of getting at Donnchad mac Briain, king of Munster (r. 1014–63), he was slain by the community (*muintir Imlecha*) itself.[105] In 1038, Orc Allaid, king of Uí Echach, was killed within Armagh itself by its rulers, Uí Shínaig, because he had treacherously killed Eochaid mac in Abbad ('son of the abbot') and profaned Armagh eight years before.[106] In 1124, the

---

102 CLH 968, 993; Standish H. O'Grady (ed. & tr.), 'Aided Dhiarmada', in idem, *Silva gadelica*, (London, 1892), i 72–82, ii 76–88; Whitley Stokes (ed. & tr.), 'The Boroma', *Revue Celtique*, 13 (1892), 32–124; Dan M. Wiley (ed. & tr.), An edition of *Aided Diarmata meic Cerbaill* from the Book of Uí Maine (PhD, Harvard University, 2000). 103 A.T. Lucas, 'The plundering and burning of churches in Ireland, 7th to 16th century', in Etienne Rynne (ed.), *North Munster studies* (Limerick, 1967), 172–229. 104 ATig, AU, AFM 1031. 105 AU, AI 1032. 106 AU 1030, 1038.

community of Derry killed Ardgar, grandson of ua Mael Sechnaill, royal heir (*rígdamna*) of Ailech, because he had outraged the church of Derry.[107] He belonged to the premier dynasty of the Northern Uí Néill: his ancestor, Niall mac Maíl Sechnaill, had been king of Northern Uí Néill (r. 1036–61). Not only earthly arms defended the churches against wrongdoers: again and again, the annalists note with satisfaction the deaths of those who had plundered churches, and attribute their violent ends to the vengeance of the patron saints they had outraged.[108]

As elsewhere in contemporary Europe, the church elite was itself involved in violence. Clerics regularly went to war in the armies of secular kings: 'An expedition by Muirchertach Ó Briain and the Southern Half of Ireland, lay and cleric' in 1113 was yet another campaign against his rival, Domnall (mac Ardgair) Mac Lochlainn, king of Ailech (r. 1083–1121).[109] There could be bitter struggles over the ownership of churches: in 1055 there was a battle between Dub Dá Leithe, coarb of Patrick, and Murchad ua Maelechlainn, superior of Clonard and Kells, a royal pluralist. Murchad's father may have been Loingsech *sapiens* (†1042) who had been lector of Clonard and belonged to a declining branch of the royal family of Meath. The battle took place at Martartech (Martry, nearly 6.5 km north-west of Navan, Co. Meath) and it was over Martartech itself, an Armagh proprietary church and estate that Murchad had seized. He was defeated by Dub Dá Leithe, however, and the annals state that many people fell in that battle.[110] Dub Dá Leithe was again at 'great war' in 1060, against a rival abbot, Cummascach Ó hErudáin, and was again victorious. He won back his position, and died in 1064 as 'coarb of Patrick' and was immediately succeeded by his nephew Máel Ísa. His rival, now described as 'head of the poor of Ireland', died in 1074, 'after an excellent penitence'; but he, too, was a nobleman, a member of Clann Chonchobair of Uí Bresail, and a kinsman of a previous coarb of Patrick.[111] In Iona, abbot Mac Meic Báethíne was slain by the son of his immediate predecessor, 'the coarb of Colum Cille in Ireland and Scotland', in what was plainly a succession struggle.[112] Mugrón, superior of Cork, bishop and lector, was killed at the church of Rosscarbery in 1057, while

---

107 AU 1134. **108** CGG 32 §29 [867]; ATig 881, AFM 881 (878); AU 942, AFM 942 (940), AC 942 (935); ATig 983, AFM 984 (983); AFM 987 (986); AU 985; AFM 1004 (1003); AU 1007, AFM 1007 (1005); AI 1013, AFM 1013 (1012); AFM 1019 (1018); ATig 1026; AFM 1034; AU 1035; ATig 1041; ATig 1043 (bis); ATig 1044, CS 1044 (1042); ATig, AI, AFM 1045; ATig 1046, CS 1046 (1044); ATig 1052, CS 1052 (1050); AFM 1059; AT 1060, CS 1060 (1058); AI 1061; AU 1065; ATig 1065; AU 1066; ATig, AFM 1069, CS 1069 (1066); AFM 1069; AU 1070; AU, AI 1076; AFM 1080; AFM 1081; AU 1102; ATig 1108, CS 1108 (1104); ATig, AFM 1109; AI 1122. **109** AU, AFM, ATig 1113. **110** AU, ATig 1055; cf. NHI ix 259, which gives Murchad a descent that conflicts with AU. **111** AU, AI 1060; CS 1060 (1058); AU 1064, 1075; H.J. Lawlor & R.I. Best (ed.), 'Ancient list of the coarbs of Patrick', *Proc Roy Ir Acad (C)*, 25 (1919–20), 316–62: 330; CGH 183, 415, 418. **112** AU 1062, 1070.

coming from nocturns. The killers belonged to a local lordly family, but the motive was ecclesiastical: Rosscarbery's violent resistance to being taken over by Cork.[113] Southern clerics, led by Senóir mac Mael Mo Lua (who ended his days as 'chief anchorite of Ireland' in the church of Down), mounted a military expedition in 1076 to expel the superior of Clondalkin, Co. Dublin, who, they believed, had wrongfully seized the office.[114]

The annals record many killings of clerics. Some are simply noted, not explained: for example, the erenagh of Leighlin who was killed in the doorway of the church in 1045, the erenagh of Swords who was slain in the middle of the church complex just before Easter 1048.[115] In 1128, Gilla Pátraic mac Tuathail, coarb of St Kevin of Glendalough, was killed by Uí Muiredaig, the local ruling dynasty, 'in the middle of Glendalough'. A successor, Cathassach, coarb of St Kevin, was blinded in 1031 by Domnall mac Dúnlaing.[116] Domnall belonged to Uí Muiredaig, he was son of a king of Leinster, and four of his brothers held the same office. His gruesome act (normally reserved for secular dynastic rivals) was one of several violent incidents in his dynasty's successful attempt to seize Glendalough for its members. One of the remote beneficiaries of that achievement was St Laurence (Lorcán) Ó Tuathail, of Uí Muiredaig, abbot of Glendalough (*sed.* 1154–62; archbishop of Dublin, *sed.* 1162–80).

In the early twelfth century, the annalists express outrage at attacks on clerics. In 1117, Aed Ó Ruairc, king of Breifne, killed Mael Brigte mac Rónáin, the coarb of Kells, and many members of the community. The annalist cites Ps 33:17: 'The face of the Lord be against those committing these wickednesses, that He may wipe out their memory from the earth'. A more powerful expression of horror occurs in 1128 when Tigernán Ó Ruairc, king of Breifne, attacked Cellach, coarb of Patrick and archbishop of Armagh:

> A detestable and unprecedented deed of evil consequence that merited the curse of the men of Ireland, lay and cleric, the like of which was not previously found in Ireland, was committed by Tigernán Ó Ruairc and Uí Briúin, namely, the coarb of Patrick was outraged to his face, that is, his retinue was robbed and some of them were killed, and a young cleric of his own household who was carrying the *flabellum* was killed there. The aftermath of this evil deed is that no protection exists in Ireland that is secure for anybody henceforth until that wickedness is avenged

---

113 ATig, AI 1057; CS 1057 (1055). 114 AFM 1076, AI 1095; Charles Doherty, 'Cluain Dolcáin: a brief note', in Smyth, *Seanchas*, 182–8. 115 AU 1045, AFM 1048. 116 AU, AFM 1031; CS 1031 (1029); A.S. Mac Shamhráin, *Church and polity in pre-Norman Ireland: the case of Glendalough* (Maynooth, 1996), 91, 93, 146–7.

by God and man. The insult offered the coarb of Patrick is an insult to the Lord, for the Lord himself said in the gospel: 'He who despises you, despises me; he who despises me, despises Him who sent me' (Lk 10:4).[117]

In the same year, Conchobar Mac Lochlainn, king of Ailech (r. 1132–8, 1129–36), raided Brega 'and committed a great crime before God and man, namely, the burning of Trim with its churches, and a large number of people were martyred in them. They returned home, without having obtained peace from God or man'.[118] These entries suggest that in the early twelfth century the churches perceived attacks on themselves as intolerable, that they protested with increasing vigour against lay violence, and that they called, with some success, on the major kings for protection.

SECULAR IMPOSTS

From much earlier times, some churches were free but others were *sub censu*, that is, bound by economic obligations to secular lords, or even owned by them.[119] In the tenth and eleventh centuries, if we may judge from a few annalistic entries, the greater churches were trying to extricate themselves from lay control and secular imposts. Sometimes, this came about as compensation for the outrages committed against them by kings and lords, sometimes kings conferred liberty on churches, from whatever motive, pious or politic. One might cite the following as an early example: 'The freedom of Clonard granted by Congalach mac Mael Mithig [r. 944–56], no king or prince having claim to quartering upon it'.[120] In the course of an expedition into Mag Muirthemne in 1012, Brian Bóroime 'granted complete freedom [from secular imposts] to the churches of Patrick on that expedition'.[121] Both Congalach and Brian were new men who could expect to benefit more than most from the support of the church and a reputation for good works.

Others had to make good their failings. In 1044, Donnchad mac Briain, king of Munster (r. 1014–63), made a grant of freedom to Clonmacnoise as compensation for a very serious offence: it had been plundered by his troops in his absence. His compensatory grant is described as follows:

---

117 AU 1128. 118 AU 1117, 1128. 119 Hib 29:6. 120 AFM 951 (949): 'Soere Cluana Ioraird ó Chongalach, mac Maoile Mithigh, gan choinnimh righ nó flatha fuirre'; cf. CS 951 (950), AC 951 (964). 121 AU 1012.2: 'Slogad la Brian i Magh Muirteimhne co tuc og-shoere do chellaibh Patraicc dont shluagad-sin'.

Donnchad afterwards gave satisfaction to the church, to wit, perfect free-dom to God and to St Ciarán till the day of judgement, and forty cows to be given by him immediately; and he put his curse on any Munsterman that should ever inflict any injury on the clergy of St Ciarán.[122]

In a charter dated 1033×1049 Conchobar ua Maelechlainn, king of Meath (r. 1030–73), again in compensation for the outraging of Kells and its coarb, Mael Muire Ó hUchtáin, granted the church of Kildalkey, Co. Meath, 'with its terri-tory and land to God and Colum Cille forever, without rent or tribute, without expedition or hosting, without quartering of king or lord upon it, as it was not previously'.[123] This implies that it was his proprietary church and thus Kildalkey, the early foundation of St Mo Luóc, was a church in royal ownership in the early eleventh century. In 1108, the community of Clonmacnoise fasted against the deposed king of Meath, Muirchertach ua Maelechlainn (r. 1105–6), to obtain the freedom of the church of Kilmore 'and God soon took vengeance upon him' – a retribution that included the plundering of Meath and his own dis-honour.[124] The freeing of churches and their estates from secular imposts was still in progress in the mid-twelfth century. In 1161, Muirchertach Mac Lochlainn, king of Ireland (r. 1156–66), came on an expedition into Meath and took the hostages of Meath. He held a royal council of laity and clergy at Áth na Dairbrige (Dervor, Co. Meath) and 'on that occasion the churches of Colum Cille in Meath and Leinster were freed by Flaithbertach Ó Brolcháin, of a Cenél nÉogain clerical family, coarb of Colum Cille (therefore head of the Columban federation) and he was granted their tribute and jurisdiction, for they were unfree before that'.[125] Ó Brolcháin (abbot of Derry from 1150; personal episco-pal chair, 1158; †1175), the senior cleric of the northern half of Ireland, was acting with, and on behalf of, the king, and of course on his own behalf. Next year, Flaithbertach and the king undertook a large building programme in Derry, and in 1164 the king was closely associated with Ó Brolcháin in the building of a great church at Derry.

The *First Vision of Adomnán* (s. x/xi), a colourful and imaginative text, par-ticularly eloquent on the fearful punishments of hell, is a commentary closely linked to social and church reform.[126] It gives a sharp flavour of the thinking of

---

122 AFM 1044: 'Cluain Mic Nóis do indreadh do Muimhneachaibh i n-éccmhais Donnchadha mic Briain. Donnchadh iarsin do thabhairt a riara don eacclais .i. óghshaoire do Dia & do Chiarán co lá mbratha, & da fichet bó fo chedóir uadh, & do-rad a mhallachtain for gach n-oen do Mhuimhnechaibh do-bheradh nach ndochar for shamhadh Chiaráin co bráth'; cf. AC 1044. 123 G. Mac Niocaill (ed.), *Notitiæ as Leabhar Cheanannais, 1033–1161* (Dublin, 1961), 10–12, §1. 124 ATig 1108 = CS 1108 (1104). 125 AU 1161. 126 Ernst Windisch (ed.), 'Die Vision des Adamnán: Fís Adamnáin', in idem (ed.), *Irische*

some clerical circles. In 1096, the Irish were seized with a great fear of a plague that had been prophesied. To ward off the heavenly fire, pestilence and calamity that their evil deeds appeared to deserve, the churchmen, led by Mael Pátraic, coarb of Patrick, prescribed fasts, abstinence, and alms-giving. For their part, 'the kings of Ireland granted freedom (*saoire*) to very many churches that were under tribute'.[127] The *Second Vision of Adomnán* is closely connected with this threat of plague. In fact, its apocalyptic warning, probably relayed by popular preachers, that a heaven-sent plague was on its way because of the sinfulness of the people may have sparked off the general panic. It is a fundamentalist call to penitence and moral reform:

> Woe, woe to the men of the island of Ireland who transgress the Lord's commandments. Woe to the kings and erenaghs because they do not love the truth and they love iniquity and rapine. Woe to the teachers because they do not teach the truth but agree to the falsehoods of the ungodly. Woe to the whores and sinners who will be burned like hay-grass and stubble.

The people are accused of great sins: 'wounding, theft, adultery, parricides and manslaughter; violence to churches and clerics; greed and perjury, lies and false judgement; and the destruction of God's church …'. Their own saints have abandoned them, and no longer intercede for them in heaven or visit their earthly foundations. The text demands that Sunday be observed, that people fast, that boys be sent for religious study, and that 'each church should have two ordained clerics to administer baptism and communion and sing requiem masses'.[128] Note the insistence on pastoral care.

Here there is a broad pastoral strand of moral and organisational reform directed mainly towards the laity, and the church's demand for freedom from lay imposts and violence is evidently part of that reform. Worse than secular taxes was *coinnmed* 'quartering', sometimes *coinnmed écne* 'quartering by vio-

Texte, i (Leipzig, 1880), 165–96; C.S. Boswell (tr.), *An Irish precursor of Dante: a study on the vision of heaven and hell ascribed to the eighth-century Irish saint Adamnán, with translation of the Irish text*, Grimm Library, 18 (London, 1908; repr. New York, 1972), 28–47; Máire Herbert (tr.), 'The vision of Adomnán' in Máire Herbert & Martin McNamara (ed.), *Irish biblical apocrypha: selected texts in translation* (Edinburgh, 1989), 137–48; John Carey (tr.), *King of mysteries: early Irish religious writings* (Dublin, 1998), 261–74, 280. **127** CS 1096 (1092), AFM 1096. **128** Whitley Stokes (ed. & tr.), 'Adamnan's Second Vision', *Revue Celtique* 12 (1891), 420–43: 422 §1, 424–6 §9, 428 §§16, 18; Nicole Volmering (ed. & tr.), 'The Second Vision of Adomnán', in John Carey, Emma Nic Cárthaigh & Caitríona Ó Dochartaigh (ed.), *The end and beyond: medieval Irish eschatology*, Celtic Studies Publications 17, 2 vols (Aberystwyth, 2014), ii 647–84.

lence', that is, billeting troops on churches and on their property by force. In this way, the soldiers of an increasingly militarist society were lodged on the church and their bad behaviour and offences, which included killings, gave rise to various kinds of compensations and grants of freedom.[129] In effect, *coinnmed* appears to be military occupation of churches and their estates: the same term is used in the annals for the military occupation of whole territories. The churches' hostility to such practices is eloquently reflected in contemporary literature. For example, the twelfth-century *Aided Diarmada meic Fergusa Cerrbeoil* states:

> Bad kings and bad royal heirs and soldiers will quarter themselves on your churches ... there will come a time when the church will be enslaved to the state; there will be no privilege of churches but they will be billeted on by all. From this, evil will come upon the kingdom; and son and father and kinsman will mutually slay each other, and all men's weapons will be red with their blood.[130]

The evidence, then, points to an indigenous general movement by the church leaders to free themselves and their lands from secular taxes and burdens, and lesser kings and lords may have followed the example of the great, who alone are mentioned in the annals.

ASCETICISM AND RELIGIOUS PRACTICE

Contrary to the general impression of corruption and decay, conveyed broadly but without detail, by modern historians, asceticism flourished in Ireland in the tenth and eleventh centuries. Indeed, the ascetic piety and religious scholarship of Irish emigré monks were admired in Lotharingia and elsewhere in Europe. There are references to over twenty anchorites in the annals for the tenth century and to a significant number in the eleventh. Since anchoritism by its nature is private and retiring, most lived lives of quiet obscurity and only a tiny minority of ones famous for their sanctity are likely to be recorded in the annals. Corcrán Cléirech (†1040), an anchorite of Iniscaltra (Holy Island on Lough

---

129 ATig, AFM 1045 = CS 1045 (1043); AI 1045; AFM 1072; CS 1111 (1107); Mac Niocaill (ed.), *Notitiæ as Leabhar Cheanannais, 1033–1161*, 10, 34.   130 CLH 968; Standish H. O'Grady (ed. & tr.), *Silva gadelica* (2 vols, London, 1892), i 78–9 (text), ii 83–4 (tr.); Dan M. Wiley (ed. & tr.), An edition of *Aided Diarmata meic Cerbaill* from the Book of Uí Maine (PhD, Harvard University, 2000), 110–64; idem, 'Stories about Diarmait mac Cerbaill from the Book of Lismore', *Emania*, 19 (2002), 53–9.

Derg) who is described as the 'head of western Europe in holiness and learning' and who died at Lismore as a pilgrim penitent,[131] is a good example of strict asceticism. He sent Anmchad, a member of his community, into overseas exile as penitence for a tiny fault – being a little too generous as host with the community's wine – and Anmchad subsequently died as a revered and saintly *inclusus* in Fulda.[132] One is not surprised that such strictness in a superior could co-exist with marriage in some instances. For example, Tigernach Boirchech (†1061), superior of Movilla (Co. Down), sent Marianus Scottus the Chronicler into penitential exile for a trivial fault in 1056 as he himself reports.[133] But Tigernach, who is described in his obit as 'chief spiritual director of Ireland', had a son Flaithbertach who succeeded his father as superior of Movilla and died in religious retirement in 1098.[134] Conn na mBocht of Clonmacnoise (†1060), anchorite, superior of the Céli Dé (evidently a house of stricter observance), and a wealthy man famous for his charity, belonged to a rich and well-established clerical lineage. Four of his sons held high office at Clonmacnoise, and he was grandfather of the great scribe Mael Muire (†1106), son of bishop Céilechair.[135] Evidently, a cleric could play many parts in his lifetime.

The annalistic record varies: some are recorded as simple anchorites, without local association, such as Faílbe (†925) or Mael Mórda (†1032).[136] Two eleventh-century persons, not associated with any monastic house, are give the title 'anchorite of God': Anmchad ua Dúnchada (†1058) and Cormac ua Mael Dúin (†1074).[137] These may have been solitaries, living the true hermit life in the wilderness and noted for their sanctity. Others probably belonged to small communities of anchorites:[138] for example, Gormgal (†1018) of Ardailén (High Island), a church off the west coast of Galway; and another Gormgal (†1056), 'principal anchorite' of Inis Dar Caircrenn (Ram Island on Lough Neagh), which has a round tower and therefore may have had a community of anchorites. Others are associated with major monastic houses: Diarmait (†957), anchorite of Glendalough; Aengus ua Robartaig (†969), anchorite of Derry; Cétfaid (†1056), anchorite of Lismore. Still others held office as teachers or scholars in major houses: *fer léigind* or lector (head of the monastic school), scholar (*sapiens, saí*), canon lawyer (*scriba*) or the like. Two – Dub Scoile ua Mancháin (†967) of Glendalough and Dúnchad (†1006) of Clonmacnoise – are described as *cenn*

---

131 AFM, AU, AI 1040. **132** CLH 656; G. Waitz (ed.), *Mariani Scotti Chronicon*, MGH SS 5 (Hannover, 1844), 481–564: 557 (s.a. 1043). **133** Ibid. **134** AU, AFM 1098. **135** CS 1059 (1057); AFM 1031; LU p xii; D. Ó Corráin, 'Mael Muire the scribe: family and background', 1–28: 28. **136** AFM 925 (923), 1032. **137** AI 1058, 1074. **138** AU 1018.1, 1056.3; Jenny White Marshall & Grellan D. Rourke, *High Island: an Irish monastery in the Atlantic* (Dublin, 2000), esp. 7–11; Brian Lalor, *The Irish round tower: origins and architecture explored* (Cork, 1999), 104–5.

riagla 'head of the rule'.[139] It is uncertain what this means, whether an authority on the rule of the house or dean of discipline, probably the former. Very commonly, those described as anchorites had held senior administrative offices: superior, abbot, bishop, often enough as pluralists; for example, Cairbre mac Feradaig, anchorite, superior of Castledermot (Dísert Diarmata) and Timahoe (Tech Mo Chua), and 'head of piety of Leinster', who died in 921 at a great age.[140] The various titles of Mael Brigte ua Mael Finn (†1041)[141] – priest, anchorite, bishop – suggest that men spent a portion of their lives as anchorites, before being called to high office as bishops, abbots, or superiors, or after they had retired from such offices to prepare themselves for eternity.

This kind of retirement is very common: bishops and church superiors, and some of the greatest of these, resigned their offices and the wealth, status and worldliness that went with them, and set off 'on their pilgrimage' to another house, with which they had no former administrative connections, where they lived apart from the community as simple ascetics, but were maintained by it and participated, at some remove, in its religious devotions. A busy high-status ninth-century cleric expresses a longing for such a retreat from the world in a polished lyric.

Ba sí báes fom-themadar	Let the folly which protects me
eter lissu lann	amid enclosures of churches
locán álainn eladglan	be a pleasant little plot, holy
	with memorial stones,
os mé m'óenur ann.	and that I should be all alone there.
Céim íar sétaib soscéla,	Following the pathways of the gospel,
salmchétal cach thráth,	psalm-singing every canonical hour,
crích fri rád, fri roscéla,	an end to talk, to news mongering,
filliud glúine gnáth.	constant genuflexion.[142]

The hermit's plot and strict devotions rather than the rich mansion and lax practices of a lordly superior may be folly in the eyes of his more worldly peers, but this is what he truly desires, at least at the end of his career.

Very often, the anchorite belonged to one of the great church foundations, but evidently lived apart from the community in his own cell and enclosure. In texts of the Old-Irish period he is listed among the ecclesiastical dignitaries –

---

139 AFM 967 (965), 1006 (1005). Dúnchad was ancestor of Meic Cuinn na mBocht at Clonmacnoise. 140 AFM 921 (919). 141 AFM 1041. 142 Murphy, *Early Irish lyrics*, 22 §9.13, 179.

scribe, bishop and superior of a great church[143] – and his presence lends status to his host institution. Here he may function as scholar, scribe, legal expert and teacher: Dúnchad (†1006), *fer léigind* of Clonmacnoise, was a historian as well as an anchorite; Cenn Faelad in tSabaill (†1012) was anchorite, bishop, pilgrim and choice confessor;[144] and there were many like them. This was nothing unusual in the Western church. Some continental Benedictine monasteries (among them Cluny) had small communities of anchorites, set apart from the main monastery, as did Cassiodorus many centuries before. The Irish practice appears no different.

The role of the Irish anchorites as scholars, teachers and scribes within the church community and its schools suggests the life of the *inclusus*, a form of eremetism that goes back to early Christianity and continued into the twelfth century. The *inclusus* was an anchorite who lived within the precincts of a monastery (or attached to a secular church), subject to the abbot, but not to the ordinary rule. According to the *Regula solitariorum* of Grimlaicus[145] (*c*.AD 900, Metz), the *inclusus* had a cell, a little oratory and a small garden, all surrounded by a high wall. After a probationary period, the postulant went through a formal ceremony presided over by the bishop or the abbot, was led to his quarters, and the door sealed up. The *inclusus* could never again leave his quarters without the permission of his superior. But he was not cut off from society entirely. His oratory was so close to the church that he could participate, through an aperture, in the regular devotions of the brethren. Through another, he was provided with his needs and conducted his teaching and spiritual counselling.[146] The life of the anchorite in an Irish church, where he lived apart in his own cell and enclosure, may not have been so formally organised, but when Irish monks came to the Continent in the tenth and eleventh centuries, they found something familiar in the life of the *inclusus* and adopted it with enthusiasm. Among them were Fínán (†878) of Rheinau, Anmchad (†1043) of Fulda, Padernus (†1058) of Paderborn, Muirchertach († post 1070) of Regensburg, Marianus Scotus the Chronicler (†1082) of Fulda and Mainz, Marianus Scotus the Scribe (†1088) of Regensburg, Eoin († post 1090) of Göttweig – all noted for their sanctity or learning or both in their adopted communities.[147]

143 CLH 583; Bieler, *Irish penitentials*, 230 §6.5; E.J. Gwynn (ed. & tr.), 'An Irish penitential', *Ériu* 7 (1914), 121–95: 170 §17; tr. D.A. Binchy, in Ludwig Bieler, *Irish penitentials*, 258–83: 273 §17. **144** AFM 1006 (1005), 1012 (1011). Cenn Fáelad belonged to the monastery of Saul, Co. Down, a dependent church of Armagh. **145** PL 103, 575–664; Andrew Thornton OSB (tr.), *Grimlaicus, Rule for solitaries* (Collegeville MN, 2011); K.S. Frank 'Grimlaicus, Regula solitariorum', in Franz J. Felten & Nikolas Jaspert (ed.), *Vita religiosa im Mittelalter: Festschrift für Kaspar Elm zum 70. Geburtstag*, Berliner Historische Studien, 31 (Berlin, 1999), 21–35. **146** DTC i 1138–40; B. Mac Carthy (ed.), *The Codex Palatino-Vaticanus No. 830*, Todd Lecture Series 3 (Dublin, 1892), 4–7. **147** Helmut Flachenecker, *Schottenklöster: irische Benediktinerkonvente im*

FOREIGN AND ROMAN CONNECTIONS

It is not correct to see Ireland as being out of contact with, even isolated from, the rest of Christendom in the tenth and eleventh centuries.[148] Irish pilgrimages indicate otherwise. Some like the pious Domnall Déisech made the pilgrimage to the Holy Land and returned to die in religious retirement at home.[149] Clemens, 'a most ardent lover of Christ and of pilgrimage', the companion in exile of Marianus Scotus the Scribe, alone of his group left Germany and went to Jerusalem where he ended his days.[150] Laymen also undertook this journey: in 1080, Ó Cinn Fháelad, king of the Déisi, went to Jerusalem.[151] Others went to Rome, not usually as officials or appellants (though some may have been) but as pilgrims to the tombs of the Apostles, some to end their lives there in penitence and religious retirement.[152] Some were wealthy and travelled in style, accompanied by a retinue and numerous servants; others were poor and begged their way.[153] The crippled Gilla Míchíl made the pilgrimage to Rome six times in search of a cure, and when he was finally cured, allegedly by Edward the Confessor, he set off a seventh time to give thanks to St Peter in Rome.[154]

Already, there is good evidence for Roman pilgrimages before and during the ninth century.[155] Céle Dabaill mac Scandail, coarb of Comgall of Bangor (Co. Down), bishop, scribe, teacher, 'apostolic doctor of the whole of Ireland' and confessor of Niall Glúndub (†919), king of Ireland, went to Rome as a pilgrim in 928 and died there in 929.[156] Fergil, abbot of Terryglass, died a Roman pilgrim in the same year.[157] The next reference to an Irish clerical pilgrim in the annals occurs in 1024: Fachtna, quondam lector and priest of Clonmacnoise and superior of Fennor (Co. Meath) and Int Eidnén (Co. Meath), abbot of the Irish (*abb na nGaoidheal*), died in Rome, after going on his pilgrimage.[158] His title 'abbot of the Irish' suggests that Fachtna may have given up his many

hochmittelalterlichen Deutschland, Quellen und Forschungen aus dem Gebiet der Geschichte NF 18 (Paderborn, 1995), 50. **148** Aubrey Gwynn, 'Ireland and the Continent in the eleventh century', *Ir Hist Stud*, 8 (1953), 193–216 (repr. Aubrey Gwynn, *The Irish church in the eleventh and twelfth centuries*, ed. Gerard O'Brien (Dublin, 1992), 34–49). **149** AI 1006.5. **150** CLH 655; 'Vita Mariani', AASS Feb. ii, 361–72: 368 (iii 15); Stefan Weber (ed. & tr.), *Iren auf dem Kontinent. Das Leben des Marianus Scottus von Regensburg und die Anfänge der irischen Schottenklöster* (Heidelberg, 2010), 126–7 §10; Flachenecker, *Schottenklöster*, 70. **151** AI 1080.3. **152** For a general survey see Kathleen Hughes, 'The Celtic church and the papacy', in C.H. Lawrence (ed.), *The English church and the papacy in the middle ages* (London, 1965), 3–28, repr. in Hughes, *Church and society*. **153** Kenney, *Sources*, 601 §420'; CLH 469–70 (Liège pilgrim letters to bishop Franco, 854×901); Helen Waddell, *The wandering scholars* (6th ed., London, 1954), 84–5. **154** Ailred of Rievaulx, 'Vita sancti Edwardi regis', PL 195, 738–90: 754–5. **155** Simon Young, 'Donatus, bishop of Fiesole 829–76, and the cult of St Brigit in Italy', *Cambr Mediev Celt Stud*, 35 (1998), 13–26; idem, 'Brigid of Kildare in early medieval Tuscany', *Studia Hibernica*, 30 (1998–9), 251–5; Donnacán mac Máele Tuile, scriba et ancorita, died in Italy (AU 843). **156** AU 928, AFM 926 (928); AU 929, AFM 927 (929). **157** AFM 929 (927). **158** AFM 1024.

offices in Ireland to become head of an Irish house in Rome in the early eleventh century and this might help to account for the unusual frequency of clerical and royal pilgrimages to Rome. Bishop Cellach Ó Selbaig, abbot of Cork, who died in 1036, had been a Roman pilgrim[159] and another distinguished Irish cleric died in Rome in 1038, namely, Coirpre ua Caímgilláin, coarb of Cainnech (i.e., superior of Aghaboe, diocese of Ossory, Queen's Co.).[160]

The annals record a string of Irish royal pilgrimages in the eleventh century: Flannacán ua Cellaig, king of Brega, and Sitric Silkenbeard, king of Dublin (r. 989–1036), in 1028; Flaithbertach an Trostáin 'pilgrim staff' Ó Néill, king of Ailech (r. 1004–30), in 1030–1 (he gave up the kingship during his pilgrimage); Amlaíb son of Sitric of Dublin in 1034 (he was killed on the way by the English); Laidcnén Ó Leocáin, king of Gailenga, and his wife in 1051; and Donnchad mac Briain, king of Ireland, in 1064.[161] The annals no longer list Roman pilgrimages in the twelfth century: evidently they had become too common to be noteworthy. In any case, they record only the pilgrimages of the great: the journeys of the less exalted are unlikely to be noticed.

Clearer evidence of an Irish house at Rome is found in the late eleventh century. A liturgical work belonging to S. Maria in Palladio on the Palatino contains two lists of Irish monks who occupied the neighbouring house, Sancta Trinitas (Trinità degli Scoti), towards the end of the eleventh century – a house that was still in existence in the thirteenth century.[162] The annals record the death of its superior in 1095: Eogan, 'head of the monks of the Irish in Rome'.[163] This foundation, and these long-established contacts, provide a context for pope Gregory VII's undated letter to Tairdelbach ua Briain, king of Ireland (r. 1063–86), and to the archbishops, bishops, abbots and superiors (*proceres*), dated variously (1076, 1078, 1080, 1083), and perhaps belonging to 1074.[164] The pope concludes: 'If any matters arise among you which seem worthy of our help, do not fail to send them to us at once, and with God's help you will obtain your just demands'. This implies that the Irish clerical elite was already in close touch with the papacy and that a reliable channel of communication was open.[165] The Irish in Rome were also in touch with their colleagues at home and this made the church in Ireland more aware of contemporary trends.

---

159 AI, AFM 1036. **160** AFM 1038. **161** AU 1028, 1030, 1034, 1051, 1064; AI, AFM, AT 1164; AC 1064 (1063); Waitz, *Mariani Scotti Chronicon*, 559 (1164). **162** André Wilmart, 'La Trinité des Scots à Rome', *Revue Bénédictine*, 41 (1929), 218–30; 44 (1932) 359–61; Anselmo M. Tommasini, *Irish saints in Italy*, tr. J.F. Scanlan (London, 1937), 95–9. **163** AI 1095. **164** Maurice P. Sheehy (ed.), *Pontificia hibernica: medieval papal chancery documents concerning Ireland, 640–1261* (2 vols, Dublin 1962–5), i 7–9. There is serious doubt about its claim to authenticity (Kenney, *Sources*, 768). **165** Aubrey Gwynn, 'Pope Gregory VII and the Irish church', *Ir Ecclesiast Rec*, 58 (1941), 97–109; idem, 'Ireland and the Continent', 200–3; Sheehy, *Pontificia hibernica*, i 7–8.

CONTINENTAL AND ENGLISH RELATIONS

Irish pilgrims and emigré clerics of the ninth century and later used long-established routes and traditional institutional connections, religious and intellectual, in Lotharingia, the Rhineland, Bavaria and further afield. Most were admired for their learning and piety but there was a predictable minority of Irish clerical wanderers (*clerici vagantes*), wastrels, itinerant monkish troublemakers (*gyrovagi*), chancers (*deceptores*) and gleemen, as the condemnations of church councils make clear.[166]

Irish pilgrim monks played an important role in the tenth-century monastic reform in Lotharingia, between the Rhine and the Aisne; the reformers were in close touch with the many Irish teachers and pilgrims in this area between the ninth and eleventh centuries; and Irish monks were often chosen as abbots because of their remarkable learning and asceticism.[167] There is little evidence for their direct involvement with the Cluniac reform, but Irish monks came under Cluniac influence indirectly, especially through Fleury, where Cluniac practices were observed, and some of their associates and patrons had strong Cluniac connections.[168] In 945 bishop Rudolf of Laon handed over the monastery of St-Michel-en-Thiérache and the convent of Bucilly to Irish monks and nuns. Among leading Irish figures were the bishop Forannán and the monks Forannán and Cathróe (a Scottish Gael educated at Armagh,[169] who got a like training at St-Benoît-sur-Loire). In 946, count Eilbert and his wife, Hersindis (who was a patroness of Irish pilgrims), founded the Benedictine monastery of Waulsort in the Ardennes and Otto I's foundation charter specifies that its lands are to belong to the Irish in perpetuity and its abbot is to be chosen from the Irish members of the community. Cathróe was selected as its first abbot and when he declined his place was taken shortly after by Mael Callann, who later moved to St-Michel-en-Thiérache. Another Mael Callann (†978), who had associations with Fleury, and later with Laon, is said to be the author of *Dialogus de statu sanctae ecclesiae* (961×965).[170] Some time before 953

---

166 Waddell, *Wandering scholars*, 76–7, 267–76. 167 Felim Ó Briain, 'Irish missionaries and medieval church reform', *Miscellanea historica Alberti de Meyer* (Louvain, 1946), 228–54; Josef Semmler, 'Iren in der Lothringischen Klosterreform', in Heinz Löwe (ed.), *Die Iren und Europa im früheren Mittelalter* (Stuttgart, 1982), 941–57. 168 Aubrey Gwynn, 'Irish monks and the Cluniac reform', *Studies* (Dublin), 29 (1940), 409–29 (repr. Aubrey Gwynn, *Irish church*, 1–16); N. Bulst, 'Irisches Mönchtum und cluniazensische Klosterreform', in Löwe, *Iren*, 958–69. 169 Alexander Boyle, 'St Cadroe in Scotland', *Innes Rev* 31 (1980), 3–6; D.N. Dumville, 'Saint Cathróe of Metz and the hagiography of exoticism', in John Carey, Máire Herbert & Pádraig Ó Riain (ed.), *Studies in Irish hagiography: saints and scholars* (Dublin, 2001), 172–88. 170 BCLL 195 (§725); Bulst, op. cit., 959–60; Dumville, op. cit. 185, denies his authorship of this tract.

the bishop of Metz, who ruled one of the richest ecclesiastical establishments in the Empire, appointed Cathróe abbot of St Felix-St Clement in Metz. When he died, probably in 971×976, he was succeeded by a distinguished Irish abbot, Fíngen. Some time between 1000 and 1005 bishop Adalbert II of Metz appointed Fíngen abbot of St Symphorion in Metz and finally bishop Haimo of Verdun appointed him abbot of St Vannes, making him abbot of three monasteries in two different dioceses. He died in 1005 and his virtues are commemorated in an anonymous poem, probably by an Irishman, written shortly after his death.[171] In Metz, too, in the tenth century, a shortened version of Adomnán's *Vita Columbae* (which concentrated on angelic visits and the saint's holy death) was written by an Irish scholar who carefully modernised the ancient name-forms of Adomnán's text, and this must mean that he was writing for Irish emigré readers.[172] Lotharingia had a taste for Irish Otherworld and wonder tales: there are several tenth- and eleventh-century Lotharingian manuscripts of the *Vitae Fursei* and the *Navigatio sancti Brendani*, two of the most famous examples of the genre.[173]

There were Irish associations with Cologne from the end of the eighth century and Sedulius Scottus had friendly relations with the bishop of Cologne in the mid-ninth. The monastery of Gross St Martin was founded by archbishop Bruno (*sed.* 955–65) and according to Marianus Scottus the Chronicler, who left Ireland in 1056 as a 'pilgrim for the kingdom of heaven and became a monk at Cologne on Thursday the first of August of that year', it was granted in perpetuity to the Irish in 975.[174] He lists its abbots among whom are Cillíne and Ailill (known to the German records as Elias), who came from Muckno, Co. Monaghan. Ailill also became abbot of St Pantaleon in 1019 at the request of his friend the archbishop, and ruled it until his death in 1042.[175] In 1027, Dúnchad mac Gilla Mo Chonna, abbot of Dunshaughlin and a member of the royal dynasty of Brega, described as 'the most outstanding scholar of the Irish', died at Cologne presumably as a pilgrim.[176] Bran mac Mael Mórda, king of Leinster (r. 1016–18), who was blinded by king Sitric of Dublin in 1018, ended his days in religious retirement at Cologne in 1052.[177] These Irish annalistic notices show that the Irish clergy at Cologne remained in close touch with their homeland.

171 Kenney, *Sources*, 608–10, 613 (§425–9, 437); Flachenecker, *Schottenklöster,* 47–8. 172 Jean-Michel Picard, 'The cult of Columba in Lotharingia (9th–11th centuries): the manuscript evidence', in Carey et al., *Studies in Irish hagiography*, 221–36. 173 Ibid., 233–4; MGH SRM 4, 423–51; Carl Selmer (ed.), *Navigatio Sancti Brendani* (Notre Dame IN, 1956, repr. Dublin, 1989), xxvi–l; idem, 'The beginnings of the St Brendan legend on the Continent', *Cath Hist Rev*, 29 (1943–4), 169–76. 174 Kenney, *Sources*, 529 (§336), 555, 613 (§439); Semmler, 'Iren', 946–55. 175 AFM 1042: Ailill Mucnama, cend manach na Gaoidheal, d'écc hi cColóin. 176 AU, AFM 1027.1. 177 AU, AFM 1052.

A list of relics in Holy Trinity Dublin, later Christ Church, acquired from Cologne some time after 1031, further points to intimate connections in the early episcopate of bishop Dúnán (†1074).[178]

In the tenth century, there was an Irish presence at Verdun, Toul and Trier. Cináed, Fíngen, Aed and Benedictus (probably Mael Bennachtan) were Irish clerics at Trier.[179] In the early eleventh century, an Irish monk called Carus (?Carthach), probably of St Clemens of Metz, reworked the Life of his patron in 1068 hexameters, and wrote the hymn 'Laus Cari de sancta cruce'.[180]

Würzburg is the foundation of St Kilian (in Irish, Cillíne), an Irish mission-ary monk who was martyred there in 687/89. Evidence for an Irish presence is scant thereafter. Irish manuscripts of the eighth century now preserved there,[181] may have been brought by the emigré Irish scholar, Clemens Scottus, who seems to have died there. In the eleventh century, and very likely long before, it was a place of Irish devotion. Marianus Scottus the Chronicler came on pilgrimage there in 1069 and was ordained priest 'beside the body of St Kilian'. David Scottus ('the Irishman'), an imperial propagandist in the interest of emperor Henry V (and his chaplain), was master of the cathedral school at Würzburg (1108/9–20) and was still there in 1137. He may have died in that year, some time after an Irish Benedictine house was established in Würzburg.[182] In 1161/2, Gilla na Naem Laigen, formerly reform bishop of Glendalough, died at Würzburg as abbot (*cenn manach*) of that house.[183] His namesake, Gilla na Naem (in Latin Nehemias) Ó Muirchertaig (†1149), bishop of Cloyne and friend of St Malachy, may have been a monk at Würzburg before becoming bishop.[184]

Emigré Irish ranged as far north as Hamburg. Among the evangelists sent to the pagans of the north by Adalbert, archbishop of Hamburg and Bremen (*sed.* 1043–72), was an Irish bishop called John, 'a holy and simple man', the first Christian missionary to the Wends. He was killed by them in the course of an uprising against the Christian prince Gottschalk in 1066 and is regarded as a

178 CLH 1320; John Clarke Crosthwaite (ed.), *Martyrology and book of obits of Christ Church* (Dublin, 1846), 3–4, 141; Pádraig Ó Riain, 'Dublin's oldest book? A list of saints "made in Germany"', in Seán Duffy (ed.), *Medieval Dublin*, v (Dublin, 2004), 52–72; Marie Therese Flanagan, *The transformation of the Irish church in the twelfth and thirteenth centuries*, Studies in Celtic History 29 (Woodbridge, 2010), 7–10. 179 Kenney, *Sources*, 610 (§430); Rainer Reiche, 'Iren in Trier', *Rheinische Vierteljahrblätter*, 40 (1976), 1–17; Flachenecker, *Schottenklöster*, 48. 180 CLH 482; Karl Strecker (ed.), MGH, PLAC 5/1–2 (Munich, 1937), 109–45; Gabriel Silagi (ed.), MGH, PLAC 5/3 (Munich, 1979), 659–60. 181 CLH 32, 304, 393–4, 800; CLA 9 §§1398–99, 1403, 1415–16; Ludwig Christian Stern (ed.), *Epistolae beati Pauli glosatae glosa inter-lineali* (Halle, 1910). 182 A. Gwynn, 'The continuity of the Irish tradition at Würzburg', Vorstand d. Würzburger Diözesangeschichtsvereins (ed.), *Herbipolis jubilans: 1200 Jahre Bistum Würzburg* (Würzburg, 1952), 57–81; Flachenecker, *Schottenklöster*, 165. 183 AFM 1160/61 (1085). This and the obits of three other bishops are misplaced (NHI ix 313). The annalists use *cenn manach* 'superior of monks' as the title for Irish Benedictine abbots on the Continent. 184 I owe this suggestion to Dr Ó Riain-Raedel.

martyr.[185] In the far south and east, at Melk, there was a lively devotion, under imperial patronage, to Colmán, an Irishman, tortured and executed as a spy at Stockerau in 1012 on his way to the Holy Land and whose tomb was erected by emperor Henry II.[186]

In the eleventh century, Regensburg, the political and commercial capital of the south, became the most significant Irish centre in Germany.[187] Already, about 1040, an Irish pilgrim, Muirchertach, arrived there from Aachen and the nuns of Obermünster permitted him to take a cell attached to their convent. Here he became famous for his sanctity. A generation later, a much more famous Irishman arrived, Muiredach mac Robartaig (fl. 1067–c.1080), known as Marianus Scottus the Scribe, a member of a distinguished Irish ecclesiastical family. He belonged to a group of three pilgrim monks whose original destination was Rome. They left Ireland in 1067, stayed a year at St Michael in Bamberg (where they appear to have become Benedictines) under the protection of the pro-imperial bishop Hermann and then moved on to Regensburg where they were welcomed by Willa, abbess of Obermünster (she is called 'mother of pilgrims') and, with the permission of the bishop, they were given a dependent church of her convent, Weih St Peter and its cells, on the outskirts of Regensburg.

Here, in return for the hospitality they received they became *inclusi* and laboured as scribes. In fact, three of the many manuscripts produced by Marianus and his companion, Eoin, survive. The first, Vienna, Österreichische Nationalbibliothek cod. lat. 1247, contains a copy of the Pauline epistles with a copious commentary, written by Marianus in caroline minuscule and signed by him. It was completed in May 1079. The second, now Edinburgh, NLS, Acc. 11218/1 olim Fort Augustus, Benedictine Abbey, Ratisbon 1 (AD 1080–3), contains eight ascetical treatises in Latin, six in the hand of Marianus (who died in 1080) and two in the hand of Eoin, who gives the year of writing as 1083. The third manuscript, now Princeton, University Library, Robert Garrett Collection 70, in the hand of Eoin, dated to 1081–2, is a copy of the *Dialogues* of St Gregory the Great.[188]

185 I.M. Lappenberg (ed.), *Adami Gesta Hammaburgensis ecclesiae pontificum*, MGH SS 7 (1845) 267–389: 355 §50; B. Schmeidler (ed.), *Adami Gesta Hammaburgensis ecclesiae pontificum*, MGH SRG us (Hannover & Leipzig, 1917), 193–4, 225; Bellesheim, *Geschichte*, i 334–5; Kenney, *Sources*, 614 (§442); John Ryan, 'Early Irish-German associations', *Capuchin Ann*, 36 (Dublin, 1969), 148–59: 157.   186 'Passio Cholomanni', 'De miraculis sancti Choromanni martyris', MGH SS 4, 674–8; Louis Gougaud, 'Les saints irlandais dans les traditions populaires des pays continentaux', *Revue Celtique*, 39 (1922), 199–226, 355–8: 223–4.   187 What follows is based mainly on P.A. Breatnach, *Die Regenburger Schottenlegende – Libellus de fundacione ecclesie consecrati Petri* (Munich, 1977); idem, 'The origins of the Irish monastic tradition at Ratisbon', *Celtica*, 13 (1980), 58–77; Flackenecker, *Schottenklöster*, 59–282; Frank Shaw, 'Karl der Grosse und die schottischen Heiligen', *Medium Ævum*, 45 (1976), 164–86; 'Vita Mariani', 361–72.   188 Mark Dilworth, 'Marianus Scotus – scribe and monastic founder', *Scott Gael Stud*, 10 (1965), 125–48; Françoise

A steady flow of Irish pilgrim monks came to Regensburg, originally from the north of Ireland, but from the beginning of the twelfth century postulants and financial support came mainly from the south. Weih St Peter and its Irish community was taken under the protection of the emperor Henry IV in February 1089 – and thus became independent of the bishop and free of dues and taxes. However, Weih St Peter had become too small for its community and about 1090 St James was founded. The precise date cannot be established: it is first mentioned in 1091 in a letter to Wratislaw II, king of Bohemia (a supporter of Henry V), with whom the Irish community at St James had a close relationship. In a formal diploma issued in March 1112 the emperor Henry V took the new church of St James under his protection as an imperial monastery, and this was soon followed by a series of papal privileges that put the monastery under the direct protection of the pope. From St James, other Irish Benedictine monasteries were founded elsewhere: St James at Würzburg (c.1134×1139), St James at Erfurt (c.1136), St Egidius at Nürnberg (c.1140), St James at Constance (c.1142), St Marien in Vienna (1155), the priory of Heilige Kreuz in Eichstätt (c.1155). Bishop Embricho of Würzburg consecrated the Irish Benedictine foundation of St James of Würzburg in 1138 and its first abbot was a saintly Irish monk called Macarius, who came with a small community from Regensburg.[189] St James at Erfurt was the most northerly and the only one in Thuringia. St Egidius at Nürnberg was a royal foundation, by emperor Conrad III and his queen, and here the Irish Benedictines took over the existing church of St Egidius and it flourished under Hohenstaufen patronage. Bishop Hermann of Constance (sed. 1138–65), a loyal follower of Conrad III, may have founded the Irish Benedictine house at Constance, at the suggestion of the emperor, in 1142.[190] It will be evident that Irish contacts were principally with the great imperial centres – in Lotharingia (Ghent, Liège, Toul, Verdun), in the valleys of the Rhine and the Main (Cologne, Mainz, Würzburg, Fulda, Bamberg), in Bavaria (Nürnberg, and notably Regensburg and Passau on the Danube) and in the Alpine lands (Constance, Reichenau, St Gall) – and Irish sympathies were often but not always with the German emperors in the late eleventh and early twelfth centuries.[191]

Henry & Geneviève Marsh-Micheli, 'A century of Irish illumination (1070–1170)', Proc Roy Ir Acad (C), 62 (1962), 101–64: 124–5; Ludwig Hammermayer, 'Die irischen Benediktiner "Schottenklöster" in Deutschland und ihr institutioneller Zusammenschluss vom 12. bis 16. Jahrhundert', Studien und Mitteilungen zur Geschichte des Benediktinerordens und seiner Zweige, 87 (1976), 249–338; Breatnach, 'Monastic tradition at Ratisbon', 63–4. **189** Flachenecker, Schottenklöster, 165–80. **190** Ibid., 180–205. **191** Denis Bethell, 'English monks and Irish reform in the eleventh and twelfth centuries', in T.D. Williams (ed.), Historical Studies, 8 (1971), 111–35.

The Irish in continental Europe remained in contact with their homeland. They needed a steady flow of the right kind of postulants from Ireland, in piety and scholarship, if their foundations were to survive, and this required that they maintain an intimate relationship with their communities of origin and with their former superiors in Ireland. Besides, the annals reflect the Irish domestic interest in the émigrés, some of whom held high office in Ireland before their departure, and the necrologies, annals and calendars of the Irish continental foundations provide evidence for the émigrés' continuing interest in their homeland.[192] The Irish Benedictine congregation sought financial aid in Ireland and won the patronage of Irish kings and bishops, some at least of whom were kinsmen. For example, Gilla Críst (in Latin Christianus) Mac Carthaig, abbot of Regensburg, died in Ireland a little before 1158 while collecting funds; and his successor, Gregory, was in Ireland about 1166 and returned to Germany with hagiographical texts as well as money. There was, then, a two-way flow of people, texts (literary and ecclesiastical) and ideas that kept the Irish church and some of the more important kings in close contact with circles in continental Europe, reform-minded and conservative, Gregorian and imperialist. Contrary to what some historians have believed, the Irish church was not an institution isolated from continental Europe, inward looking, even entropic, mindlessly conservative, and taken unawares by eleventh- and early twelfth-century developments originating on the Continent.

Neither were the Irish isolated from England, but their connections were with the English Benedictine houses of the tenth-century reform and, in post-Conquest times, this meant Evesham, Worcester, Glastonbury, Winchester, Durham, Canterbury and the like, but principally with houses in the west and north. Worcester manuscripts of the tenth and eleventh centuries show familiarity with Irish learning and indicate close contacts – through pilgrims, teachers and traders – between Worcester and Ireland.[193] Of the two 'noble cenobites', monks of 'outstanding probity' of the church of St Mary at Worcester who died in 1113, one was the Irishman Colmán.[194] Irish saints were celebrated in English

192 CLH 261; Alban Dold, 'Wessobrunner Kalendarblätter irischen Ursprungs', *Archivalische Z* 58 (1962), 11–33; Dagmar Ó Riain-Raedel (ed.), 'Das Nekrolog der irischen Schottenklöster: Edition der Handschrift Vat. lat. 10100 mit einer Untersuchung der hagiographischen und liturgischen Handschriften der Schottenklöster', *Beitr Gesch Bistums Regensburg*, 25 (1992) 7–119 (and cf. Ernst Hochholzer, 'Bemerkungen und Ergänzungen zu ein missglückten Edition', *Studien und Mitteilungen zur Geschichte des Benediktinerordens und seiner Zweige*, 106 (1995), 333–76); Dagmar Ó Riain-Raedel, 'Aspects of the promotion of Irish saints' cults in medieval Germany', *Z Celt Philol*, 29 (1982), 220–34; idem, 'Twelfth- and thirteenth-century Irish annals in Vienna', *Peritia*, 2 (1983), 127–35; idem, 'The travels of Irish manuscripts: from the Continent to Ireland', in Toby Barnard, Dáibhí Ó Cróinín & Katharine Simms (ed.), '*A miracle of learning*': *studies in manuscripts and Irish learning: essays in honour of William O'Sullivan* (Aldershot, 1998), 52–67. **193** Bethell, 'English monks', 116–18. **194** W. Stubbs (ed.), *Chronica magistri*

liturgy and Irish prayers and devotions influenced English prayer-books.[195] Until the eleventh century, Irish learning was well regarded in England. In addition, English-German contacts – ecclesiastical and commercial – were, like those of the Irish, with Lotharingia and the Rhineland, and Lotharingian bishops ruled several English sees before the Conquest. Notable Irish clerics became Benedictine monks in England and long before the Gregorian reform there were cultural and ecclesiastical exchanges and personal relationships between clergy in the Irish and English churches.

These became more formal on the establishment of the dioceses of Dublin and Waterford. The bishops of Dublin from 1074 to 1121 were Irishmen, trained as Benedictine monks in the province of Canterbury: Gilla Pátraic (in Latin Patricius), bishop of Dublin (*sed.* 1074–84), is said to have been formed at Worcester (but this is doubtful); his successor, Donngus (in Latin Donatus), bishop of Dublin (*sed.* 1085–95), was a Benedictine at Canterbury; and his successor and nephew, Samuel Ó hAindlide (*sed.* 1096–1121), was a Benedictine monk at St Alban's. Máel Ísu Ó hAinmire (in Latin Malchus), first bishop of Waterford (*sed. c.*1047–1135), had been a Benedictine monk at Winchester. What some historians see as the earliest stage of the reform, namely the creation of the earliest urban dioceses in Dublin and Waterford, represents, in some senses, an anglicisation of the Irish church, and Irish clerics were well aware of movements of thought and political conflicts within the English church.

IRISH ROYAL COUNCILS AND SYNODS

There had been mixed synods of clergy and laity in the ninth century but there are no references to synods in the Irish church in the tenth and eleventh centuries – very likely because the Irish records have been lost. However, kings engaged in legislation in mixed assemblies of laymen and clerics, and this legislation is marked by religious concerns. A few are mentioned in the annals in the eleventh century. The first is 'a law and ordinance' enacted by Donnchad mac Briain (r. 1014–63) in 1040: 'that none should dare to steal or do feats of arms on Sunday, or go out on Sunday carrying any load'.[196] Clerical inspiration must lie behind this insistence on Sunday observance – a long-standing con-

Rogeri de Houedene, RS 51 (4 vols, London 1868–71), i 168. **195** Robert Bartlett, 'Cults of Irish, Scottish and Welsh saints in twelfth-century England', in Brendan Smith (ed.), *Britain and Ireland, 900–1300: Insular responses to medieval European change* (Cambridge, 1999), 67–86; Kathleen Hughes, 'Some aspects of Irish influence on early English private prayer', *Studia Celtica*, 5 (1970), 48–61. **196** AI 1040.6.

cern that had been legislated on *c*.700 and later.[197] The legislation against war and violence on Sunday seems to reflect the contemporary peace movement in Aquitaine and other parts of France.[198] In 1050 the lords and clergy of Munster assembled under their king at Killaloe, at a time of famine and social disorder when 'no protection was extended to church or fortress, gossipred or mutual oath' and 'they enacted law and a restraint upon every injustice, from small to great'.[199] Here the annalist implies that there was a serious law-making programme on issues concerned with crime and social order.

It is likely that there were many other legislative assemblies of kings, lords and clerics in the eleventh century, and these may pre-figure the reforming synods of the early and mid twelfth century. These synods, the high points of a much more general and continuous local synodal activity, were at first mixed assemblies of kings and clerics, as Irish synods had usually been, but when the reformers became more confident of their powers, as they did in the fourth decade of the twelfth century, the kings were excluded.

These reformers proposed a revolution in the administration of the Irish church that affected the mission, personnel and property of every ecclesiastical institution from the humblest parish church and hermit's cell to the greatest foundations. Concurrently, they proposed a root-and-branch reformation of marital law and sexual mores that was intended to bring Irish social life into full consonance with what they thought was the ideal model of Christian social life, however impractical, as set out in canon law that looked back to the age of Jerome and Augustine. The attitudes of the reformers and specifically their censorious representations of their own church and society to others, and especially to the reforming papacy and its agents, activities at once hypercritical and unrealistic, were to have far-reaching consequences for Ireland.

197 CLH 625–6; Vernam E. Hull (ed. & tr.), 'Cáin domnaig', *Ériu*, 20 (1966), 151–77; J.G. O'Keeffe (ed. & tr.), 'Cain domnaig, 1. The epistle concerning Sunday', *Ériu*, 2 (1905), 189–214; Máire Herbert (tr.), 'Letter of Jesus on Sunday observance' in Máire Herbert & Martin McNamara (ed.), *Irish biblical apocrypha: selected texts in translation* (Edinburgh, 1989), 50–4 §16.   198 H.E.J. Cowdrey, 'The peace and the truce of God in the eleventh century', *Past & Present* 46 (1970), 42–67; Thomas F. Head & R.A. Landes, *The peace of God: social violence and religious response in France around the year 1000* (Ithaca NY, 1992); Thomas F. Head, 'The development of the peace of God in Aquitaine (970–1005)', *Speculum*, 74 (1999), 656–86.   199 AI 1052.2, AFM 1050.

CHAPTER II

Reforming lay society: Irish marriage and divorce

IRISH MARITAL AND SEXUAL BEHAVIOUR is the main, almost the exclusive, preoccupation of the reformers when it came to their programme for the betterment of the lives of the laity and this insistent concern runs as a leitmotiv through the entire period of the reform. Other crimes and serious sins – parricide, murder, treachery, rapine and theft, eloquently denounced by Irish religious writers and teachers[1] – are largely ignored. The marital and sexual practices encountered by the Gregorian reformers, and repeatedly condemned by them, are complex ones and need to be discussed here in some detail for several reasons: they reveal a great deal about the structure of Irish society in the eleventh and twelfth centuries, they help us understand the minds of the reformers, and they have not been well understood by modern historians. What is more significant, these charges soon brought the Irish, Scottish and Welsh churches and peoples into disrepute in the eyes of English and continental observers and had serious consequences for the English racial and religious perception of the Irish, including the allegation of barbarism – even paganism – down to the Protestant Reformation and beyond[2] and its use as a justification for aggression, expropriation, colonisation and religious repression. The principal charges made against the Irish are that they divorce and remarry, that they exchange wives, and that they do not observe the church's incest prohibitions.

We begin with an admonition in pope Gregory VII's letter to archbishop Lanfranc of Canterbury, dated July 1073, not long after the pope's consecration and previous to Lanfranc's letters to the Irish kings:

> that you strive by every means open to you to ban the wicked practice which we have heard rumoured of the Irish (*Scotti*): namely, that many of them not only desert their lawful wives but even sell them.[3]

1 CLH 170, 175; J.G. O'Keeffe (ed. & tr.), 'A poem on the day of judgment', *Ériu*, 3 (1907), 29–33; Stokes, 'Adamnan's Second Vision', 422–8; 'Fís Adomnán', LU 67–76: 74. 2 John Gillingham, *The English in the twelfth century: imperialism, national identity and political values* (Woodbridge, 2000), 15–18, 43–4, 102–9, 145–50; N.P. Canny, *The Elizabethan conquest of Ireland: a pattern established* (Hassocks & New York, 1976), 123; Hiram Morgan, 'Giraldus Cambrensis and the Tudor conquest of Ireland', in idem (ed.), *Political ideology in Ireland, 1541–1641* (Dublin, 1999), 22–44. 3 Helen Clover & Margaret Gibson (ed. & tr.), *The letters of Lanfranc archbishop of Canterbury* (Oxford, 1979), 64–7 (letter 8) = Philip Jaffé (ed.),

Evidently, the pope has been given an overstated and misleading account of divorce and sexual mores in Gaelic society, written by an outsider or by a fervent domestic reformer. This widely disseminated text, with some additions and modifications, lies behind the standard set of charges levelled at the Irish throughout the period of the Gregorian reform and beyond, as we shall see.

Lanfranc, with concerns more than merely pastoral, takes up the matter with the Irish kings. In his letter to Gofraid mac Amlaíb, king of Dublin (r. ?1072–4), written in 1073/4, he states:

> There are said to be men in your kingdom who take wives from either their own kindred or that of their deceased wives; others who by their own will and authority abandon the wives who are legally married to them; some who give their own wives to others and by an abominable exchange receive the wives of other men instead. For the sake of God and your own soul command that these offences and any others like them be corrected throughout the land which you rule, and with God's help so treat your subjects that those who love good may cherish it the more and those who lust after evil may never venture to do wrong.[4]

Lanfranc expands on some of the pope's charges and adds the matter of canonical incest and the strange allegation of exchanging wives (which is, as one expects, without foundation). In his letter to Tairdelbach ua Briain, king of Ireland, sent about the same time, he writes:

> But among many things which are commendable certain reports have reached us which are quite the opposite: namely that in your kingdom a man abandons at his own discretion and without any grounds in canon law the wife who is lawfully married to him, not hesitating to form a

Monumenta gregoriana (Berlin, 1865), 520–1. Clover & Gibson take it that *Scotti* refers to the Irish. Aubrey Gwynn ('Lanfranc and the Irish church', *Ir Ecclesiast Rec* 57 (1941), 481–500: 495) thinks it means Scots, and perhaps also Irish; in a revised version of the paper (A. Gwynn, *Irish church*, 68–83: 73) he had become sure that Scots were meant. W.D.H. Sellar, 'Marriage, divorce and concubinage in Gaelic Scotland', *Trans Gaelic Soc Inverness*, 51 (1978), 464–93: 470 thinks the letter refers to Ireland. In fact, both countries had much the same social structure and the pope's further instruction to stamp out like vice in 'insula Anglorum' also seems to indicate that Ireland is intended. The strange notion of selling wives may be a misunderstanding of the terms governing divorce in Irish law which require that all the divorced wife's assets that she brought into a marriage and her share in the profits generated within the marriage must be handed back to her (*Cáin lánamna* §§9–18 = Rudolf Thurneysen (ed. & tr.), 'Cáin lánamna', in D.A. Binchy & Myles Dillon (ed.), *Studies in early Irish law* (Dublin, 1936), 1–80: 27–39, repr. Thurneysen, *Gesammelte Schriften*, i–iii, ed. De Bernardo Stempel & Ködderitzsch (Tübingen, 1991), iii 287–366. **4** Clover & Gibson, *Letters of Lanfranc*, 66–9 (letter 9) = PL 150, 535–6 (letter 37).

criminal alliance – by the law of marriage or rather by the law of forni-
cation – with any other woman he pleases, either a relative of his own or
of his deserted wife or a woman whom someone else has abandoned in
an equally disgraceful way.[5]

The same kind of charges are repeated by Anselm, archbishop of
Canterbury, obviously depending directly on the correspondence of his predecessor kept in the Canterbury archives, in two letters to Muirchertach Ó Briain,
king of Ireland, written in 1095–6:

> It is reported among us that marriages are dissolved in your kingdom
> without any reason, and wives are given in exchange; and that kinsmen
> are not ashamed to have intercourse either under the name of marriage
> or in some other way, publicly and without rebuke, against all the pro-
> hibitions of canon law.[6] ... It has been said to us that men exchange their
> wives for the wives of others as freely and publicly as a man might
> exchange his horse for a horse or any other property; and that they
> abandon their wives at will and without any cause. How evil this is any
> man who knows the law of Christ will understand.[7]

Here Anselm adds little apart from inflated rhetoric and some exaggeration.

St Bernard's *Life of St Malachy*, written in 1149 and based on his conversa-
tions with Malachy, with four Irish monks who had studied at Clairvaux, and
on a document supplied by abbot Comgán of the Cistercian house of
Inislounaght, Co. Tipperary, added something quite new to the current descrip-
tions of Irish society and its church. This tedious and tendentious hagiography,
essentially an *exemplum* of the truly holy man intended for his continental contemporaries, brimming with pious platitudes and heavy with biblical ballast, is
nonetheless an essential source for the twelfth-century church because of the
quality of the information that lies behind it. A widely-read text, it made
Malachy a saint but did his country grave wrong. Bernard is loud (as ever) in
self-righteous denunciation of what he does not quite understand, particularly
the organisation of the Irish church, and high-flown in a rhetoric that points
up the outstanding holiness of his hero: the godly man came from a barbarous
and wicked people and thus his sanctity was truly remarkable – in fact, a divine
miracle – that all the more redounded to his credit.

5 Ibid. 70–3 (letter 10) = PL 150, 536–7 (letter 38).   6 Ussher, *Whole works*, iv 520–1; A. Gwynn, 'St Anselm
and the Irish church', *Ir Ecclesiast Rec*, 59 (1942), 1–14: 13–4.   7 Ussher, *Whole works*, iv 523–4.

Our Malachy was born in Ireland of a barbarous people, was brought up
there, and there received his education. But from the barbarism of his
birth he contracted no taint, any more than fishes of the sea from their
native salt. But how delightful to reflect that uncultured barbarism
should have produced for us so worthy a fellow-citizen with the saints
and members of God's household ... Malachy instituted anew the
wholesome usage of confession, the sacrament of confirmation, the marriage contract – of all of which they were either ignorant or negligent ...
It was when he was just entering the thirtieth year of his age that he was
consecrated bishop and brought to Connor; for that was the name of the
city. But when he began to administer his office, the man of God understood that he had been sent not to men but to beasts. Never before had
he known the like, in whatever depth of barbarism; never had he found
men so shameless in regard to morals, so dead in regard to rites, so impi-
ous in regard to faith, so barbarous in regard to laws, so stubborn in
regard to discipline, so unclean in regard to life. They were Christians in
name, in fact pagans. There was no giving of tithes or first fruits; no
entry into lawful marriage, no making of confessions: nowhere could be
found any who would either seek penance or impose it. Ministers of the
altar were exceedingly few. But indeed what need was there of more
when the few were almost in idleness and ease among the laity? There
was no fruit which they could bring forth from their offices among a
people so vile. For in the churches there was not heard the voice of the
preacher or singer. What was the athlete of God to do?[8]

Malachy was appointed bishop of Connor against his will. It is evident from
Bernard's narrative that it still rankled deeply with him that he had to resign as
archbishop of Armagh (1132–6) for political reasons. Evidently, he thought that
as leader of the reform he should be primate, and here ambition can be clothed

---

8 *Vita S. Malachiae*, §§1, 16 = H.J. Lawlor (tr.), *St Bernard of Clairvaux's Life of St Malachy of Armagh*
(London & New York, 1920), 6, 36–7. For this text, see J. Leclercq, C.H. Talbot & H.M. Rochais (ed.),
Sancti Bernardi opera (8 vols, Rome 1957–77), iii (1963) 307–78 (the best edition) = Jean Mabillon (ed.),
Sancti Bernardi abbatis Claræ-Vallensis Opera omnia (4th ed. rev. Paris, 1839), ii 1465–1524, repr. PL 182,
1073–1118; AASS Nov. ii/1, 135–66; Lawlor (tr.), *St Bernard of Clairvaux's Life of St Malachy of Armagh*
(London & New York, 1920). With the exception of AASS, which has its own system of paragraph numbering (given in parentheses by Lawlor), all the others use Mabillon's paragraph numbering, and reference is here made only to that numbering. The Life of St Lorcán Ua Tuathail (s. xiii[1]) is textually
dependent on Bernard's Life and opens with the same charge of barbarism: Lorcán lived 'in the middle
of a depraved and perverse nation'; 'he drew no more from the barbarism of his land than a sea-fish
draws salt from the brine' (Charles Plummer (ed.), 'Vie et miracles de S. Laurent, archêveque de Dublin',
Analecta Bollandiana, 33 (1914), 121–86: 128).

in perceived duty. His continuing embittered and unforgiving attitude to the vanquished Uí Shínaig and his need to paint them blacker than they were reveal his injured pride and his self-righteousness. He was persuaded, against his will and with great reluctance, to take Connor by his teacher Ímar Ó hAedacáin and by the archbishop of Armagh, Gilla Meic Liac (*sed.* 1137–74).[9] Here Bernard's text is based directly on Malachy's own account of the conditions of the diocese of Connor on his becoming bishop, and that, in turn, is conditioned by his dislike of Connor. Here, for the first time, the charges of barbarism, and of being Christians in name but pagans in fact, enter the record. The originator is the injudicious Malachy, the propagator the credulous Bernard who knew nothing of Connor but what Malachy had told him. Whether Malachy, on his arrival in Rome, was equally imprudent with pope Innocent II, we do not know, but we may suspect.

There are serious inconsistencies. How, for example, could a cleric brought up in Armagh be quite unaware of the cultural and spiritual condition of the people of Connor a mere 52 km away? How could Connor, but evidently not Armagh or other dioceses, have fallen into such a state? How could an allegedly barbaric Irish society produce learned and ascetic abbots such as Ó hAedacáin, on whom Bernard lavishes praise? How could such a deep lapse from religion and civility be put right in Connor by Malachy in a few years, as Bernard asserts?

But Bernard, despite his windy rhetoric and contradictions, was taken at his word and read all over Europe. The new charges of barbarism and of being Christians in name but pagans in fact were now applied to the whole people. These subsume the perceived sexual irregularities of the Irish laity and clergy – now mere further symptoms of barbarism – and were soon taken up and reappear in three very significant places: in the papal letter *Laudabiliter satis* issued to Henry II by pope Adrian IV in 1155/6, in the three letters of pope Alexander III (1172), and in the widely disseminated writings of Giraldus Cambrensis, a court clerk, and an ambitious and disappointed political churchman. In these latter, Bernard's happy ending, the triumph of Malachy's pastoral care and reforms over all evils, is notably absent.

Pope Adrian IV commends Henry II for 'striving, as a true catholic prince should, to enlarge the boundaries of the church, to reveal the truth of the Christian faith to peoples still untaught and barbarous …'.[10] Remarkable as this extreme statement may be, it is more subdued than those of his successor. The

---

9 *Vita Malachiae* §16 ; Lawlor, *Life of Malachy*, 36. **10** Sheehy, *Pontificia*, i 15–16 §4; A.B. Scott & F.X. Martin (ed. & tr.), *Expugnatio hibernica: the conquest of Ireland by Giraldus Cambrensis* (Dublin, 1978), 144–5; David C. Douglas & George W. Greenaway (ed.), *English historical documents* ii (2nd ed., London, 1981), 828–30.

charge of barbarism, that orginated from Malachy and his coterie of advanced reformers, and such chosen successors as Gilla Críst Ó Con Áirge, was spread far and wide by the detractive eloquence of Bernard.[11] It now entered the vocabulary of the papacy and the records of the papal chancery.

The letter of pope Alexander III to Henry II of England, written at Tusculum, 20 September 1172, contains the final set of sexual charges, embedded in a context of allegations of barbarism and filth.[12]

The spurious *Quoniam ea* or 'Privilege of Alexander III' in some manuscripts of Giraldus Cambrensis (it is not certain whether he concocted it himself) echoes the words of Bernard:

> This we do in order that, once the vile practices of that land have been stamped out, this barbarous nation, Christian only in name, may by your diligent efforts take on a new comeliness in the sphere of morals, and that after the church of that land, hitherto undisciplined, has been reduced to order, thanks to your efforts, that race may in the future really earn the name of Christian which they now profess.[13]

Giraldus sums up:

> This is a filthy people, wallowing in vice … They do not … contract marriages. They do not avoid incest … Moreover, and surely this is a detestable thing, and contrary not only to the Faith but to any feeling of honour – men in many places in Ireland, I shall not say marry, but rather debauch, the wives of their dead brothers. They abuse them in having such evil and incestuous relations with them. In this (wishing to imitate the ancients more eagerly in vice than in virtue) they follow the apparent teaching, and not the true doctrine, of the Old Testament.[14]

11 Diarmuid Scully, 'The portrayal of Ireland and the Irish in Bernard's Life of St Malachy', in Damian Bracken & Dagmar Ó Riain-Raedel (ed.), *Ireland and Europe in the twelfth century: reform and renewal* (Dublin, 2006), 239–56. **12** Sheehy, *Pontificia*, i 21–2 §6; Edmund Curtis & R.B. McDowell (ed.), *Irish historical documents, 1172–1922* (Dublin, 1943), 20–1; Douglas & Greenaway, op. cit. 832. **13** Scott & Martin, *Expugnatio*, 146–7; Maurice P. Sheehy, 'The bull *Laudabiliter*: a problem in medieval diplomatique and history', *J Galway Hist Archaeol Soc*, 29 (1961), 45–70: 64–6. **14** *Topographia hibernica*, iii 19 (J.S. Brewer, J.F. Dimock & G.F. Warner (ed.), *Giraldi Cambrensis Opera*: v. *Topographia hibernica et Expugnatio hibernica* (London, 1867), 164–5; J.J. O'Meara (tr.), *The history and topography of Ireland* (London, 1982), 106 §98); Thomas O'Loughlin, 'Giraldus Cambrensis and the sexual agenda of the twelfth-century reformers', *J Welsh Relig Hist*, 8 (2000), 1–15. By about 1170 confused claims of Irish depravity, heresy, and apostasy, mixed up with Rhineland anti-semitism, occur in the writings of Hildegard of Bingen (1098–1179), the German mystic ('Vita Disibodi', i 2=PL 197, 1099–1100; Louis Gougaud, *Christianity in the Celtic lands* (London, 1932, repr. Dublin, 1993), 72).

Giraldus had a distasteful interest in bestiality and his salacious and credulous tales of two alleged instances of this in Ireland, on the same level as his account of the bearded lady, witches in the form of hares, and the wolf who talked with a priest, still served to convey to his readers an image of outlandish depravity among the Irish.[15]

The understandings of Irish marital and sexual mores, as set out by the archbishops of Canterbury, Bernard, popes Adrian IV and Alexander III and others, are based to a degree on real differences of behaviour but mostly on differences of perception.

It needs to be pointed out that Old Irish is the first European vernacular to have a legal technical term for *sponsus, sponsa (coniunx)*, the canonical marriage partner, namely, *cétmuinter*. This is attested c.AD 650. Ideally, this marriage is life-long,[16] and in the law tract *Cáin lánama* it comes first as the primary and most privileged form of marriage.[17] Though privileged, a *cétmuinter* may not contract independently of her husband.[18] If a man gives bridewealth to a secondary wife (*adaltrach* lit. 'adulteress') it falls forfeit to his *cétmuinter*.[19] A child of a *cétmuinter* marriage is the ideal heir to kingship. However, society, as usual, fell far short of clerical lawyers' ideals and Irish law permitted divorce and remarriage (some of the reasons are allowed in canon law, for example non-consummation), secondary wives and concubines and the offspring of such unions were generally regarded as legitimate and heirs.

Marriage within the forbidden degrees of kindred posed a major problem for the churchmen who, in their bid to control marriage and reproduction, set out to establish new norms and increasingly strict rules of exclusion that had no warrant in scripture, patristics or custom. All over Europe lineages tended towards endogamy, namely, to marry their close relatives in order to preserve family estates and foster the ideology of kinship on which they based their power; equally, the church opposed the marriage of close relatives and extended the bounds of incest prohibitions. Marriage within the sixth degree according to canonical computation, that is, between second cousins or closer, was widely

---

15 *Giraldi Opera*, v 108–10 (ii 21, 23); O'Meara, *Topography*, 73–5 §§54, 56; for Giraldus's specious later defence of his unseemly preoccupation and his absurd insistence that his accounts were true, see Yves Lefèvre, R.B.C. Huygens & Brian Dalton (ed. & tr.), *Giraldus Cambrensis: Speculum duorum* (Cardiff, 1974), 168.   **16** CIH vi 2231.1–8 (*Bretha nemed*): '… ar us [=is] e triar nad scara comudh co bas: ceile fri tigerna iar ndigbail tsed do dernuind, manach fria airchindech, cetmuinter dligthech fria ceile iar n-urnaidm'.   **17** *Cáin lánama* §§3–28.   **18** Rudolf Thurneysen, 'Irisches Recht', *Abh Preuss Akad Wiss*, philhist Kl, Jhrg 1931, Nr 2 (Berlin, 1931), 25 §38; repr. *Gesammelte Schriften*, 3 vols (Tübingen, 1991), iii 175–262; cf. 'Irisches Recht' §§28–9; *Cáin lánama* §§21–2; D.A. Binchy (ed.), *Críth gablach*, MMIS 11 (Dublin, 1941), 16 line 410 ('Cétmuinter co córus lánrechta lánamna comcheniúil', wife of the *aire túise*); CIH i 7.29 ('fuil fearus cétmuinter oc etach techta'); ii 401.14 ('folach cétmuintiri') for other provisions. **19** *Cáin lánama* §23.

forbidden in the sixth century. In Irish terms, this ruled out members of one's *gelfhine* and *derbfhine,* the basic property-owning kin, respectively the male descendants of a common grandfather and great-grandfather. This made it very difficult to consolidate family lands by strategic marriage. This arose particularly in the case of inheriting females (in default of male heirs) who took a life-interest in family estates and could transmit an interest to their children only by marrying one of the patri-lateral heirs, usually a first or second cousin. A way out was found in the parallel cousin marriage of the Old Testament, and Irish canonists explicitly quote as a precedent the marriage of the daughters of Salphaad, with God's approval, to their father's brother's sons. This enabled Irish lawyers to justify, with cogent arguments drawn from the bible, marriage to first and second cousins, which had been condemned by earlier church councils.[20]

In continental Europe, legal thinking set off in the opposite direction. Beginning in the first half of the ninth century and for reasons that have never been satisfactorily explained, the forbidden degrees came to be increased from six (in some areas from four) to seven, and the way of calculating them was completely changed: relationship was now determined by counting back to the common ancestor and thus marriage was forbidden between all those who were seventh or less in descent from a common ancestor, that is, one could not marry one's sixth cousin or closer – and this absurd rule was expressly formulated in a canon of pope Alexander II in 1076.[21] Only royals and aristocrats (if they) are likely to know who their fifth and sixth cousins are; and illiterate commoners were totally at sea (if anyone cared about them). In practical terms, these rules of consanguinity were impossible to observe (the forbidden degrees were reduced to four at the Fourth Lateran Council in 1215 in an attempt to bring some sense into things) and in continental Europe royal lineages found it very difficult to get suitable wives who fell outside the prohibited relationships and could, therefore, produce the legitimate offspring that alone could inherit.[22] However, the new rules were accepted as authoritative by the reforming churchmen who attempted to impose them on royalty and aristocracy, with some limited success in the tenth and eleventh centuries. When they encountered Irish practices they were aghast at what they saw as flagrant incest and degeneracy and a public flouting of the laws of the church. In fact, Irish practices were

---

20 Nm 26:28–34, 36:10–12; Hib 32:20. D. Ó Corráin, 'Irish law and canon law', 157–61. Giraldus's disparaging reference to the Irish use of the Old Testament (cited above) suggests that he encountered this justification of Irish practices while in Ireland. 21 Joseph Freisen, *Geschichte des kanonischen Eherechts* (Paderborn, 1963), 371–439; Constance B. Bouchard, 'Consanguinity and noble marriage in the tenth and eleventh centuries', *Speculum,* 52 (1981), 268–87: 269–71; Jack Goody, *The development of the family and marriage in Europe* (Cambridge, 1983), 134–46. 22 Bouchard, 'Consanguinity', 273–86.

every bit as well founded as continental ones, but that did not matter: what was in question was an apparent authoritative teaching and the reformers were determined to impose it, regardless of practical difficulties.

Marital prohibitions were also based on affinity, the relationship established by sexual intercourse, licit or illicit, consensual or not.[23] Here, too, Irish society was found deficient by the reformers. Jewish law, for example, forbade a man to marry his step-mother, step-daughter, mother-in-law or daughter-in-law. Over time, the medieval church extended the prohibitions based on affinity to the same limits as consanguinity. The reformers held rigidly to this view and it caused great problems and doubts in the arrangement of dynastic marriages. The difficult eighth canon of the first synod of Cashel (1101) deals with marriage prohibitions that arise from affinity, and only those. The canon states: *gan ben a athar ná a senathar, nó a siúr nó a <h->inghean, do beith 'na mnaoi ag fear i nÉirinn, nó bean a dhearbhráthar, nó bean ar bith chomh fogus sin i ngaol do* 'that no man in Ireland shall have to wife his father's wife or his grandfather's wife, or her sister or her daughter, or his brother's wife, or any other woman so near related'.[24] What is in question here, in the first instance, is a prohibition of marriage with one's step-mother or one's step-grandmother – a prohibition well-founded in St Paul's severe condemnation of a case in Corinth (1 Cor 5:1–8; cf. Lv 18:8). I understand 'her sister or her daughter' as a prohibition against marrying the sister or daughter of either of these women. Some scholars have interpreted this part of the canon as forbidding brother-sister and father-daughter marriage (notably Standish H. O'Grady and D.A. Binchy).[25] This is very improbable because incest of this kind is likely to be as unusual and as socially abhorrent in Ireland as elsewhere in Western Europe: it hardly needs to be legislated against in a church council and, besides, it is never laid as a charge against the Irish. Further, the entire thrust of this canon is against unions forbidden because of affinity, not consanguinity. Next, the canon forbids a man to marry his brother's (or half-brother's) wife. Finally, a man is forbidden to marry any woman as closely related to him by affinity as all the foregoing – a rule that probably excludes all non-consanguine direct descendants of these women.

---

23 DTC i 518–27. 24 Tadhg Ó Donnchadha (ed.), *An Leabhar Muimhneach* (Dublin, 1940), 341 (my text is from Ó Donnchadha's edition; I emend his *shiúr* to *siúr*); Standish H. O'Grady (ed. & tr.), *Caithréim Thoirdhealbhaigh*, ITS 26–7 (2 vols, London, 1929, repr. Dublin, 1988), i 174–5 (text), ii 185 (translation); A. Gwynn, 'The first synod of Cashel' *Ir Ecclesiast Rec*, 66 (1945), 81–92; 67 (1946), 109–22 (rev. repr. in Gwynn, *Irish church*, 155–79). 25 O'Grady, op. cit., ii 185; Binchy, cited in Kathleen Hughes, *The church in early Irish society* (London, 1966), 264 (Binchy's argument is linguistic, not legal, and is intrinsically weak); Gwynn, *Irish church*, 167–70.

In fact, the canon addresses precisely the practices later complained about
by pope Alexander III in 1172, as we have seen. True, the pope makes an additional charge: 'many of them abandon the mother and marry the daughters';
this is not to be understood as father-daughter incest but the offence against
affinal prohibitions committed by a man who marries the daughter of his
divorced wife by another man. The fathers of the synod of Cashel in 1101 were
both courageous and trendy – courageous because they tackled a central ele-
ment in royal and aristocratic social life, trendy because their ruling was based
on contemporary continental canonical thinking though it does not, explicitly
at least, insist on the now current extent of the affinity prohibition. The circumstances in which a man might marry his step-mother, his grand-step-
mother, or their sisters or daughters arise in a society that practises polygynous
marriage, divorce and dynastic alliances by marriage within a relatively narrow
aristocratic elite. Here older aristocrats tend to marry, as later wives, women as
young as their sons and grandsons by earlier wives, and these women (and their
female descendants) become sexually available again, licitly or illicitly, usually
as widows or divorcées, when they are still quite young. The socio-sexual tension created by such marriages is the theme of the superb Old-Irish tale, *Fingal
Rónáin*.[26] Add to this other considerations – aristocratic marriage involves
property and political strategies among men of power – there is a limited pool
of high-status women who can be used diplomatically in forming alliances
between dynasties, and the Irish divorced and remarried freely. For the eleventh
and twelfth centuries the Lecan prose *Banshenchas* lists royal and aristocratic
marriages between about fifty families, many of whom intermarry repeatedly
over and between generations.[27] One can see at once how the niceties of affinal
prohibitions, especially the extremist rules now being pushed by the reformers
on the Continent, were not likely to be observed at the higher levels of Irish
society. Given that the fathers of Cashel legislated against breaches of the rules
governing affinity, it is hardly credible that they failed to legislate also against
incestuous marriage between consanguines: it is thus likely that some of the
decrees of the synod of Cashel have been lost.

In the matter of divorce and remarriage, the prudent tolerances of the very
early middle ages came to be displaced by the stricter teaching of St Augustine
on indissolubility and the prohibition of re-marriage. In fact, the Augustinian

26 CLH 1056; Kuno Meyer (ed. & tr.), 'Fingal Rónáin: how Rónán slew his son', *Revue Celtique*, 13 (1892),
368–97; David Greene (ed.), *Fingal Rónáin and other stories*, MMIS 16 (Dublin, 1955), 2–15; T.M. Charles-
Edwards, 'Honour and status in some Irish and Welsh tales', *Ériu*, 29 (1978), 123–41; Tomás Ó Cathasaigh,
'The rhetoric of *Fingal Rónáin*', *Celtica*, 17 (1985), 123–44. 27 CLH 795; Margaret E. Dobbs (ed. & tr.),
'The Ban-Shenchus', *Revue Celtique*, 48 (1931), 189–200.

position became the cornerstone of the Carolingian reform programme (itself more aspirational than effective), and by the twelfth century it had triumphed in the Western church – as an objective, not a reality.[28] Reformers insisted that marital regulations fell solely within the competence of ecclesiastical jurisdiction and they required that marriage should be monogamous, indissoluble, consensual and exogamous. Only within marriage was sex licit, and there only if procreative; and concubinage, which was tolerated in the early christian period, was forbidden.[29] This is the theory: the practice was different. The church might make rules as it wished, but human nature and social practice did not change, and this is especially true of royalty and aristocracy whose privileged economic and social position gave them access to many women. The Merovingians had been genuinely polygynous.[30] The Carolingians were less so: they mostly practised serial monogamy, which was enabled by easy divorce and remarriage, and they mated polygynously, though in Carolingian times the sons of concubines did not tend to succeed. Elsewhere in Europe, in Norway for example, polygyny continued and the children of concubines were not excluded from succession.[31] What happened in Western Europe generally in the eleventh and twelfth centuries was that upper-class men (women had less freedom) married monogamously and mated polygynously, that it to say, they had one lawful wife, more-or-less in accord with the rules of the church, and relative ease of annulment made new licit wives possible. Besides that they had what were, in the eyes of the church, seriously sinful illicit relationships with other women – many were concubines within the lordly household, many more were casual contacts outside it. In the eyes of the church these were sinful acts, not marriage partnerships. This represented a formal change, an altered perspective that did not change sexual activity as such but regulated it in a way that was different from that of early medieval Europe. While marriage became more-or-less monogamous and at least formally indissoluble, men of power – political or economic – continued to have sexual access to many women, and the best efforts of the church had little effect on this practice throughout the middle ages, on the laity or on its own clergy, higher or lower.[32] In effect, the church-

---

28 Theodulf of Orleans (†818), PL 105, 213; Council of Friuli (796×797), MGH Concilia ii 192–93; Council of Paris (AD 829), MGH Concilia ii 671; pope John VIII (sed. 872–82), PL 126, 746; P.L. Reynolds, *Marriage in the western church: the christianization of marriage during the patristic and early medieval period* (Leiden, 1994), 214–9. 29 James A. Brundage, *Law, sex and christian society in medieval Europe* (Chicago, 1987), 183; idem, 'Sex and canon law', in Vern L. Bullough & James A. Brundage, *A handbook of medieval sexuality* (New York & London, 1996), 33–50. 30 See for example the marriages of Chilperic (Gregory of Tours, *History of the Franks*, iv 28); Pauline Stafford, 'Sons and mothers: family politics in the early middle ages', in D. Barker (ed.), *Medieval women* (Oxford, 1978), 79–100. 31 Jenny M. Jochens, 'The politics of reproduction: medieval Norwegian kingship', *Am Hist Rev*, 92 (1987), 27–49. 32 Laura

men were much more concerned with lawful marriage than with illicit mating[33] – the first was seen to be a fundamental Christian institution, founded on the Gospels and the teaching of the Fathers of the church; the second was a mortal sin that could be forgiven. Their most significant success was in making marriage more-or-less indissoluble (and where soluble, subject to their own canonical rules) and in establishing that only the children of the canonical wife could be heirs. How the church and its lawyers managed to impose this rule on the lineages of kings and lords remains obscure. It was, however, matched by a corresponding leniency in the rules for nullity, at least in the case of the great – and here the church claimed sole competence.

In the light of these developments, the Irish reformers, who had adopted current canonical thinking, now came to see the practices of their fellow-countrymen as seriously immoral. In a way, this was not something new: the rigorist canonists of the *Hibernensis* had laid down a strict Augustinian line in the eighth century and before,[34] the widely diffused Irish penitentials and their continental derivatives promote the same strict sexual ethic,[35] and indeed Irish canon-law texts contributed significantly to Carolingian teachings. The naive Irish reformers succeeded in conveying their righteous horror to the papacy – and to anybody who was prepared to listen to them – at least as early as the beginning of Gregory VII's pontificate, and the story lost nothing in each telling. For the Irish of the eleventh and twelfth centuries, marriage, in practice, remained a secular contract, not an ecclesiastical one. It was not indissoluble: men married and divorced readily, and aristocrats and evidently well-off commoners, practised polygynous mating as did their continental European peers.[36] It is worth noting that *Cáin lánamna* (*c.*650), the principal vernacular law tract on marriage, is the work of churchmen, distinguishes clearly between *sponsus/sponsa*, Irish *cétmuinter* 'first wife' and all other kinds of marital relationship. However, the offspring of all relationships (except those with slaves and very low-class women) were usually considered legitimate heirs, belonged to their father's lineage, and bore his name. Already, by the eleventh century, surnames had come into existence in Ireland and this gave the multiple offspring of polygynous lords a clear

Betzig, 'Medieval monogamy', *J Family Hist*, 20/2 (1995), 181–286. **33** Ibid.; Georges Duby, *Medieval marriage: two models from twelfth-century France* (Baltimore MD, 1978); idem, *The knight, the lady and the priest: the making of modern marriage in medieval France* (Harmondsworth, 1985); idem, *Mâle moyen âge: de l'amour et autres essais* (Paris, 1988), 11–33. **34** Hib 46. **35** Bieler, *Irish penitentials*, 76–80, 82, 86–92 (Vinnian §§10–21, 27, 36–46), 112–6, 126–8 (Cummean, II §§1–31; X §§1–18), 160 (Canones Hibernenses I, §§4–8), 178 (Canones Adomnani §16), 194–6 (Synodus II Patricii §§xxv–xxix), 204, 218–22 (Bigotianum §37, II §§1–11), 262–5 (Old Irish penitential §§11–36). **36** Thurneysen, 'Cáin lánamna', 1–80 = *Gesammelte Schriften*, iii 287–366; Thurneysen, 'Heirat', ibid. 108–28; repr. 367–86; CIH vi 2301, lines 21–4; cf. iv 1483, lines 8–9; D.A. Binchy (ed. & tr.), 'Bretha crólige', *Ériu*, 12 (1938), 1–77: 44–5 §§6–7, 73–4.

social identity obvious to all. Their continental equivalents lacked surnames for centuries to come: thus their polgynous offspring are almost invisible in the record. Irish marital customs were not an inheritance from paganism, but a *modus vivendi* worked out in the sixth and seventh centuries, side by side with the more rigorist prescriptions of the *Hibernensis* and the penitentials. Thus the practices of the Irish aristocracy (and they rather than the ordinary people are what mattered to the reformers), openly differed from the current thinking on marriage in regard to indissolubility and legitimacy, consanguinity and affinity. Though the objects (at least in Ireland) of well-developed pastoral care, the lower orders did much as they pleased: illicit relationships with women were repeatedly denounced, and the repetition alone shows that the denunciations had little effect, in Ireland or anywhere else. In Ireland, as in England, there was nothing unusual about a well-to-do commoner having a wife and a concubine – and this may be a long-established North European practice.[37] The Irish, then, were not more debauched than their continental peers nor more vicious in their social mores: they were just differently organised, confident in their own institutions, and reluctant to change them. In the case of the nobility, this reluctance was closely tied in with lineage structures, strategies of heirship and politically significant alliances between dynasties. The rules governing their practices are clearly set out in the texts of a legal tradition that goes back to the mid-seventh century – texts that were studied and glossed within church schools in the eleventh and twelfth centuries, that is, throughout the reform period, as authoritative sources of law.[38]

There is no good reason to believe that the proposed reform of non-canonical marriage practices – divorce, remarriage and sexual or marital relationships within the forbidden degrees of kindred, not to mention concubinage – was likely to be easily or quickly achieved (and this is as true of continental Europe as it is of Ireland). The annals, genealogies and sagas provide the evidence for this and only a few examples can be cited here. Magnus Mac Duinn Shlébe, king of Ulaid (r. 1166–71), who was killed in Downpatrick by his brother Donn Slébe in 1171, had the following crimes to his name: desertion of his own wife, the abduction of his foster-father's wife (who was the former wife of his brother Aed, †1158), the rape of the wife of his other brother

37 Jean Scammell, 'Freedom and marriage in medieval England', *Econ Hist Rev*, 27 (1974), 523–7; Margaret Clunies Ross, 'Concubinage in Anglo-Saxon England', *Past & Present*, 108 (1985), 3–34. 38 CIH ii 502–19, iii 903, v 1804–1112, vi 1947–9; Binchy & Dillon, *Studies in Early Irish law*, 1–80. The second recension of *Táin bó Cuailgne* (CLH 1103), usually dated to the first third of the twelfth century, demonstrates that *Cáin lánamna*, the tract on marriage law (of c.650) and its glosses were still studied in clerical circles (BL ii 261–3; Cecile O'Rahilly (ed. & tr.), *Táin bó Cúalgne from the Book of Leinster* (Dublin, 1967), 1–3).

Eochaid, king of Ulaid (r. 1158–66), and the outraging of the church and its clergy.[39] Magnus's deeds are recorded in the annals as shocking acts that gravely offended his contemporaries, but they do indicate what a violent and ruthless king might do. The marriages of the great Tairdelbach Ó Conchobair, king of Connacht (r. 1106–56) and king of Ireland at the height of the reform, reveal the patterns of dynastic marriage and the breaches of the rules of affinity in the interest of political alliances that the reformers deplored. The annals and the *Banshenchas*[40] record that he was married seven times, but it is not possible to discover the sequence of his marriages. He married two daughters of Domnall (mac Ardgair) Mac Lochlainn, the powerful king of Ailech (r. 1083–1121), namely, Mór (†1122) and Derbfhorgaill. He married Caillech Dé, daughter of Ó hEidin, a Connacht lord, but she also married Tairdelbach Ó Briain, king of Munster (r. 1142–52; †1167). She was mother of Ruaidrí, king of Ireland (1166–83; †1198), and of Muirchertach Ó Briain, king of Munster (r. 1167–8).[41] He was also married to two sisters (or daughters) of Murchad Ó Maelechlainn, king of Meath (r. 1106–63), namely Órlaith and Taillte. A sixth wife, Dubchoblaith, was daughter of a Connacht nobleman, Mael Sechlainn Ó Mael Ruanaid.[42] A seventh marriage is reported in the genealogies in a context so interesting that it is worth quoting:

> *Tairrdelbach Mor mac Ruaidrí immorra aird-rig Ereand ro badar meic imda aici .i. Ruaidrí rig Erenn beos, Cathal Croibdearg, rig Condacht, Domnall Mor tanaisti na Breifne … A tri meic re mnai fosta [.i. ingen Meic Diarmada] .i. Mael Issa .i. comarba Comain (sindser a cloindi & a oigri), Aed Dall &Tadc Alainn …*

> Tairdelbach Mór son of Ruaidrí, however, high-king of Ireland, had many sons i.e. Ruaidrí king of Ireland also, Cathal Crobderg king of Connacht, Domnall Mór *tánaise* of Breifne … His three sons by his permanent wife [i.e., the daughter of Mac Diarmada] i.e. Mael Ísu, coarb of Commán (the eldest of his family and his heir), Aed Dall and Tadc Álainn …[43]

---

39 AU 1171. **40** CLH 795; Dobbs, 'Ban-Shenchus', 191, 234. **41** AFM 1168. **42** AFM 1168; Muireann Ní Bhrolcháin, 'The *Banshenchas* revisited', in Mary O'Dowd & Sabine Wichert (ed.), *Chattel, servant or citizen: women's status in church, state and society*, Historical Studies, 19 (Belfast, 1995), 70–81: 75–6. **43** Lec. facs. f. 63vb9–17 (L); An Lebar Donn al. Dublin, RIA, 23 Q 10 (1233) 13a1–15 (Q); O Clery Book of Genealogies, *Analecta Hibernica* 18 (1951) 75–6, §894 (C). The identity of his 'permanent wife', given above in brackets, occurs in QC; the statement in parentheses, probably a gloss, occurs only in L. For L's *fosta* QC read *phósta* 'married'. For *ben fosta* see DIL s.v. fosta. The genealogist lists eighteen sons; daughters are not recorded.

Evidently, the genealogist considered his first and 'permanent' wife (or at least the mother of his eldest son) to be his canonical wife. Her son Mael Ísu was superior of the church of Roscommon. The other wives, canonical or concubinary, represent the complex dynastic marriages of a great king. They are of two kinds: strategic marital alliances with the daughters of important provincial kings from which he could expect some benefit as king of Ireland; and marriages with the daughters of the leading nobility of his own kingdom that helped consolidate his power within. The niceties of canon law were not allowed stand in the way and the contemporary demands of the reforming clergy made little impact on these socio-political concerns. Nonetheless, there are some subtle literary references that suggest that Tairdelbach was seen by at least some of his contemporaries as overdoing it.[44]

These dynastic marriage patterns are taken for granted by the genealogists and by Gilla Mo Dutu Ó Casaide (fl. 1143×c.1153), the historian and hagiographer who compiled the *Banshenchas*, an account of the famous women of Irish literature and history. Ó Casaide was a cleric who came from the church of Ardbraccan in Co. Meath and who composed his metrical version of the *Banshenchas* in the church of Devenish in 1147.[45] He was, therefore, writing when the reform was in full swing[46] and he recounts the multiple and non-canonical marriages of recent and contemporary kings, as well as those of heroes of remoter times, without a word of reproof. He piquantly declares: 'Whores, base folk and wicked women, the badly bred masses: I have omitted these from my arrangement'[47] – lest he should bring dishonour on kings by recounting their defective descent. Many of his reform-minded contemporaries could not concur and would be quick to put some of the noblest women in the land in the category Ó Casaide thought he had excluded. Effective marriage reform meant setting aside much of the social structures of Irish royal and lordly society – in effect, the replacement of one type of aristocratic society by another – and the Irish reformers are unlikely to have been in a position to put through a fundamental change of this kind, in the short term, or the long.

44 The tale of Áed mac Muiredaig, king of Connacht, and his fairy lover (Whitley Stokes (ed. & tr.), *Acallam na senórach*, in Whitley Stokes & Ernst Windisch (ed.), *Irische Texte*, 4th ser., 1 (Leipzig, 1900), 176–8) may be a subtle allusion to Tairdelbach's married life. 45 Dobbs, 'The Ban-Shenchus', *Revue Celtique*, 47 (1930), 282–339 (unsatisfactory edition). 46 Muireann Ní Bhrolcháin, 'The manuscript tradition of the Banshenchas', *Ériu* 33 (1982), 109–35; Charles Doherty, 'Some aspects of hagiography as a source for Irish economic history', *Peritia*, 1 (1982), 300–28: 322–4. 47 Translated from the late Dr Muireann Ní Bhrolcháin's edition of the Metrical *Banshenchas* (§269) which she kindly made available to me.

CHAPTER III

The intervention of Canterbury

THE CAREER CLERIC Lanfranc of Pavia (1005/10–1089), Benedictine monk and prior of Bec and master of its school, was suitably appointed archbishop of Canterbury (*sed.* 1070–89) by William the Conqueror. He was the king's friend, counsellor and imperious overseer of the English church, often responsible for secular government, even for military matters. His expansionism as a church leader may reflect the secular ambitions of his patron as much as pretensions inherited from tenth-century English kings and any ancient claims of Canterbury to a primacy of the British Isles. By 1074, a mere four years after his appointment, he was making his presence felt in the Irish church. The criticisms of the Irish institutions voiced by Lanfranc and later by his successor Anselm must be seen in the light of eleventh-century continental and Norman-French attitudes to practices different from their own, and from those prescribed by the new canon law and the reforming papacy. What was different was all too quickly condemned as barbarous or immoral or both. Ireland, Wales and Scotland were outside what became the Angevin Empire, the French kingdom, the German Empire and northern Spain and Italy, thus outside the Romance and German lands, the seats of the European powers. What was remote was very likely to be seen as barbaric, even savage. And England, in the eleventh century, was on the edge, if not beyond. Such attitudes are evident in Lanfranc's letter of 1072/3 to pope Alexander II, in reference to his professed reluctance to accept appointment as archbishop of Canterbury. Here he describes 'the native races' of Britain as 'barbarous' (*gentiumque barbararum*) and he finds the decadence of the English church and the depravity of its people wearisome.[1] The same attitudes recur in the work of the historian William of Malmesbury (†1141/3) who condemns the ignorance and immorality of the pre-Conquest English clergy.[2] Ordericus Vitalis (†*c.*1143), the son of a French priest reared in England, is eloquent about the avarice, lust and drunkenness of the English, lay and cleric, and the debauchery of their monks.[3] The work of modern historians lends no support to these intem-

1 Clover & Gibson, *Letters of Lanfranc*, 30–2 (letter 1). 2 W. Stubbs (ed.), *Willemi Malemesbiriensis De gestis regum*, RS 90 (2 vols, 1887–90), ii 304–6; John Gillingham, 'Civilizing the English? The English histories of William of Malmesbury and David Hume', *Hist Res*, 74 (2001), 17–43. 3 Le Prévost & Deslisle (ed.), *Historia ecclesiastica* (Paris 1840–5), ii 208; Marjorie Chibnall (ed.), *The ecclesiastical history of*

perate judgements of outsiders, conquerors, or would-be conquerors, who claimed authority over those whom they described as morally inferior and – more important – thought they had a superior title to their assets, as the English bishops quickly learned to their loss. And what was true of English church and society was also true of attitudes towards the Irish.[4]

From the consecration of Gilla Pátraic (in Latin, Patricius) of Dublin in 1074 until the synod of Kells in 1152, the diocese of Dublin was a suffragan of Canterbury. This submission is formally expressed in the professions of the five bishops who ruled Dublin in that period, made on the occasion of their consecration at Canterbury, though the form of the oath of obedience varied. Besides, the first bishop of Waterford, Mael Ísu Ó hAinmire (in Latin, Malchus), consecrated by Anselm in 1097, took a like oath of obedience. By these oaths they bound themselves to full obedience to the see of Canterbury, but the oaths stand alone. The other usual signs of the dependence of suffragan bishops – for example, attendance at provincial synods and the use of appellate jurisdiction – are not in evidence, and do not seem to have been ever demanded.[5] Indeed, the letter of the Dubliners to Canterbury in 1121, requesting the consecration of Gréine (in Latin, Gregorius) as their bishop, ends with a certain note of desperation as if Canterbury was not doing enough to hold on to Dublin: they ask Ralph, archbishop of Canterbury, to consecrate their candidate Gréine 'if you want to retain longer that diocese that we have long preserved for you'.[6]

Canterbury's claim to Dublin was part of its claim to primacy over Ireland, and that, in turn, was expressed as subsidiary to its wider claim to primacy over the whole island of Britain which Lanfranc (*sed.* 1070–89) began to make in 1070. So much for its expression: its reality in Lanfranc's eyes was not less than that of his immediate and insistent claim to primacy over York, and both were founded on the same partial reading of the historical record. The first piece of evidence was a reading of Bede, put by Lanfranc to the council of Winchester in 1072 and carefully recorded in his report of its proceedings to pope Alexander II: 'from the time of St Augustine, the first archbishop of Canterbury, until the last years of Bede himself, which is a period of almost 140 years, my predecessors exercised primacy over the church of York and the whole island which men call Britain, and over Ireland as well; they extended pastoral care to all: they ordained

---

Orderic Vitalis, 6 vols, Oxford Medieval Texts (Oxford, 1968–80); A. Gwynn, 'Lanfranc and the Irish church', *Ir Ecclesiast Rec*, 57 (1941), 481–500: 484–7 (rev. repr. Gwynn, *Irish church*, 68–83). 4 John Gillingham, *The English in the 12th century: imperialism, national identity and political values* (Woodbridge, 2000), 57. 5 J.A. Watt, *The church and the two nations in medieval Ireland* (Cambridge, 1970), 217–18. 6 Ussher, *Whole works,* iv 532–33; Martin Rule (ed.), *Eadmeri Historia novorum in Anglia,* RS 81 (London, 1884), 297.

bishops …'.⁷ In fact, only Bede gave any basis for a claim to Ireland. The immediate Bedan text (and one with which Lanfranc could righteously identify)
appears to be pope Gregory I's instruction to Augustine: 'we commit to you, my
brother, all the bishops of Britain that the unlearned may be instructed, the weak
strengthened by your counsel, and the perverse corrected by your authority',⁸ but
this was not much help unless one could read Britain as including Ireland,
something Lanfranc did when he entitled himself *Brittaniarum primas* 'primate
of the Britains' in 1074 when he consecrated Gilla Pátraic bishop of Dublin.⁹ A
second passage in Bede offered something more, even if it fell far short of
canonical title. Writing of Augustine's successor, Laurentius, Bede says 'he
endeavoured to bestow his pastoral care upon the older inhabitants of Britain as
well as upon those Irish who live in Ireland, which is an island close to Britain.
He came to realize that in Ireland, as well as in Britain, the life and profession of
the people was not in accordance with church practice in many things' – a passage which Lanfranc, again happily able to see himself in Bede's words, para-
phrases creatively in a carefully crafted legalistic argument for primacy over both
islands.¹⁰ Lanfranc's claim over York was full of difficulties, his claims to rights
in Ireland were flimsy, and for all his eloquent urgings, the papacy dragged its
feet about the first and ignored the second. But this did not put a stop to
Canterbury's notion that it had an almost patriarchal authority that included a
responsibility for Ireland and, with varying degrees of vigour and conviction, it
continued to push its case for more than eighty years.

Pushing his primacy to the utmost (a common concern of contemporary
archbishops) was only one strand in Lanfranc's policy towards Ireland. As the
leader in Norman England of what soon became the Gregorian reform (though
far too supportive of the king's rights in Gregorian eyes), and in constant touch
with the papacy, his concerns for theological and liturgical orthodoxy and discipline, and for correct canonical procedures and administration, may be genuine: he consecrated bishops to Dublin, he made gifts of books, he admonished
Irish kings and clergy, and his interventions in these matters had the support of
the Irish churchmen who respected him as a scholar, theologian and adminis-
trator. And Tairdelbach ua Briain, the most powerful king in Ireland, who got
control of Dublin in 1072, seems to have supported his interventions.

7 Clover & Gibson, *Letters of Lanfranc*, 50–1 (letter 4); Watt, *Church*, 221. 8 HE i 27 (viii); Bertram
Colgrave & R.A. B. Mynors (ed. & tr.), *Bede's Ecclesiastical history of the English people* (Oxford, 1969),
88–9. 9 Profession of Gilla Pátraic, in Ussher, *Whole works*, iv 564; Michael Richter (ed.), *Canterbury
professions*, Canterbury & York Society, 67 (Torquay, 1973), 67; Gwynn, 'Lanfranc and the Irish church',
498 (Gwynn, *Irish church*, 75). 10 HE ii 4; Colgrave & Mynors, *Ecclesiastical history*, 144–7; Clover &
Gibson, *Letters of Lanfranc*, 50–1 (letter 4); Gwynn, 'Lanfranc and the Irish church', 491.

IRISH SUFFRAGANS OF CANTERBURY

It is uncertain where, when and by whom Dúnán (†1074), the first recorded bishop of Dublin, was consecrated, perhaps Cologne. On his death, Gilla Pátraic (in Latin, Patricius), was sent in the same year to be consecrated as his successor by Lanfranc in St Paul's in London. Gilla Pátraic, to whom some literary texts have been wrongly attributed, had, it is said, been trained at Worcester.[11] We do not know what motivated his recourse to Canterbury. Perhaps he wished to be sure of canonical consecratation, a concern that would imply some familiarity with contemporary canon law. Lanfranc made the most of the opportunity and extracted a consecration oath from him that gave full expression to his primatial claims and flattered Dublin at the same time (it was written, of course, by Lanfranc's chancery):

> I Patrick, who has been chosen to rule Dublin, the metropolis of Ireland (*metropolis Hiberniae*), do hand to you, my reverend father, Lanfranc, primate of the British Isles (*Britanniarum primas*) and archbishop of the holy church of Canterbury, this charter of my profession; and I promise that I shall obey you and your successors in all things …

This formula implies a metropolitan role for Dublin under the primacy of Canterbury. It is unlikely that Gilla Pátraic went to Canterbury without the consent of Tairdelbach ua Briain (r. 1063–86); Gofraid, who ruled Dublin as his sub-king, had (Lanfranc himself says) sent Gilla Pátraic to him for consecration.[12] On this occasion Lanfranc wrote Tairdelbach a letter, delivered by Gilla Pátraic. In grossly flattering terms, he addressed him as 'magnificent king of Ireland', praised his great wisdom, humility and justice (as related to him, he says, by the new bishop of Dublin), and expressed his deep affection for him. This is a diplomatic prelude to advice and criticism. He pointed out, as we have seen, the marital failures of the Irish and he made four other points: 'bishops are consecrated by a single bishop; many are ordained [bishops] to villages or

11 Elizabeth Boyle, 'The authorship and transmission of *De tribus habitaculis animae*', *J Mediev Latin*, 22 (2012), 49–65; idem, 'On the wonders of Ireland: translation and adaptation', in Elizabeth Boyle & Deborah Hayden (ed.), *Authorities and adaptations: the reworking and transmission of textual sources in medieval Ireland* (Dublin, 2014), pp 233–61. 12 CLH 658; A. Gwynn (ed. & tr.), *The writings of bishop Patrick, 1074–84*, SLH 1 (Dublin 1955) = idem, 'The first bishops of Dublin', *Reportorium Novum*, 1 (1955), 1–26, repr. in H.B. Clarke (ed.), *Medieval Dublin: the living city* (Dublin, 1990), 37–61; Marie Therese Flanagan, *Irish society, Anglo-Norman settlers, Angevin kingship: interactions in Ireland in the late twelfth century* (Oxford, 1989), 12–20; Martin Holland, 'Dublin and the reform of the Irish church in the eleventh and twelfth centuries', *Peritia*, 14 (2000), 111–60: 111–19; Ussher, *Whole works*, iv 488 (= PL 150, 534–5, letter 36), 564; ASMD 1074; Richter, *Canterbury professions*, 68.

towns; infants are baptised without the use of consecrated chrism; holy orders are conferred by bishops for money'. Lanfranc asks him to call together a council of bishops and religious, at which he himself should attend with his advisors, and legislate against these evils.[13] There is no record of any such assembly, but some church synods may have met.

Gilla Pátraic and his companions were drowned in the Irish Sea in October 1084, while sailing to England. In August 1085, Lanfranc consecrated Donngus (in Latin, Donatus) bishop of Dublin. He did this at the request 'of Tairdelbach, king of Ireland, of the bishops of the region of Ireland, and the clergy and people of the aforesaid city'. This indicates that Tairdelbach had summoned a council of clergy and laity to select a candidate and this may well have been urged by a reform party emerging within the Irish church as a whole, of which Tairdelbach appears supportive. Donngus Ó hAindlide was an Irish Benedictine monk of Christchurch, Canterbury, but in his consecration oath, unlike his predecessor, he simply swears canonical obedience as bishop of Dublin to Lanfranc as 'archbishop of the holy church of Canterbury'.[14] Clearly, there is a formal change, or at least tension, in the relationship between Canterbury and Dublin. There may be an echo of this in the title Lanfranc uses in his reply to a letter from bishop Domnall Ó hÉnna (†1098) and his fellow bishops. He addresses Ó hÉnna as 'venerable bishop of Ireland', giving him precedence over the others. Ó hÉnna was bishop of Killaloe and, more importantly, Tairdelbach's court bishop and kinsman, whose status was directly linked to that of his patron.[15] When archbishop Anselm wrote a careful and diplomatic letter to the canonical Irish bishops some time after his consecration in December 1093 – and it can be read as an assertion of his metropolitan status in Ireland – Ó hÉnna is given seniority over Donngus and the other bishops, and a similar precedence is accorded him in the *decretum* prepared in 1096 for the consecration of Mael Ísa Ó hAinmire (in Latin, Malchus) as bishop of Waterford.[16] One could perhaps deduce that Tairdelbach was no unqualified supporter of Dublin as a metropolitan see and Lanfranc and Anselm, treading prudently, were careful not to push their luck.

When Donngus died in November 1095 he was succeeded by his nephew, Samuel Ó hAindlide, who was consecrated by Anselm in Winchester cathedral in 1096.[17] He ruled the see until his death in 1121. Samuel, it is said, was a Benedictine monk of St Albans. He was chosen at a council, held in Dublin, by

---

13 Clover & Gibson, *Letters of Lanfranc*, 70–3 (letter 10) = PL 150, 536–7 (letter 38).   **14** Ussher, *Whole works*, iv 564; ASMD 1085.   **15** Clover & Gibson, *Letters of Lanfranc*, 154–61 (letter 49) = PL 150, 532–3 (letter 33); Holland, 'Dublin and the reform', 117–8; Ó Corráin, 'Dál Cais – church and dynasty', *Ériu*, 24 (1973), 57.   **16** Holland, 'Dublin and the reform', 121–3.   **17** Rule, *Eadmeri Historia*, 73–4 = PL 159, 393.

Muirchertach Ó Briain, son of Tairdelbach, and king of Ireland, who had succeeded on his father's death in 1086.[18] As far as Canterbury was concerned,
Samuel soon proved to be an awkward and undiplomatic suffragan. He
returned with a letter from archbishop Anselm to Muirchertach Ó Briain
whom he addresses, with notable flattery, as 'glorious king of Ireland by the
grace of God'. It repeats Lanfranc's complaints of two decades before and urges
the king to correct the abuses.[19]

Meanwhile, Muirchertach held a council at Waterford, which chose Mael
Ísa Ó hAinmire (in Latin, Malchus), who had been a Benedictine monk under
bishop Wachelin at Winchester and sent him to Anselm to be consecrated
bishop of Waterford. His *decretum* was signed (in sequence) by Muirchertach
Ó Briain; Diarmait Ó Briain, the king's brother and ruler (*dux*) of Waterford;
Domnall Ó hÉnna, bishop of Killaloe; Mael Muire Ó Dúnáin, a court bishop,
who came originally from Ardbraccan in Meath;[20] Samuel, bishop of Dublin;
and Ferdomnach, 'bishop of the Leinstermen', all of whom will have been the
most important people to attend the council and the makers of policy.[21] Now
Canterbury had two suffragan bishops in Ireland and its policy of discreetly
pushing forward its claim to primacy appeared successful. The return of Mael
Ísa from Canterbury is likely to have been the occasion of archbishop Anselm's
second letter to Muirchertach Ó Briain, though Gwynn suggests a date as late
as 1100.[22] Anselm first addresses the sexual and marital mores of the Irish. Then
he refers again to the canon law governing the appointment of bishops: a
bishop must be consecrated by three bishops, a bishop cannot be consecrated
canonically without a fixed see, one cannot have a pastor without a flock; and
he urges the king to remedy all these defects.

Some time after 1096, reformers in the Irish church changed direction: led by
Muirchertach Ó Briain and his advisors, they moved towards an Irish-centred
programme for reform, and Canterbury's plans for Ireland began to unravel.
How this came about is obscure, but it may be connected with Ó Briain's grow-
ing self-assurance, and political rivalry between him and Henry I in the Irish Sea
area.[23] The change of policy becomes evident at the synod of Cashel.

---

18 Gwynn, 'First bishops of Dublin', 17–20; idem, 'St Anselm and the Irish church', *Ir Ecclesiast Rec*, 59
(1942), 1–14 (repr. Gwynn, *Irish church*, 99–115); Holland, 'Dublin and the reform', 123–14. 19 Ussher,
Whole works, iv 520–1; Gwynn, 'St Anselm and the Irish church', 13–4. 20 D. Ó Corráin, 'Mael Muire Ua
Dúnáin (1040–1117), reformer', in P. de Brún, P. Ó Riain & S. Ó Coileáin (ed.), *Folia gadelica: essays presented to R.A. Breatnach* (Cork, 1983), 47–53. 21 Ussher, *Whole works*, iv 518–9; Rule, *Eadmeri Historia*,
76–7 = PL 159, 395–96; Holland, 'Dublin and the reform', 124–8; A. Gwynn, 'The origins of the diocese of
Waterford', *Ir Ecclesiast Rec*, 59 (1942), 289–96. 22 A. Gwynn, 'The first synod of Cashel' *Ir Ecclesiast Rec*,
66 (1945), 81–92; 67 (1946), 109–22: 120–1. 23 Edmund Curtis, 'Murchertach O'Brien, high king of
Ireland, and his Norman son-in-law, Arnulf de Mongomery, circa 1100', *J Roy Soc Antiq Ire*, 20 (1921), 116–

Ó Briain and the other kings who supported the reformers were quick enough to see the advantages for themselves in the proposed new order. They observed the powers of the kings of England, the German emperors, and the European feudal rulers and they readily grasped that what was proposed might give them power over the churches, their personnel, and their enormous landed resources that they could never otherwise get. The Irish church was, for the most part, ruled by ecclesiastical lineages that were (even when closely related to the royal dynasty) largely independent of royal control and protected by ancient rights and usages. As we have seen, the church had been successful in progressively freeing itself of lay imposts in the eleventh and early twelfth centuries, and this further diminished royal claims on them. It is likely that the clerical advisors of the kings calculatedly held out to them the prospect of increased prestige and greater influence in church affairs to win them to the cause of reform. That, and the promise of success as the reward of godliness in this world and eternal happiness in the next, was a heady cocktail: sanctity and self-interest could be served together. The flattering attentions of popes and foreign archbishops urged them in the same direction, and the status to be won from their ostensibly high-minded and disinterested support of the Gregorian reform gave them a moral authority in Irish political struggles, useful in cowing their rivals and advancing their own political ambitions. In a word, reform favoured kings, and they knew it.[24] Ó Briain was first in – and spectacularly so – but others followed, tardily at first, but more quickly as the reform gathered pace. Some Irish kings were doubtless pious, from time to time at least, but their ruthlessness in contemporary political and military struggles indicates that this view must not be pushed far. None put religious zeal before prudence, as did king David I of Scotland,[25] and some of the most violent and calculating, such as Diarmait Mac Murchada, king of Leinster (who had flattering correspondence from St Bernard that does the saint no credit),[26] strongly supported the reformers, more from policy than piety. An interesting eleventh-century poem of advice to a king, 'Cert cach ríg co réil', urges the king to have good but firm relations with the clergy. He is to cherish the churchmen – 'Have contented and wealthy clergy, who want not for clothing nor food nor drink, in every church' – but he is to keep control of them.[27]

24. **24** Benjamin T. Hudson, 'Gaelic princes and Gregorian reform', in Benjamin T. Hudson & Vickie Ziegler (ed.), *Crossed paths: methodological approaches to the Celtic aspect of the European middle ages* (Lanham MD & London, 1991), 61–82. **25** G.W.S. Barrow, 'Scottish rulers and the religious orders, 1070–1153', *Trans Roy Hist Soc*, 5th ser., 3 (1953), 77–100. **26** G.-G. Meersseman, 'Two unknown confraternity letters of St Bernard', *Cîteaux in de Nederlanden* 6 (1955), 173–8 = Jean Leclercq, *Recueil d'études sur saint Bernard et ses écrits* (3 vols, Rome 1962–69), ii 313–18. **27** Tadhg Ó Donnchadha (ed. & tr.), 'Cert cech ríg co réil', in Osborn J. Bergin & Carl Marstrander (eds.), *Miscellany presented to Kuno Meyer* (Halle a. S., 1912), 258–72.

CHAPTER IV

Synod of Cashel, 1101

THE SYNOD HELD AT CASHEL in 1101 under the presidency of Muirchertach Ó Briain, king of Ireland, has often been depicted as the proceeding of conservative and isolated Irish clergy, who had just woken up to the Gregorian reform that had been going on for decades and, blinking in the new light of a papally directed re-organisation of the Western church, moved somewhat bumblingly to make ameliorative adjustments to their own eccentric Irish establishment.[1] In fact, Cashel was the first major reforming synod of the twelfth century, and the fathers of Cashel, though no reckless pioneers, knew well what they were about: 'An assembly of the men of Ireland, lay and cleric, at Cashel under the presidency of Muirchertach Ó Briain, and it was on that occasion that Muirchertach Ó Briain gave Cashel of the kings as a grant to St Patrick and to the Lord'.[2] The *Annals of the Four Masters* give a further significant detail that clearly reveals the Gregorian programme: the grant was made 'without the claim of any individual layman or cleric upon it, but the religious of Ireland in general' – terms that indicate that it was to be free from any secular exaction and that it was a grant to the church in Ireland as such, namely, that it was not to become the property of any individual, group of clerics, or any single religious institution.

This was an astute political and ecclesiastical move on the part of Ó Briain who, by this time, was keen to counter Canterbury's ambitions. Cashel had been the historical possession of the Eóganacht kings of Munster whom Dál Cais (Uí Briain) had displaced, and it remained a potent historical symbol of the kingship of Munster. Significantly, Ó Briain maintained a residence there.[3] It had ecclesiastical associations: Cashel had an early church, perhaps since c.700, and a succession of later ones. His grant had a double effect. In the first place, it demonstrated Muirchertach's position as a great reforming king of Ireland who granted the church its second major ecclesiastical centre under Gregorian conditions and it allowed him to make overtures about its primacy

---

1 Aubrey Gwynn, 'The first synod of Cashel', *Ir Ecclesiast Rec*, 66 (1945), 81–92; 67 (1946), 109–22, rev. repr. A. Gwynn, *The Irish church in the eleventh and twelfth centuries*, ed. Gerard O'Brien, 155–79. K. Hughes, *The church in early Irish society* (London, 1966), 263–6. **2** ATig 1101 = CS 1101 (1097). Its new status took time to be recognised: it was burned by Éile in 1102. **3** AFM 1091 = AC 1091 (1089); ATig 1090.

to a still-conservative Armagh in the cause of reform.[4] In the second place, it deprived the Eoganacht dynasty of its ancient historic centre forever.

A summary and imperfect record of the decrees of the synod has been preserved in a very late genealogical tract, *Senchas Síl Briain*.[5] The same source and the *Annals of the Four Masters* state that bishop Mael Muire Ó Dúnáin, who was to become one of Ó Briain's court bishops and a leading reformer (by origin a member of an old clerical lineage), was present at the synod. *Senchas Síl Briain* adds that he attended as papal legate, a statement that has been accepted by Gwynn and others, but the evidence of this text is otherwise unsupported and hardly convincing.[6]

The original decrees were obviously in Latin: all we possess is an incomplete Modern-Irish summary. There are eight surviving decrees.

1   *Gan ceannach eaglaise Dé do athlaochaibh ná do aithchléirc<h>ibh go bráth* 'that neither ex-layman nor ex-cleric shall practise simony in God's church for all time'. The decree is directed against simony or the purchase of church office. Two technical terms need explanation: *athláech*, literally 'ex-layman', is one who takes up the clerical vocation late in life, and the use of the term here may point to a layman who takes minor orders merely to qualify for an ecclesiastical office so that he may take its profits; *aithchléirech*, literally 'ex-cleric', is a person who has abandoned the clerical life, probably uncanonically, but it also means 'wicked cleric'.[7]

2   *Gan cíos ná cáin do rígh ná do thaoiseach ón eaglais i nÉirinn go bráth* 'that neither king nor lord be entitled to levy rent or tax on the church in Ireland forever'. This decree is broadly in accord with the Gregorian programme but it specifically legislates against secular imposts on churches and church lands. It is also in line with the freeing of church

---

4 Anthony Candon, 'Barefaced effrontery; secular and ecclesiastical politics in twelfth century Ireland', *Seanchas Ardmhacha*, 14 (1990–1), 1–25; Holland, 'Dublin and the reform', 132–3. The Munster section of the *Book of rights* was prepared for this assembly by Ua Briain's propagandists: it establishes the pre-eminence of the king of Munster as king of Ireland and subtly invites Armagh to take the lead in the reform (Candon, 'Effrontery', 14–17, 22). **5** Tadhg Ó Donnchadha (ed.) *An Leabhar Muimhneach*, 341 (critical text from Dublin, TCD, 1281 olim H. 1. 7, 105a and Dublin, RIA, 23 G 22 (486), 57; I normally use Ó Donnchadha's readings); Standish O'Grady (ed. & tr.), *Caithréim Thoirdhealbhaigh*, ITS 26–7 (2 vols, London 1929, repr. Dublin 1988), i 174–5, ii 185–6. Marie Therese Flanagan, *The transformation of the Irish church in the twelfth and thirteenth centuries*, SCH 29 (Woodbridge, 2010), 47–9, 187–8. **6** A. Gwynn, 'Papal legates in Ireland during the twelfth century', *Ir Ecclesiast Rec*, 63 (1944, 361–70; idem, *Irish church*, 116–25, 156; Aubrey Gwynn & Dermot F. Gleeson, *A history of the diocese of Killaloe* (Dublin, 1962) 109; Ó Corráin, 'Mael Muire Ua Dúnáin (1040–1117), reformer', 47–53. **7** For the semantics of *aith-*, in this context, see DIL s.v. aithben, aithchléirech, aithfer; Carl Marstrander, *Revue Celtique*, 36 (1915), 335–90: 337. Not all *aithlaích* were so regarded; cf. AI 1057.3.

lands mentioned in the annals in the tenth and eleventh centuries and
with the later legislation of the council of Cashel in 1171/2.

3   *Gan tuata do beith in' oircheanneach innte* 'that a layman shall not be superior in it [the church]'. Traditionally, the *airchinnech* or erenagh was at
least in minor orders, sometimes merely a tonsured cleric (*cléirech co
corainn*), and thus technically at least a member of the clergy.[8] It is likely
that the fathers of Cashel required more than this minimum, and they
may not have seen the sub-grades of tonsured cleric, acolyte and psalm-
singer, as holy orders at all. Here they may be insisting that superiors of
churches be always in major orders, and thus celibate. If so, this represents
a radical departure, again consonant with the Gregorian programme.

4   *<Gan> dá oircheannach do beith i n-aenchill acht ar in gcill do bheith i
gcomhrac dá chóigeadh* 'that there shall not be two superiors in one
church, except in a church where two provinces march'. The arrangement
condemned here has to do, evidently, with the division of the landed
resources of a church between rival superiors as a means of resolving conflict. The division is allowed where a church is on a border – and there
were many of these[9] – because such a church is likely to own property in
two over-kingdoms, and have clergy and superiors from both.

5   *Gan bean do bheith ag oircheannach cille ann* 'that no superior of a church
should have a woman'. The Irish is ambivalent: one could understand wife
or concubine but this is a matter of perception and makes little difference
for clerics' wives had come to be seen as concubines. The decree requires
superiors to be Continent. In Ireland, as elsewhere, such decrees were
aspirational, but an integral part of the Gregorian programme that struck
at clerical marriage, hereditary succession in church, and the alienation of
church property to support the offspring of the clergy.

6   *Gan coimirce do bheith ag in té dhéanfadh goid ann agus gan coimirce ag
fear fill ná fionghail<e>* 'that there be no sanctuary for one who commits
theft there [in church] and no sanctuary for a man who kills in treachery or commits kin-slaying'. The term *coimirce*, Old-Irish *commairge*,
usually means the protection or period of protection (also called *fóesam,
turtugud*) that a powerful person may offer another, making him

---

8 Liam Breatnach (ed. & tr.), 'The first third of *Bretha nemed*', *Ériu*, 40 (1989), 1–40: 14 §13; CIH ii 639.15–
24, ii 686.37–687.2, iii 701.2–4, 704.25–28, iv 1233.1–4; Hib 9:1–2. A church ruled by a lay superior (*airchindech laich*) unreproved by an abbot loses its privileges (CIH 2.4). According to the commentary he has
no honour price until he does penance and is tonsured.   **9** P. Ó Riain, 'Boundary associations in early
Irish society', *Studia Celtica*, 7 (1972), 12–29. For an example of two abbots see AU 877.1: Eugan & Mael
Tuile nepos Cuanach, duo abbates Cluana Moccu Nois, in pace dormierunt. However, this entry is
ambiguous.

immune from legal proceedings. It is not clear whether physical sanctuary in a church is also involved here, but it probably is. These are public-order provisions making those who plunder a church or violate it or who kill in treachery or by kin-slaying liable to the full rigour of the law.

7   *Gan cion an chléirigh, nó an fhile, do thabhairt don tuata* 'that the due of the cleric or the poet should not be given to a lay person'. Payments that belong to the clergy by right (and these include tithes and the income from church estates) should not be paid to any lay person. The reference to the poet, though reflecting long-established privilege, is likely to be a later gloss and not part of the decree.

8   *Gan ben a athar ná a senathar, nó a siúr nó a <h->inghean, do beith 'na mnaoi ag fear i nÉirinn, nó bean a dhearbhráthar, nó bean ar bith chomh fogus sin i ngaol do* 'that no man in Ireland shall have to wife his father's wife or his grandfather's wife, or her sister or her daughter, or his brother's wife, or any other woman so near related'. This decree, outlawing affinal incest, has been discussed above.

In general, the canons of Cashel reflect the Gregorian concern to draw a clear line of separation between the laity and a celibate clergy. The canons on simony, affinity and clerical celibacy are very close to contemporary canons passed elsewhere. They compare well with the decrees of the council of London of 1102, presided over by Anselm of Canterbury and Gerard of York, which forbade priests and deacons to marry, excluded priests' sons as heirs to their fathers' churches, ordered that churches and prebends must not be bought, and prohibited marriages within the seventh degree. And most of these rules were renewed – as they needed to be – in further London councils in 1108, 1125 and 1129.[10] They had been part of the programme of Urban II's much-publicised council of Clermont in 1095.[11] Similar legislation was passed at the general council held in Reims under pope Calixtus II in 1119, again at Reims in 1148 under Eugenius III, and repeatedly at many other councils.[12]

The surviving decrees have nothing to say about the constitution of a Gregorian diocesan hierarchy, demanded by Lanfranc and Anselm, much less the formal and novel structures of primate and metropolitans. This was still too delicate a political issue: Armagh had long claimed primacy in Ireland in right of St Patrick (a tenth-century annalistic entry, probably made in Armagh,

---

10 Hefele-Leclercq, *Conciles*, v/1 (1912) 476–8, 503–4, 658–60, 674–5. 11 Flanagan, *Transformation of the Irish church*, 46–9. 12 *Conciles*, 576–9, 824–7; H.C. Lea, *A history of sacerdotal celibacy in the christian church*, i 306–59.

affirms that its bishop was 'bishop of the Irish').[13] Nor did the synod touch on Canterbury's suffragan sees in Ireland over which it claimed primacy. The fact that Samuel, bishop of Dublin, had been playing the metropolitan so openly that he had to be rebuked by archbishop Anselm c.1100×1103 may have helped bring matters to a head.[14] Apparently, Ó Briain and his advisors played one off against the other, and used the threat of Canterbury to bring the conservative rulers of Armagh into the reform movement. Hereditary married coarbs, drawn from Uí Shínaig, an aristocratic lineage of Ind Airthir of Airgialla, had ruled Armagh without a break since 1001 and their influence and office-holding had long preceded that date.[15] Bernard of Clairvaux and most subsequent writers have not understood what the coarbs of Patrick had become and have condemned them for not being what they never intended to be. Bernard's ringing denunciation of them as 'an evil and adulterous generation' that 'suffered none to be bishops but those who were of their own tribe and family' is quite mistaken.[16] This, in point of fact, is the deeply hostile view of St Malachy, their most able opponent. Domnall, the married coarb of Patrick, died while brokering peace[17] between Ó Briain and Mac Lochlainn, king of Ailech, and he was buried with great pomp at Armagh in August 1105. His death opened the way for important changes, carefully noted by the annalist. Cellach (in Latin, Celsus or Celestinus), his grand-nephew, an unmarried man, was appointed to succeed him and was ordained priest 'by the choice of the men of Ireland' on 23 September 1105, the feast of St Adomnán.[18] Within a few months, Caínchomrac Ó Baígill, bishop of Armagh (*sed.* 1099–1106), died, and this left the way open for Cellach's consecration as celibate bishop of Armagh. Next year, he visited Munster as coarb of Patrick 'and on that occasion Cellach assumed the orders of noble bishop by the command of the men of Ireland' – an expression that makes it quite clear that Muirchertach Ó Briain and his advisors were behind the demand that he be consecrated bishop.[19] Bernard states that Cellach, as he was obliged if he were to be a Gregorian primate, formed a second archiepiscopal see, subordinate to Armagh.[20] He may have agreed (as it suited him) to Muirchertach's plans for Cashel and have done so on his visit to Munster in 1106.

---

13 AU 957.1: *Cathusach m. Dulgen … comarba Patraic sui-espoc Goidel, in Christo Iesu pausauit* 'Cathassach mac Dulgen … coarb of Patrick, sage bishop of the Irish, rested in Christ Jesus'. 14 A. Gwynn, 'Bishop Samuel of Dublin', *Ir Ecclesiast Rec*, 60 (1942), 81–8. 15 T. Ó Fiaich, 'The church of Armagh under lay control', *Seanchas Ardmhacha*, 5 (1969), 75–127. 16 *Vita Malachiae*, §19. 17 Negotiation of peace or cessation of hostilities was a common function of the coarb of Patrick (AU 1102.8, 1105.3, 1107.8, 1109.5, 1113.7; ATig 1120; AI 1120.5; 1126.8, 1128.9; AFM 1139, 1148). 18 AU 1105.3. 19 AU 1106.6. 20 *Vita Malachiae*, §33.

DE STATU ECCLESIAE

The next significant move is the production of *De statu ecclesiae* by Gille al. Gilla Espaig (in Latin, Gillebertus), bishop of Limerick. We know very little about his background. The first reference to him occurs in his own friendly note (which can be dated to autumn 1106) to archbishop Anselm congratulating him on his victory over 'the indomitable minds of the Normans' – this refers to Anselm's fraught relationship with Henry I and suggests that Gille was closely following church-state conflicts in England. He also sent Anselm a present of twenty-five pearls with a request to remember him in his prayers.[21] At that time, Gille was not long bishop: his letter was Anselm's first news of his new position. In his brief and somewhat formal reply, Anselm reminisces on how they had met at Rouen and had become acquainted. He urges Gille to join with his king and fellow bishops in extirpating vice, but he makes no primatial claims on behalf of Canterbury. His letter implies that Gille had been consecrated bishop in Ireland.[22] It is possible that this took place in 1106 at the assembly of reform bishops that met in council in Munster for Cellach's consecration, but we cannot be sure. What is certain is that Canterbury had nothing to do with the matter.[23] Gille wrote his *De statu ecclesiae* when he was bishop and papal legate; he composed it, as he notes in his covering letter ('De usu ecclesiastico'), at the request of his fellow-bishops; and he addresses it, as a programme for the forthcoming synod, to the bishops and clergy of Ireland.[24]

He sets out the structure of the church (and illustrates it with what he calls a pyramidal diagram) from the obedient and good-living laity, to lower clergy, priests, bishops, archbishops, the primate and the pope. He describes the duties of each grade. For the laity, he sets out clearly the church's current rules about consanguinity and affinity. He separates monks and their monastery from the secular clergy and their parishes: 'it is not for monks to baptise, give communion, or provide any other church service unless perchance they should be obliged to do so under the instructions of the bishop. Their purpose is, having abandoned the world, to devote themselves in prayer to God alone'. Thus he curtly dismissed the long-established pastoral role of traditional Irish monas-

---

21 Ussher, *Whole works*, iv 511. **22** Ibid. 513. **23** A. Gwynn, 'The diocese of Limerick in the twelfth century', *N Munster Antiq J*, 5 (1946), 35–48; idem, *Irish church*, 125–9. **24** CLH 659; preserved in three English MSS: (i) Cambridge, Corpus Christi College Library 66, 98; (ii) Cambridge, University Library, Ff. I. 27, 51–8; and (iii) Durham, Cathedral Chapter Library, B. II. 35, 36v–38r; on the MSS, see D.N. Dumville, 'Celtic-Latin texts in northern England, *c*.1150–*c*.1250', *Celtica*, 12 (1977), 19–49: 43–4; edited Ussher, *Whole works*, iv 500–10, repr. PL 159, 995–1004; re-edited and translated (both unsatisfactorily) by John Fleming, *Gille of Limerick (c.1070–1145) architect of a medieval church* (Dublin, 2001) 142–64; Michael Richter, 'Gilbert of Limerick revisited', in Smyth (ed.), *Seanchas*, 341–7.

ticism. The bishop has rule over monks and secular clergy, and he has at least
ten and at most a thousand churches under his government. The archbishop
has at most twenty suffragans, at the least three. He equates the emperor with
the pope, the king with the primate, the duke (*dux*) with the archbishop, the
count (*comes*) with the bishop, the knight (*miles*) with the priest. These equa-
tions work well within vernacular Irish legal ideas of rank and already in an
Old-Irish law tract ('Cia neimed is uaisli fil i talmain?') we find a comparison
between the dignity of the pope and that of the emperor (though there the
pope takes precedence).[25] The Irish grades of rulers fit better with *dux, comes*
and *miles* than many scholars think. *De statu ecclesiae* – carefully but simply
structured, clear and preachy – is the blueprint for the revolutionary changes in
church organisation now proposed by the reformers. It is a practical programme, not a theoretical exercise, and those who seek learning there are wasting their time.[26] It is the only direct evidence we have for the increasingly radical
thinking of the reformers in the first decade of the twelfth century: what they
sought was nothing less than the overthrow, from within, of the traditional
Irish church, an institution whose unbroken history stretched back over nearly
700 years to the early centuries of christianity in Ireland, to a unique age of the
saints, and that had created (and continued to create) a remarkable literary and
artistic Christian culture. This inherited ecclesiastical order, however venerable,
however celebrated its missions and its schools, was to be replaced by a conventional contemporary episcopal hierarchy, and this hierarchy was to be independent of Canterbury and its claims. We know nothing of the intense local
negotiations throughout much of Ireland that preceded the synod nor of the
arguments that convinced pope Paschal II of the merits of the plan and led him
to appoint Gille as papal legate to preside at the forthcoming synod.

25 CIH ii 588.1 = ALI iv 362; cf. the discussions of the relative status of the emperor, the king of Ireland,
and the primate of Ireland in twelfth-century glosses in ALI ii 224 = CIH v 1779.23–32. 26 Richter, loc.
cit.

CHAPTER V

Synod of Ráith Bresail, 1111

T HE *ANNALS OF INISFALLEN*, and here we have the Munster view, report the event as follows: 'A great assembly of the men of Ireland, clergy and laity, in Fiad Mac nAengusa i.e. Ráith Bresail presided over by Muirchertach Ó Briain, high-king of Ireland, and Ó Dúnáin, eminent bishop of Ireland, Cellach, coarb of Patrick, and the nobility of Ireland besides, and they enacted discipline and law better than any made in Ireland before their time', and they add a verse: 'The number of the pure clerical order, in the synod of Ráith Bresail, three hundred priests – a perfect assembly – and a fair fifty of bishops'.[1] The other annals report the event with varying nuances and differ somewhat in the number of those who attended and the precedence the leaders are accorded. The synod took place at Mag Mossaid, within sight of Cashel.[2] The real president of the synod was Gille, bishop of Limerick and papal legate. None of the annals reports the actual decisions taken. Fortunately, the seventeenth-century historian, Geoffrey Keating, had access to the lost Annals of Clonenagh and copied a detailed account of the diocesan arrangements made at the synod into his great history of Ireland, *Forus feasa ar Éirinn*.[3]

No canons survive, but we can get an inkling of some of the more important ones. Keating, summarising his source, states: 'It was at this synod that the churches of Ireland were given entirely to the bishops, and secular princes were not to have jurisdiction over them or rent from them forever'. Two things are involved here; first, the Irish churches and their estates were made over to the bishops; and second, any jurisdiction or rights to income claimed over the churches by secular lords were extinguished. The first proposed to endow the bishops, at the expense of the hereditary clerical families, with the property necessary to establish an episcopal hierarchy, that is, the new bishops, who had little

---

1 AI 1111.3; cf. AU 1111.8 (which place Cellach first); AT 1111; CS 1111 (1107). For the synod see Lawlor, *Malachy*, pp xxxvii–liii; Aubrey & Dermot F. Gleeson, *A history of the diocese of Killaloe* (Dublin, 1962), 116–27; Gwynn, *Irish church*, 180–92; Watt, *Church*, 14–18, Holland, 'Dublin and the reform', 141–7. 2 Diarmuid Ó Murchadha, 'Where was Ráith Bresail?', *Tipperary Hist J* (1999) 151–61. A.G. van Hamel (ed.), 'A poem on Crimthann', *Revue Celtique*, 37 (1917/9), 325–44. 3 AI 1111.3; cf. AU 1111.8 (which place Cellach first); AT 1111; CS 1111 (1107); David Comyn & P.S. Dinneen (ed. & tr.), *Forus feasa ar Éirinn: History of Ireland by Geoffrey Keating*, ITS 4, 8, 9 15 (4 vols, London 1908–14, repr. Dublin 1987), iii 298–306 (hereafter Keating, *History*). For a critical text of Keating's record of the synod, see John Mac Erlean, 'Synod of Ráith Bresail: boundaries of the dioceses of Ireland', *Archivium Hibernicum*, 3 (1914), 1–33.

or no resources, were to be funded by giving them ultimate legal ownership of all ecclesiastical property within their newly constituted dioceses. This transfer of property is likely to have been painfully slow and imperfect. The second, in true Gregorian fashion, condemned lay investiture and all kinds of lay impositions on the church or its estates. Both decrees were momentous in intent, and equally difficult to put into effect.

Keating then gives an account of the setting up of the dioceses and a list of them. And here the Munster–Armagh basis of the synod becomes clear. Canterbury's primatial claims on Dublin and Waterford were set aside and its larger ambitions in Ireland were quietly thwarted. Ireland was divided into two provinces, Armagh in the north, Cashel in the south, each with twelve suffragan dioceses. Keating states that this was done in imitation of the English church – this may refer to Gregory the Great's original (and unfulfilled) instructions to Augustine of Canterbury, preserved by Bede and thus well known to the Irish.[4] The Anglo-Norman church of Lanfranc and Anselm was ignored. The ideal Ps-Isidorean model was that each archiepiscopal province should have twelve episcopal sees.[5] This was as good a way as any of finding an appropriate precedent and answering the tricky question: how many dioceses? At the same time, the north–south division in Ireland was a long-established historical tradition and a contemporary political reality that any diocesan carve-up must reflect. Besides, the synod had to take provincial kingdoms, local lordships and competing ecclesiastical claims into account, a matter made more difficult by the evident absence of senior representatives of Connacht and Leinster. Some important decisions had to be provisional. For example, the synod divided Connacht into five dioceses but added the rider: 'If the clergy of Connacht are agreeable to this division we desire it, but if they do not agree to it, let them make whatever division they choose, and we approve the division that pleases them, provided there be in Connacht five bishops only'. There is a like provision about the division of Leinster, again into five dioceses.[6]

The next important matter dealt with was the defining of diocesan extents. In the case of the papal legate's own diocese of Limerick, its cathedral is named and its boundaries are carefully delimited by reference to fourteen points, with

4 HE i 29. This was still a matter being chewed over in the Canterbury–York dispute: see, for example, the letter of archbishop Ralph to pope Calixtus II, AD 1119 (James Raine (ed.), *The historians of the church of York* ii (London, 1886), 228–51: 241) and Irish bishops no doubt knew about it.   5 Horst Fuhrmann, 'Provincia constat duodecim episcopatibus: zum Patriarchsplan Erzbischof Adalberts von Hamburg-Bremen', *Studia Gratiana*, 11 (1967), 391–404. The Ps-Isidorian schema 'may have been more influential than any supposed analogy with the English church where the balance between Canterbury and York was very uneven, and certainly not twelve and thirteen episcopal sees' (Marie Therese Flanagan, private comm.)   6 Keating, *History*, iii 302–4, 306; MacErlean, 'Ráith Breasail', 9, 11.

the addendum that 'whoever transgresses these boundaries does so in violation of the Lord, the apostle Peter, St Patrick and his successor, and the Christian church'. Evidently, Limerick, which existed before the synod, was the model the others should follow, but they are delimited by a mere four named points. There are thirteen dioceses in the ecclesiastical province of Armagh (Ulster, Meath and Connacht): the primates's archdiocese of Armagh and twelve suffragans: Clogher, Ardstraw, Derry or Raphoe, Connor, Down, Duleek, Clonard, Clonfert, Tuam, Cong, Killala, Ardcarne or Ardagh. There are twelve dioceses in the ecclesiastical province of Cashel (Munster and Leinster): the archdiocese of Cashel and eleven suffragans: Lismore or Waterford, Cork, Ratass, Killaloe, Limerick, Emly, Kilkenny, Leighlin, Kildare, Glendalough and Ferns or Wexford. The symmetry of the original plan was not achieved: Cashel is a suffragan short, but the reason is evident. Dublin, under bishop Samuel (almost certainly absent from the synod), held back, but it was not ignored. The delimitation of Glendalough (from Greenock in Co. Meath to Begery Island in Wexford Harbour, and from Naas to Lambay) made Dublin an island within the diocese of Glendalough, much smaller than the territory of the kingdom of Dublin, and signalled the intention of the fathers of Ráith Bresail to make it a suffragan of Cashel, when the opportunity arose, if it was to survive as a diocese at all. The decrees of the synod are signed, in order, by Gille, the papal legate; Cellach, coarb of Patrick and primate of Ireland; and Mael Ísa Ó hAinmire, now archbishop of Cashel and no longer a suffragan of Canterbury; and the bishops duly anathematise those who transgress their ordinances.

Dean Lawlor states that the synod of Ráith Bresail 'gave to Ireland a paper constitution of the approved Roman and Catholic type'.[7] This is true, but its achievements were also revolutionary. Despite some marks of impermanence and uncertainty, it laid down the future model of a hierarchical and diocesan structure, itself a radical departure in Irish church organisation, and the essentials endured. However, adjustments began immediately. In the very year of Ráith Bresail, the clergy of Meath met in synod at Uisnech and re-divided their territory between Clonmacnoise and Clonard.[8] It was the first of many. The process worked itself out over the next four decades as hundreds of local claims and counterclaims, clashes of jurisdiction, conflicts and disputes were resolved.

Dublin, too, was subjected to the wishes of the fathers of Ráith Bresail. On the death of bishop Samuel of Dublin in 1121, the primate moved quickly to enforce his authority and this brought about a sharp conflict within the city. The partisan *Annals of Ulster* record that 'Cellach, coarb of Patrick, took the

---

7 Lawlor, *Malachy*, p. xlviii. 8 CS 1111 (1107), ATig, AB 1111.

episcopacy of Dublin by choice of the Foreigners and the Irish'.[9] What this means is not that Cellach had himself made bishop of Dublin (that would be uncanonical), but that he entered Dublin, had his primacy recognised by a majority of the clergy and people, and took charge of the diocese for the time being. There was, however, strong opposition from some of the clergy and burgesses who were supported (for his own political ends) by Tairdelbach Ó Conchobair, king of Connacht and new overlord of Dublin.[10] They chose their own candidate, sub-deacon Gréine (in Latin, Gregorius), and despatched him to be ordained priest and consecrated bishop by archbishop Ralph of Canterbury. Cellach may have sent an emissary to put the objections of the Irish bishops, but if so Canterbury ignored his protest. Gréine was consecrated bishop of Dublin in Lambeth in October 1121 and returned to Dublin within the month, but he found Cellach in possession, and was expelled. However, the competing parties presently came to an arrangement, though not a resolution of the problem. Archbishop Ralph died in 1122, and was succeeded by William of Corbeil (*sed.* 1123–36), who may have fudged the issue. Some time, probably between 1123 and the death of Cellach in 1129 Gréine got possession of his see, though there is no record that Dublin became a suffragan of Cashel.[11]

9 AU 1121; cf. ASMD 1120, 1122. 10 Ussher, *Whole works*, iv 534; Flanagan, *Irish society*, 30. 11 Ussher, *Whole works*, iv 532 (Dublin letter to Ralph of Canterbury); Gwynn, 'Bishop Samuel of Dublin', 81–8; idem, 'First bishops of Dublin', 20–5; H.B. Clarke, 'Conversion, church and cathedral: the diocese of Dublin to 1152', in James Kelly & Dáire Keogh (ed.), *History of catholic diocese of Dublin* (Dublin, 2000) 19–50: 40–1, 44–5, 50; A.S. Mac Shamhráin, 'The emergence of the metropolitan see: Dublin, 1111–26', ibid. 51–71: 51–5; Holland, 'Dublin and reform', 135–6, 144–53.

CHAPTER VI

St Malachy and Armagh

THE NEXT REMARKABLE FIGURE in the history of the reform is Mael M'Aedóc Ó Morgair, better known as St Malachy of Armagh.[1] Our chief difficulty with Malachy and his career is that the principal witness is Bernard's Life of Malachy – hagiographical, political, inaccurate on what we can check, biased. This must be borne in mind at all times. Malachy was born in 1095, the son of Mugrón Ó Morgair, *aird-fher léigind* or principal of the schools of Armagh and a distinguished scholar, who died in Mungret in 1102. Thus Malachy belonged by birth to the elite of Armagh, but not to its highest echelon. He received his strict early formation from Ímar Ó hAedacáin – 'a holy man of great austerity, the pitiless chastiser of his body', Bernard says – the ascetic abbot of the monastery of SS Peter and Paul[2] in Armagh, who died as a pilgrim in Rome in 1134. Malachy was ordained deacon about 1118, priest about 1119. Though only in his mid-twenties, he was already prominent – clear evidence of ability and ambition. When bishop Cellach went to Dublin in 1121 to deal with the problem of succession there, he made Malachy his *vice gerens* in Armagh. It is truly remarkable that a man who was a simple priest, ordained about two years before, and still in his twenties, should be given so important an office. It is evident that Malachy was both unusually able and conspicuously ambitious. Already a keen reformer, as vicar 'he ordained the apostolic sanctions and the decrees of the holy fathers, and especially the customs of the Roman Church'; and this, if Bernard's words mean anything, may indicate that he was attempting to enforce the norms of the new canon law in Armagh. This may suggest that he had access – and this is hardly surprising – to one or other of the late eleventh- and early twelfth-century canon-law collections then current on the Continent – for example, the reformist collections of Anselm of Lucca (1036–86).[3]

---

1 A. Gwynn, 'St Malachy of Armagh', *Ir Ecclesiast Rec*, 70 (1948), 961–78; 71 (1949), 134–48, 317–31 (rev. repr. Gwynn, *Irish church*, 193–217); Lawlor, *Malachy*, pp lii–lviii. However, Malachy's prominence may be due to the survival, outside of Ireland, of evidence on him and his coterie. Something the same may be said of Lorcán Ó Tuathail, archbishop of Dublin. 2 No rule of the monastery of SS Peter and Paul has survived. We thus have no idea whether the rule of this house was Irish or Benedictine. 3 Andrey Mitrofanov, *L'ecclésiologie d'Anselme de Lucques (1036–1086) au service de Grégoire VII: Genèse, contenu et impact de sa "Collection canonique"*, Instrumenta Patristica et Mediaevalia, 69 (Turnhout, 2015).

When Cellach returned to Armagh, Malachy was free to pursue his monastic vocation. His formation had hitherto been wholly Irish but he now came into contact with one formed in English Benedictine monasticism. He went to Lismore, with Cellach's permission, and placed himself under the direction of bishop Mael Ísa Ó hAinmire for about two years. Then he was summoned back to Armagh by Cellach and Ímar. While Malachy was still at Lismore, Aengus Ó Gormáin, bishop of Down and coarb of Bangor, retired and died as a pilgrim there. His successor handed over Bangor and its properties to Malachy: 'the *princeps* (i.e., the superior) made over to him the actual place of Bangor (from which he took his title), that he might build or rather rebuild a monastery', as Bernard puts it. It seems possible that the superior was Malachy's maternal uncle, Muirchertach Ó hInnrechtaig, who died at Armagh in 1131. Malachy took ten monks of Ímar Ó hAedacáin's monastery of SS Peter and Paul in Armagh and re-established Bangor as a monastery of strict observance. Malchus (in Irish Máel Ísa), brother of the notable reformer Gilla Críst Ó Con Áirge, was a member of that community.[4] Malachy gave the vast properties of Bangor to be managed by a traditional coarb elected in the usual way and, presumably, he obliged him to support the new monastery and its community with its income. In 1124 Malachy was appointed bishop of the dioceses of Down and Connor and ruled these dioceses and Bangor until a period of very violent warfare in 1127. He withdrew to Lismore with many of his followers, and here he encountered and became a warm friend of Cormac Mac Carthaig, king of Munster (r. 1123–38), who had been defeated in local struggles and who had retired to Lismore for the time being. Cormac's reluctant religious phase did not last long, but his friendship with Malachy endured and he endowed a new monastery for him. Bernard calls it *monasterium Ibracense*: its identity is disputed and, though patronised by Cormac Mac Carthaig, it did not last long. It may have been in Uí Braccáin, a small territory in the east of the territory of Eóganacht Chaisil.[5] Malachy remained here as head of a community of monks until his return to the north in 1132.

Cellach, archbishop of Armagh, died in the Armagh house of Ardpatrick, in Co. Limerick, in April 1129 and he was buried, on his own instructions, at Lismore. Why he chose Lismore remains uncertain. The florid entry on his death in the *Annals of Ulster* vividly conveys the regard in which he was held, certainly in his own diocese of Armagh:

> Cellach coarb of Patrick, a virgin and the chief bishop of western Europe and the only head whom Irish and foreigners, lay and clergy, obeyed,

---

4 *Vita Malachiae*, §§14, 52. 5 BL vi 1374 (line 41151); CGH 195, line 16 ('Dedad a quo Uí Dedaid id est Uí Braccáin); 223 (Uí Dedaid).

having ordained bishops and priests and all kinds of cleric besides, having consecrated many churches and cemeteries, having bestowed goods and valuables, having imposed rule and good conduct on all, laity and clergy, after a life of singing the hours, celebrating mass, fasting and praying, after extreme unction and an excellent repentance, sent forth his soul to the bosom of the angels and archangels in Ardpatrick in Munster, on Monday, the first of April, the twenty-fourth year of his abbacy and the fiftieth of his age. His body was brought on the third of April to Lismore of Mo Chutu in accordance with his own testament, and it was waked with psalms and hymns and canticles, and he was buried in the tomb of the bishops on the fourth of April.

His dying wish (*quasi testamentum*) was that Malachy succeed him as archbishop of Armagh and he sent this instruction to the kings of Munster and to the magnates of the land. His plea was immediately ignored by his own family, Uí Shínaig: the day after his burial, Muirchertach (*sed.* 1129–34), the son of Cellach's predecessor, was installed as traditional coarb of Patrick,[6] and this led to serious conflict and an immediate crisis for the reformers, all the more critical because Conchobar Mac Lochlainn (r. 1129–36), the powerful king of Ailech and overlord of Airgialla and Ulaid, and thus of Armagh, supported Uí Shínaig. Despite his professed reluctance and urged on by bishop Mael Ísa and bishop Gille, the papal legate (who, saintly though they may have been, were prepared to use force to gain their ends), Malachy was elected and consecrated archbishop of Armagh in 1132. He left the temporalities to Muirchertach, lived outside the town, and got on with the administrative and spiritual tasks of an archbishop. Muirchertach died in September 1134 and another member of Uí Shínaig, Niall, the brother of Cellach, was installed as traditional coarb of Patrick. Malachy got possession of his see in the same year, perhaps with the help of his brother, Gilla Críst, bishop of Clogher, and his brother's patron, Donnchad Ó Cerbaill, king of Airgialla, in whose kingdom Armagh lay. Niall and his party surrendered the Bachall Ísa ('Staff of Jesus') and the other insignia of St Patrick in 1135, and he resigned his coarbship in 1137. Malachy resigned his archbishopric in 1136 and Gilla Meic Liac (in Latin, Gelasius), the aristocratic abbot of Derry, was elected and consecrated archbishop of Armagh in 1137 and ruled the see until his death in 1174.

The period of reaction in Armagh was now over, but one must not underestimate its seriousness or the sincerity of its leaders. It is important to note that

6 AU 1129.3.

Bernard's embittered rhetoric about the traditional coarbs, which reflects the views of Malachy and the reformers, is strongly partisan: for example, he describes Muirchertach as 'not a bishop but a tyrant' (though he made no claim to be bishop), Niall as the issue of 'a damned lineage'.[7] Far from using such intemperate language, the annals treat these Uí Shínaig coarbs as venerable ecclesiastical figures. The death of Muirchertach in 1134 is reported as having taken place 'after the victory of martyrdom and penance';[8] the accession of Gilla Meic Liac in 1137 is recorded succinctly as: 'a change of abbots in Armagh i.e. the erenagh of Derry [Gilla Meic Liac] in the place of Niall son of Aed'. This notice pointedly ignores Malachy's canonical claim to the primacy, and may represent the view of one faction. Niall's own death-notice in 1139 describes him as 'coarb of Patrick for a time' who died 'after intense penitence'.[9] Evidently, pious intentions and canonical process were not enough. Malachy's resignation in 1136 was motivated by calculation rather than by saintly humility: if the reformers were to succeed, their candidate for the primacy needed to be a great ecclesiastical grandee, and Gilla Meic Liac, former abbot of Derry and a scion of Uí Néill,[10] had the lineage and ecclesiastical status required to give them credibility.

Malachy resumed his position as bishop of Down. Working from a monastic community, probably in Bangor, and observing the monastic life (so says Bernard), Malachy laboured pastorally to better his diocese.[11]

But his perspective was much wider than Bangor, and we can infer that he saw himself as the leader of reform and one who ought be archbishop of Armagh. Reformers are none other than those who want one's position, power and property because of an absolute conviction that they can and will devote them to proper ends. The uncompassionate sacrifice of individuals and institutions is part of the business – loss of property, status and reputation. Malachy was a man of steely ambition and unquestioning self-confidence. He felt he could dismiss the leadership of powerful churches, reject all forms of Irish monasticism, transfer enormous assets from one institution to another, reshape the whole of the Irish church, and if possible society at large. Like nearly all political leaders he was charismatic, political, persuasive, conciliatory, coercive, manipulative, subtle and disingenuous; he was one who could dissimulate, and if necessary bully. Bernard's image of the shy, withdrawn holy man is a pious fiction.

Apparently unhappy that the two Irish archbishops had yet to be granted the pallia,[12] and perhaps in the second half of 1138 or early in 1139, Malachy

---

7 *Vita Malachiae*, §§20, 22. 8 AFM 1134 (based on the lost entries of the lacunose AU). 9 AFM 1137, 1139. 10 Lec. facs. 56rd3–16; Séamus Pender (ed.), *The O Clery Book of genealogies* = *Analecta Hibernica* 18 (Dublin, 1951), 42. 11 *Vita Malachiae*, §§31–2; H.J. Lawlor, 'Notes on St Bernard's Life of St Malachy, and his two sermons on the passing of St Malachy', *Proc Roy Ir Acad (C)*, 35 (1919), 230–64. 12 The *pallium*

decided to go to Rome and seek them from pope Innocent II (*sed.* 1130–43). He may also be responding to Innnocent II's Second Lateran Council (2–17 April 1139), convoked in 1138 (and Irish bishops may have been summoned), or to its decrees which set out afresh the programme of the reformers.[13] Through the good offices of Bernard, the pope was without opposition, and that news would have quickly reached Ireland. In regard to Malachy's proposed visit to Rome, Bernard states that at first, his decision was opposed by clergy and magnates 'because all judged that they could not endure so long an absence of the loving father of them all ... Therefore, all with one voice opposed him, and would have used force but that he threatened them with divine vengeance'. Malachy resolutely faced them down and, reluctantly, they finally consented. Behind Bernard's pious palaver one can discern a serious rift among the reformers. There may be more. Malachy's opponents may have distrusted his attempt to solve Irish problems by an appeal to the pope; they may have considered him undiplomatic and extreme in his views about the Irish church; they may not have shared his enthusiasm for foreign religious orders; but the details of these disagreements are hidden from us. Besides, they may have learned of, and greatly disliked, his proposal to set aside Irish monasticism wholly and to introduce foreign orders into Ireland. In fact, they may have thought he was too big for his boots. Malachy's threatening his opponents with divine vengeance is in character. The Irish problems, as he saw them, were that there were two metropolitans, no primacy in the strict Roman sense (other than a largely unwanted offer from Canterbury), and the ambiguous position of Dublin was still unresolved. Some may have prudently felt that the time was not yet ripe for radical changes; and if they did, they were proved right.

Malachy adamantly set out for Clairvaux and Rome. He crossed over from Bangor to Scotland, late in 1139 or very early in 1140, and he went by Carlisle to York where he met Waltheof, abbot of the Cistercian monastery of Melrose (founded in 1136). Together with his large retinue, including five priests and other clerics, he travelled on foot (they had three or four pack-horses between them), and progress was slow, perhaps 150 km per week. His route southwards from York would bring him to London and Canterbury, and he probably sailed from Dover to the French coast at Wissant. His next major stop, evidently care-

---

(plural *pallia*) is a circular band of lamb's wool, with hanging strips and dark crosses, granted by the pope to metropolitans and signifying the legal powers the metropolitan has in his province. The synod of Ravenna (877) required metropolitans to seek the pallium, in person or by deputy, within three months of their consecration. Shortly thereafter that rule was established throughout the West, apart from Ireland. **13** Decrees 1–2 (against simony), 6–8, 21 (against clerical marriage), 10, 25 (lay ownership of churches, or disposal of churches by laymen, and that all churches have the means to have priests), 17 (marriage with the forbidden degrees of consanguinity) were important issues for Irish reformers).

fully planned in advance, was Clairvaux, about 425 km away. Here he was received by Bernard in spring 1140. Clearly, Malachy was well-informed about Bernard's role in healing the recent schism and his consequent influence with Innocent II (*sed.* 1130–43). His purposes in going to Clairvaux, well prepared by previous contact by letter, if not by envoy, were at the least twofold: his interest in the monastic practices of Clairvaux and to get Bernard's support for his mission. Malachy spent a month in Rome. Though Innocent II treated him with kindness, appointed him papal legate in place of the ailing Gille, and papally confirmed the new metropolitan sees of Armagh and Cashel, he temporised about the pallia, and ruled (so Bernard records): 'In regard to the pallia, however, more formal action must be taken. You must call together the bishops and clergy, and the magnates of the land and hold a general council, and so with the assent and common desire of all you shall demand the pallium by persons of honest repute and it shall be given to you'.[14] This decision was deeply disappointing for Malachy. Bernard offers no explanation but the pope's reasoning is apparent. By the time Malachy reached Rome, Theobald, the newly consecrated archbishop of Canterbury, who had gone to Rome with four of his suffragans to get the pallium and to attend the Second Lateran Council (2–17 April 1139), had been and gone. Anxious to protect Canterbury's metropolitan relationship with Dublin and other Irish suffragans, and keen to defend its claim to primacy over Ireland, Theobald used all his efforts and the rising influence of the English at Rome to obstruct Malachy.[15] Besides, he very likely saw the erection of a single British church for the whole of the British Isles under the primacy of Canterbury as the best way forward for reform, as well as for a fraught Canterbury also menaced by Welsh and Scottish manoeuvres against its primacy. Faced with the irreconcilable claims of Canterbury and the wishes of Malachy (backed by Bernard), indebted to both sides for support in the recent schism and anxious to avoid another, the pope dissembled. He offered to give Malachy what he wanted on conditions he thought would never be met, namely, a united demand from the divided Irish church; and he was able to assure Theobald that Canterbury's interests would be respected.[16] As Bernard relates, the pope 'then took the mitre from his own head and placed it on Malachy's, and

---

14 *Vita Malachiae*, §§33–8. 15 R.L. Poole, *Studies in chronology and history* (Oxford, 1934), 287–97; Avrom Saltman, *Theobald, archbishop of Canterbury* (London 1956, repr. New York 1969), 14–15; Flanagan, *Irish society*, 32–6. 16 The pope's reassurance helps explain Theobald's dealings with an Irish diocese, the first direct Canterbury intervention in Ireland for nearly twenty years (Flanagan, *Irish society*, 31–3). When Gille resigned his see in 1140, Theobald immediately consecrated one Patrick to Limerick. This Patrick witnessed an agreement at St Paul's, London, in 1145 and was one of the four assistant prelates at episcopal consecrations at Canterbury in 1148. It is not likely that he got possession of his see (Gwynn, 'Diocese of Limerick', 39–40).

he gave him the stole and maniple he used in the offering as well. He saluted him with the kiss of peace and dismissed him, strengthened with the apostolic blessing and authority'[17] – empty if charming tokens that masked the pope's real intent, judicious procrastination. Malachy returned via Clairvaux, where he again spent time with an admiring Bernard whom he appears to have completely captivated, and he was back in Ireland by autumn 1140.

MALACHY AND THE CISTERCIANS

By training and inclination Malachy was a monk, and he worked diligently and tirelessly to promote his vision of monastic reform and innovation. His programme for monasticism was the introduction of foreign religious orders to replace the indigenous forms of the monastic life, in which he appears to have quite lost faith. Apparently, he first turned to the Savigniacs who were reformed Benedictines. The Savigniac house of Tulketh in Lancashire, founded in 1124 (the community moved to nearby Furness in 1127), may have been visited by Malachy. In September 1127, Niall mac Duinn Shlébe, king of Ulaid (r. 1113–27), founded a Savigniac monastery at Erenagh, Co. Down (it was, it appears, given the name Carrick). Thus, French or Anglo-French monks were now introduced to Ireland and a succession of four abbots is recorded until Savigny fused with Cîteaux and Carrick became a daughter-house of the English Cistercian abbey of Furness.[18] It was destroyed by John de Courcy about 1177 and re-built by him at Inis Cúscraid (Inch, Co. Down).[19] Malachy joined Gréine, bishop of Dublin, about 1148 in consecrating the grounds of St Mary's Abbey Dublin, a Savigniac house.[20]

The Cistercian foundations in Ireland derive directly from Malachy's meeting with Bernard in 1140. On his return journey from Rome, he left four of his companions, including Gilla Críst Ó Con Áirge and probably Comgán, to be trained as Cistercian monks at Clairvaux. He sent more candidates to Clairvaux in 1141 and these brought Bernard the present of a walking-stick. They also brought Bernard a letter from Malachy, ever anxious to bring the Cistercians to Ireland as quickly as possible, asking him to send two monks to find a place for a monastery in Ireland. Bernard replied that they were not yet ready, but he

17 *Vita Malachiae*, §38; for Malachy's disappointment, ibid., §67.   18 H.G. Richardson, 'Some Norman monastic foundations in Ireland', in J.A. Watt, J.B. Morrall & F.X. Martin (ed.), *Medieval studies presented to Aubrey Gwynn SJ* (Dublin, 1961), 29–43; A. Gwynn & Neville Hadcock, *Medieval religious houses: Ireland* (London, 1970, repr. Dublin, 1988), 132.   19 Flanagan, *Transformation of the Irish church*, 159. 20 H.J. Lawlor, 'Notes on the church of St Michan's, Dublin', *J Roy Soc Antiq Ire*, 56 (1926), 11–21: 12; idem, 'The foundation of St Mary's Abbey, Dublin', ibid., 22–8; Holland, 'Dublin and the reform', 154.

asked Malachy to find a site 'far removed from the turmoil of the world'.[21] He did, about 8 km north-west of Drogheda, in the valley of the Mattock, on lands donated for the purpose by Donnchad Ó Cerbaill, king of Airgialla, friend of Malachy and supporter of reform. Here the monastery of Mellifont was founded in 1142,[22] by a pioneer community of four Irishmen and nine Frenchmen. The second batch of Irish monks trained at Clairvaux arrived later. Malachy was in constant correspondence with Bernard who wrote warmly in 1143/4 congratulating him on the progress with the building, but there were conflicts between the Irish and the French monks (some went back to Clairvaux) and Bernard had doubts about monastic discipline in the new house. He sent back to Mellifont abbot Gilla Críst Ó Con Áirge 'whom we have instructed more fully, as far as we could, in the observances of our Order and we hope that he will be more careful about them in future'.[23] Despite these problems, the venture flourished. Gilla Críst became bishop of Lismore in 1151 but Mellifont contined to prosper.

The abbey was completed in 1157 and its dedication was a splendid occasion in church and state that demonstrates the reformers' remarkable influence and their ability to organise. One wonders who paid for the ostentation. The abbey was consecrated by Gilla Meic Liac, primate and archbishop of Armagh, assisted by Gréine, archbishop of Dublin, Aed Ó hOisín, archbishop of Tuam, and the papal legate.

An assembly of seniors was convened by the clergy of Ireland and by some of the kings at the monastery of Droichet Átha [Mellifont], the church of the monks. There were present seventeen bishops with the legate [Gilla Críst Ó Con Áirge] ... The number of other personages of every degree was without count. Among the kings were Muirchertach Mac Lochlainn [king of Ireland]; Tigernán Ó Ruairc [king of Breifne]; [Cú Ulad] Ó hEochada [king of Ulaid]; Donnchad Ó Cerbaill [king of Airgialla]. ... Muirchertach Mac Lochlainn presented seven score cows and three score ounces of gold to God and to the clergy as an offering for the welfare of his soul. He also granted them a townland at Droichet Átha, namely Finnabair na nIngen.[24] Ó Cerbaill gave them three score ounces of gold. And the wife of Tigernán Ó Ruairc, daughter of Ó

---

21 Mabillon, *Bernardi Opera*, i 633–5 (letter 341); Lawlor, *Malachy*, 131–3; Bruno Scott James (tr.), *The letters of St Bernard of Clairvaux* (London, 1953, repr. Stroud, 1998), 452–3. **22** ASMD 1142. **23** Mabillon, *Bernardi Opera*, i 653–4 (letter 357); Lawlor, *Malachy*, 134–7; James, *Letters of St Bernard*, 454–5. **24** Fennor (478 acres), in parish of Donore, nr Drogheda, on S. side of the Boyne, opposite the mouth of the Mattock river.

Maelechlainn, gave the same amount and a chalice of gold on the altar of Mary, and a cloth for each of the nine other altars in that church.[25]

Candid contemporary observers may have wondered how, on this magnificent occasion, clerical splendour, high society, displays of great wealth, and apparent monastic purgation and purification could sit well together, and constitute reform.

One is not surprised, then, that there was a strong flow of recruits into the Cistercian order and already in the lifetime of Bernard Mellifont founded five Irish daughter-houses.[26] The first was Bective (Beatitudo Dei) in the Boyne valley, founded and endowed by Ó Maelechlainn, king of Meath, in 1145. In eight years, six more foundations were made from Mellifont. The second was Inislounaght (Surium) on the Suir near Clonmel, c.1147. Three belong to 1148: Boyle (Buellium); Monasteranenagh (Magium) founded by Tairdelbach Ó Briain, king of Thomond († 1167), and patronised after his death by his son, Domnall Mór; and Baltinglass (Vallis Salutis), founded by Diarmait Mac Murchada, king of Leinster, in 1148×1151. Kilbeggan (Benedictio Dei) was founded in 1150, perhaps by a local aristocratic family, and in 1153 Newry (Viride Lignum) was established by Muirchertach Mac Lochlainn, king of Ailech and later king of Ireland. By 1154, there were ten Cistercian abbeys in Ireland, by 1171, fifteen.[27] In the third quarter of the twelfth century, the Cistercians became very influential and well endowed: they enjoyed the patronage of the kings and nobles. However, it is likely that the expansion of the Cistercians in Ireland was neither as neat, nor as easy, nor as simple as the Cistercian records have it. The foundation dates given above are those in the Cistercian filiation tables, but behind these dates lie lengthy processes. Four Cistercian monks became bishops: Gilla Críst Ó Con Áirge, bishop of Lismore (*sed.* 1151–79; †1186) and papal legate; Máel Ísu Ó Laígenáin (†1163), bishop of Emly, formerly a monk of Baltinglass; Finn Ó Gormáin (†1160), bishop of Kildare and former abbot of Newry; and Petrus Ó Mórda, bishop of Clonfert (*sed.* c.1150–71). The synod of Kells in 1152 was the high-water mark of Cistercian influence on Irish affairs.

CANONS REGULAR OF ST AUGUSTINE

A distinct order of the Canons Regular of St Augustine was fully recognised by pope Leo IX (*sed.* 1049–54) and given an official standing in the church in 1059.

---

25 AFM 1157; AU, ATig, ASMD 1157. 26 *Vita Malachiae*, §39. 27 C. Conway, *The story of Mellifont* (Dublin, 1958) 1–18; G. Mac Niocaill, *Na manaigh liatha in Éirinn* (Dublin, 1959), 1–19; Gwynn & Hadcock, *Religious houses*, 114–44; Roger Stalley, *The Cistercian monasteries of Ireland: an account of the history, art and architecture of the White Monks in Ireland from 1142 to 1540* (London, 1987).

Various kinds of canons, regular and secular, have a long history. The pope encouraged the formation of communities of canons to restore religious discipline and re-establish clerical celibacy. From their re-formation they were a weapon of church reform, indeed its cutting edge. In time, there came into being congregations of houses of canons founded from an exemplary house. Some lived a completely monastic life, some combined the monastic life with parish work and diocesan re-organisation. The Arrouaisian order was a congregation of the second kind. It was founded in Arrouaise in Flanders in 1090 but flourished under abbot Gervase (consecrated in 1121), and by 1148 the order had spread widely in Europe and was one of the best-known congregations of the Canons Regular of St Augustine. It was introduced to Ireland by Malachy.

In a document of 1179, abbot Gaultier of Arrouaise states that Malachy, in the abbacy of his predecessor Gervase (*sed.* 1121–47), visited the abbey:

> Malachy of holy memory, archbishop of the Irish, visited us, inspected and approved of our rule, and had our books and liturgical usages transcribed, and brought them with him to Ireland; and he ordered that almost all clerics in episcopal seats and in many other places in Ireland should receive and observe our order and habit and above all the divine office in church.[28]

This visit took place in 1140 when, according to Bernard, 'he left some with us, and some in other places, to learn the rule of life'. He may already have known about the rule because it had been intended (though there is no evidence for its adoption) for the cathedral of Carlisle, 1131×1148. Like rules were widespread elsewhere: by 1125 there were thirty houses of Augustinian Canons in England and Wales.

Malachy introduced the Arrouaisian rule between his return in 1140 and his death in 1148 – his obit describes him as the man 'who restored monasticism and canons regular in Ireland'[29] – perhaps first in 1142 at Louth on the site and lands of the earlier church and monastery of Louth. This may have been the head of the Arrouaisian congregation in Ireland. He established another house at Saul, Co. Down, while he was papal legate,[30] and it is likely that he introduced the rule to Bangor and Down, and one of these houses was the cathedral chap-

---

28 B.-M. Tock (ed.), *Monumenta Arroasiensia*, CCCH, 175 (Turnhout, 2000), 26–7; PL 217, 67. What follows is based on P.J. Dunning, 'The Arroasian order in medieval Ireland', *Ir Hist Stud*, 4 (1944–5), 297–315 and Marie Therese Flanagan, 'St Mary's Abbey, Louth, and the introduction of the Arrouaisian observance in Ireland', *Clogher Rec*, 10 (1980), 223–34. 29 ATig 1148. 30 AU, ALC, AFM 1170; AFM 1156. 31 CS, AFM 1148.

ter. Malachy's friend and fellow reformer, Aed Ó Caellaide, himself a canon, bishop of Louth and confessor to king Diarmait Mac Murchada, played a major role in expanding the rule of Arrouaise in Airgialla and Leinster. All Hallows, Dublin, founded by Mac Murchada about 1162, was Arrouaisian from the start and was a daughter-house of Louth. Ó Caellaide co-founded the Augustinian abbey of SS Peter and Paul at Knock (Cnoc na nApstal) with Donnchad Ó Cerbaill, king of Airgialla, and this was consecrated by Malachy in 1148.[31] Ó Cerbaill also founded a house for Augustinian canons and canonesses at Termonfeckin, Co. Louth.[32] Ó Caellaide is described in his obit as 'bishop of Airgialla and head of the canons of Ireland'.[33] Laurence O'Toole (Lorcán Ó Tuathail), elected abbot of Glendalough in 1153, was already a reformer. He may have introduced the Arrouaisian canons to Glendalough after he became arch-bishop of Dublin. As archbishop and a canon, he sought papal confirmation (perhaps in the face of local opposition) for the use of the Arrouaisian rule in his cathedral chapter in Christ Church.

According to *Visio Tnugdali* (AD 1149), which attributes the foundation of fifty-four houses to Malachy, he also established houses of canonesses.[34] St Mary's Abbey at Clonard was the mother-house of the Arrouaisian canonesses, and was dependent on St Mary's Abbey, Louth. Mac Murchada founded the convent of Arrouaisian canonesses at St Mary de Hogges in Dublin *c.*1146 and the cells of Aghade, Co. Carlow, and Kilculiheen, Co. Waterford, by 1152 at the latest. Churches, usually dedicated to St Mary, were shared by canons and canonesses at Termonfeckin, Duleek, Kells, Durrow, Clonfert and other places.

The Augustinian reform was applied in two ways: to cathedral chapters and to early Irish churches. Malachy and his followers proposed to strengthen reform and the new diocesan organisation by having Arrouaisian cathedral chapters. They succeeded in a few cases, but there was opposition from senior clergy in many, and the compromise was that separate houses of Arrouaisian canons were established close to the episcopal seats. At Armagh, the cathedral retained its original chapter, the monastery of SS Peter and Paul became Arrouaisian. Louth, Kells (near Connor, Co. Antrim), Down, Kells (Co. Meath),

32 Dublin, Trinity College, 77 olim B. 1. 1, obit of Donnchad Ua Cerbaill (George Petrie, *The ecclesiastical architecture of Ireland* (2nd. ed. Dublin, 1845) 394); Whitley Stokes (ed.), *Martyrology of Gorman*, HBS 9 (London, 1895) xx; Lawlor, *Malachy*, 170. **33** ALC, AFM 1182. **34** CLH 657; Brigitte Pfeil, *Die 'Vision des Tnugdalus' Albers von Windberg: Literatur- und Frömmigkeitgeschichte im ausgehenden 12. Jahrhundert mit einer Edition der lateinischen 'Visio Tnugdali' aus Clm 22254*, Mikrokosmos: Beiträge zur Literaturwissenschaft und Bedeutungsforschung, 54 (Frankfurt-am-Main etc., 1999) *55; Jean-Michel Picard & Yolande de Pontfarcy (tr.), *The vision of Tnugdal* (Dublin, 1989), 155.

Clonard, Ferns, Leighlin, Tuam and Clonfert appear to have been early houses of canons regular separate from the cathedral chapters.[35] Very many early Irish houses not associated with episcopal seats became Augustinian, mostly in the period from 1145 to the English Invasion, the period of rapid change when the Augustinian rule spread widely. Sometimes, the canons regular took over the whole site and lands of the pre-existing house, more commonly they appropriated part of the resources of the earlier house, in share with the diocesan bishops (to whom they paid head-rent).

Extensive lands granted to the Augustinian canons at the sites of Irish churches can be estimated, roughly, by reference to the later inquisitions and the jurors' oaths during the Henrician suppression of the monasteries. The following examples will give some impression of the size of the transfers.

> *Durrow* (Daurmag): the abbot was seized of the village of Durrow, the site of the 'abbey' ... church, hall, and other buildings, ruined castle, two rectories, several messuages and cottages, and over 1000 acres of land (Inquisition of 1569)
>
> *Greatconnell* (Condal): 1260 acres, a mill, five castles, about twelve parish churches, many messuages and cottages; prior seized of 1135 acres (Henrician jurors, 1540; 5 Edward VI). Estates complicated by extensive post-Invasion endowments.
>
> *Inistioge* (Inis Teóc): Augustinian priory of Columba: priory church parochial; with other buildings, orchards and gardens; 400 acres of land, many messuages, burgages, unmeasured gardens, salmon fishery on the Nore, two water mills, interest in about 14 rectories (Henrician jurors, 1541). Estates complicated by extensive post-Invasion endowments.
>
> *Louth* (Lugmad): priory church parochial; 1700 acres with 12 farms, many messuages, cottages &c., water mill, interest in about 36 churches (Henrician jurors, 1540)
>
> *Molana* (Dairinis Mael Anfaid): church, cloister and conventual buildings, garden and meadow, 380 acres of land, three salmon weirs, water mill, four rectories (Henrician jurors, 1541)[36]

When lands of such extent change hands, fraud and wrongful conversion are inevitable; the sources tell us nothing, as if all went in proper order without a hitch.

---

35 Gwynn & Hadcock, *Medieval religious houses,* 149. **36** Gwynn & Hadcock, *Medieval religious houses: Ireland,* 174–5, 177, 179–80, 185–6, 187

Occasionally, the earlier houses (some laicised, some not, and latterly known as communities of Culdees) continued side by side with the Augustinian house (as for example in Devenish, Co. Fermanagh, and in Monaincha, Co. Tipperary). So, too, at Clonmacnoise, the house of Culdees continued to prosper.[37] One must believe that many of the 'new' Augustinians were traditional Irish clergy of the old order in a new and trendy black habit, and that they maintained many of their old concerns and practices including an interest in scholarship, at least on the part of some.[38] At several of the houses coarbs and erenaghs continue to be recorded in the annals and, if the officer class remained, many more humbler members survived the changes. I believe that the cultural gaelicisation of the English colonists, a remarkable transformation that has yet to attract serious research, was the work of the traditional churchmen.

Nonetheless, the Augustinian rule, whether Arrouaisian or a variant, suited Irish conditions. The Irish mother houses and their ministry were, in the eleventh century and much earlier, closer to houses of secular canons, each of whom had his own endowment, than to communities of monks in the conventional sense. Individual priests, supervised by a bishop, usually connected with the mother house, served the parishes. These provided pastoral care and were maintained by the tithes and the contributions of those to whom they ministered, as well as by the dues of the tenantry of their church lands. From the point of view of reformers, the Augustinian rule was an exceptionally useful compromise: it was a good fit that matched important features of the traditional foundations and, while apparently effecting reform and prescribing celibacy, it did not do violence to more traditional concepts of church organisation and property management, and left room for adaptation to local conditions. It is regarded as one of the successes of the reform and far more important and locally influential than the grander and high-profile Cistercian foundations that soon fell into disorder and decay.[39] The early introduction of the Augustinian canons shows that Ireland was in tune with what was fashionable in continental Europe where the Arrouaisian rule, for example, was rapidly expanding, and was abreast of the contemporary European reform movement. As it proved, this was not enough.

---

37 AFM, ATig 1170: Maol Mórdha Mac Uairéirghe, sruith-senóir déshearcach, sonus, & saidhbhres Cluana Mic Nóis, cend a Chéled Dé, do écc i mí Nouember. **38** CLH 154, 255, 714,, 823, 1323, 1351–2, 1356. Apart from the Martyrology of Gorman (AD 1166×1174, CLH 255), evidence of Augustinian scholarship is mainly fourteenth/fifteenth-century and modest and slim (Saints' Island on Lough Ree, Lisgoole, Navan, Lorrha, Duleek). **39** Watt, *Church and the two nations*, 85–107; B.W. O'Dwyer, 'The problem of reform in the Irish Cistercian monasteries and the attempted solution of Stephen of Lexington in 1228', *J Ecclesiast Hist*, 15 (1964), 186–91.

MALACHY AND REFORM (1140–8)

Little is certain about Malachy's career in this period. Bernard's narrative becomes, for the most part, a formless, pietistic and uncritical recounting of Malachy's godliness and miracle-working, presumably based on Irish documentation and on hearsay and the pious imagination. Bernard had determined to seek canonisation of Malachy as a saint and therefore needed a dossier of miracles to present to the papacy and Irish Cistercians gave him one that he reworked.[40] Malachy's remarkable miracles and fine deeds are set out at length: in Bangor, Coleraine, Lismore, Saul, Antrim, Cloyne, Leinster (probably Ferns), Cashel, Cork and elsewhere.[41] Bernard does, however, state that Malachy exercised the office of papal legate, was almost constantly travelling (on foot, a well-worn humility topos) throughout the dioceses, and held synods everywhere.[42] He may have been present at the great assembly of the clergy of Connacht convened by bishop Muiredach Ó Dubthaig in 1143: the annals mention only political business, namely, the demand of the clergy that Tairdelbach Ó Conchobair, king of Ireland, should release his son Ruaidrí whom he had unlawfully imprisoned, but it is likely that ecclesiastical business was also transacted.[43] Malachy was among the eminent guarantors that forced Tairdelbach Ó Briain, king of Munster, to release his nephew Tadc Glae, whom he, too, had unlawfully imprisoned in 1147 – the occasion of another 'miracle' recounted by Bernard.[44] He was responsible for the election of the reformer Gilla Aeda (in Latin Gregorius) Ó Maigín, a canon regular of Cong, as bishop of Cork at an uncertain date, perhaps in 1148.[45] This, and his presence also at Cloyne with bishop Gilla na Náem (in Latin Nehemias), may suggest that Malachy had something to do with dividing the large diocese of Cork, as set out in the synod of Ráith Bresail (1111), into the three subsequent dioceses of Cork, Cloyne and Ross. This arrangement was confirmed in 1152.

In the period 1140–8 Malachy, as papal legate, worked hard to bring about the Irish general synod that would make a united appeal to the papacy for the

---

40 Marie Therese Flanagan (pers. comm.). 41 *Vita Malachiae*, §§42–56. 42 CLH 255. Martyrology of Gorman al. Féilire Uí Ghormáin (AD 1166×1174) commemorates Malachy (2 November) as *suí senad* 'sage of synods', Whitley Stokes (ed. & tr.), *Félire hÚi Gormáin: the Martyrology of Gorman*, HBS 9 (London, 1895), 210. Ó Gormáin, otherwise known as Marianus Gorman, was abbot of the Augustinian house of Cnoc na nApstal al. Cnoc na Sengán (SS Peter and Paul), Knock, near the town of Louth). 43 ATig, AFM, CS 1143. 44 AFM 1147; MacCarthy's Book, 1147 (1145–7); *Vita Malachiae*, §60; Mabillon, *Bernardi Opera*, iii 2226–31: §2 = Lawlor, *Malachy*, 154. 45 *Vita Malachiae*, §51; T.J. Walsh & Denis O'Sullivan, 'St Malachy, the Gill Abbey of Cork, and the rule of Arrouaise', *J Cork Hist Archaeol Soc*, 54 (1949), 41–60; Diarmuid Ó Murchadha, 'Gill Abbey and the "rental of Cong"', ibid., 90 (1985), 31–45; A. Gwynn, 'The bishops of Cork in the twelfth century', *Ir Ecclesiast Rec*, 74 (1950), 17–29, 97–109.

recognition of an Irish primacy and the grant of pallia to the metropolitans. The result of his labours was the national synod (the first from which secular rulers were wholly absent) held on St Patrick's Island (Inis Pátraic), an island off the Dublin coast, near Skerries, for four or five days in late May 1148.[46] There is a very meagre record in the annals: 'A synod was convened on St Patrick's Island by Malachy, successor of St Patrick, at which were present fifteen bishops and two hundred priests to enjoin rule and morals on all, laity and clergy, and Malachy, on the instruction of the synod, went a second time to confer with the pope'.[47] This was the formal end to a long process, and it ratified agreements that had already been reached – hence its small size.

Only major ecclesiastical and political compromises within Ireland could bring about unity, and this explains why nearly eight years elapsed before Malachy could make a second appeal to Rome. The first and most difficult matter was to detach Dublin from Canterbury: the price of that was that it should become a metropolitan see, for Dublin nursed metropolitan, even primatial, ambitions. Evidently that deal was done before the synod of St Patrick's Island, and Diarmait Mac Murchada, king of Leinster, is likely to have played a part in it. How long this had been agreed is unknown, but Gréine, bishop of Dublin, and St Malachy co-consecrated the site of St Mary's Abbey in Dublin and Malachy endowed St Michan's, perhaps early in 1148, perhaps previously.[48] This concession to Dublin meant that the archbishop of Cashel lost five suffragans. Tairdelbach Ó Conchobair, king of Ireland, had to be conciliated with a metropolitan see at Tuam, and this meant that the archbishop of Armagh lost seven suffragans. No details survive of the negotiations that led to these compromises but they are likely to have been long and tedious.

Malachy set out for Rome immediately after the synod of St Patrick's Island. He crossed from Bangor to Scotland, visited Soulseat Abbey, spent a few days with king David I, and then travelled southwards through England. At first, king Stephen refused him transit, clearly because he was aware of Malachy's purpose and regarded it as damaging to English interests. Eventually, Malachy was allowed pass over to the Continent, and he reached Clairvaux on 13/14 October. There he fell ill and died on 2 November 1148.[49] Others completed his mission to Rome.

---

46 The dating is based on Lawlor's calculations in 'Notes on St Bernard's Life of St Malachy', 249–50; Herbert Immenkötter, 'Eccclesia Hibernicana: die Synode von Inis Pádraig im Jahre 1148', *Annuarium Archivum Historiae Conciliorum*, 17 (1985), 19–69. 47 AFM 1148; CS 1148 is almost identical. 48 Holland, 'Dublin and the reform', 154. 49 *Vita Malachiae*, §§67–70.

CHAPTER VII

Synod of Kells, 1152

MANY ENGLISH CHRONICLERS NOTE the journey through England, probably in the summer of 1150, of the papal *legatus a latere* cardinal John Paparo, cardinal priest of St Laurence in Damaso, who was on his way to Ireland, bearing pallia for the Irish archbishops. Two of these chroniclers knew how many pallia he had, and Robert of Torigny states that this grant of the pallia was made 'contrary to the custom of the ancients and the dignity of the church of Canterbury from which the bishops of Ireland were wont to seek and accept the blessing of consecration'. King Stephen, embroiled in various church quarrels, mostly of his own making, refused Paparo passage unless he undertook to do nothing in Ireland to lessen the rights of the kingdom of England. Paparo refused and went back to Rome in a bad mood.[1] Delegates of the Irish kings and bishops now arrived in Rome asking that the legate be despatched to Ireland.[2] He returned, but not through England, in May 1151: he sailed from Flanders and put in at Tynemouth where he was received by William, bishop of Durham. King David I of Scotland (who had his own business to transact with him) despatched his chancellor to meet him at Hexham and the king received him with great honour at Carlisle towards the end of September. Paparo was accompanied by Gilla Críst Ó Con Áirge as *legatus natus*, former abbot of Mellifont, recently made bishop of Lismore.[3] The two legates and their retinues reached Ireland in October. They went first to Armagh where they spent a week in conference as guests of archbishop Gilla Meic Liac.[4] Then they disappear from view for over four months, very likely travelling widely in Ireland, planning a national synod, and consulting with ecclesiastical leaders and lay magnates in the winter and early spring of 1151–2.

The synod met at Kells, 6–23 March 1152.[5] It is not possible to say what business was transacted when but it seems likely that the consecration of two new

1 W. Stubbs (ed.), *Chronica magistri Rogeri de Houedene,* RS 51 (4 vols, London, 1868–71), i 212; R. Howlett (ed.), *Chronicle of Robert de Torigni,* RS 82 (London, 1890), iv 166; John of Hexham, in T. Arnold (ed.), *Symeon of Durham: historical works,* RS 75 (2 vols, London, 1882–5), ii 326; Marjorie Chibnall (ed. & tr.), *The Historia pontificalis of John of Salisbury* (Oxford, 1986), 6, 71 (§§2, 36); Herbert Immenkötter, 'Ecclesia Hibernicana: die Synode von Inis Pádraig im Jahre 1148', *Annuarium Archivum Historiae Conciliorum,* 17 (1985), 19–69: 22–3. 2 *Historia pontificalis,* §36 (Chibnall, 70). 3 John of Hexham, 326; *Historia pontificalis* §36 (Chibnall, 72); NHI ix 303. 4 AFM, ASMD 1151; AC 1151 (1141); A. Gwynn, 'The centenary of the synod of Kells', *Ir Ecclesiast Rec,* 77 (1952), 161–76, 250–64 (rev. repr. Gwynn, *The Irish church,* 218–33). 5 AFM,

archbishops, probably preceded by that of four or more bishops, and the formal grant of the pallia to the four archbishops took place at an early point. Immediately after its business was finished, on the very next day, Paparo sailed for Scotland and returned to Rome.

The synod was a very grand affair, attended by 3000 clerics, including Cistercian monks and Augustinian canons, and presided over by Paparo as *legatus a latere*. This was a most expensive event for the Irish church. Each of these 3000 clerics had an attendant cleric, and at least a servant. That makes a minimum daily round of 9000 meals, 18,000 collations, and the provision of accommodation and transport for 9000 per day. For the entire synod, about 261,000 meals, wine and proportionate accommodation were required. Thousands of horses need to be foddered, watered, stabled and gillied. The papal party were surely the guests of the Irish bishops. This estimate does not account for formal meals and feasting. Nor does it a account for new vestments, altar linen, church plate, processional and pectoral crosses, thurifers, incense and other items of expenditure. Scribes had to be provided with parchment, seals and wax to make multiple copies of the decisions and constitutions, and a certified official copy had to be prepared and dispatched to Rome to be enrolled in the papal archives. Where did the bishops raise the money and credit for this lavish event. Who paid for this? We do not know, but the cost fell ultimately on the *manaig* of the Irish church who cultivated its lands and paid its taxes, and on the contributions and tithes of the laity. Reform did not come cheap.

According to Keating's exiguous record, twenty-two bishops were present: Gilla Críst Ó Con Áirge, bishop of Lismore and *legatus natus*; Gilla Meic Liac Mac Ruaidrí, coarb of Patrick, archbishop of Armagh and primate; Domnall Ó Lonngargáin, archbishop of Cashel; and the bishops of Achonry, Ardagh, Ardfert, Clonmacnoise, Connor, Cork, Derry, Down, Dublin, Elphin, Emly, Glendalough, Kildare, Kilmore, Leighlin, Limerick, Meath and Ossory.[6] There were, if the record is at all complete, notable absentees: Aed Ó Caellaide, bishop of Clogher-Louth (*sed.* 1138–78); Tadc Ó Lonngargáin, bishop of Killaloe (*sed.* *c.*1138–61); Petrus Ó Mórda, bishop of Clonfert (*sed.* *c.*1150–71); and the bishops or bishops-elect of Cloyne, Ferns, Raphoe, Kilfenora, Killala, Kilmacduagh and Ross, whose names are either uncertain or unknown. Tuam was not repre-

ATig, AB, ASMD 1152; Keating, *History*, iii 312–16, 356 (citing the lost Annals of Clonenagh); London, British Library, Additional 4783 (S.H. O'Grady, Robin Flower & Myles Dillon, *Catalogue of Irish manuscripts in the British Museum* (3 vols, London, 1925–53, repr. Dublin, 1992), ii 524–5); Martin Holland, 'The synod of Kells in MS BL, Add. 4783', *Peritia*, 19 (2005), 164–72. Holland argues convincingly that the synod was held at Kells, though he concedes that some functions may have taken place at nearby Mellifont.   6 Keating, *History*, iii 316; NHI ix 268–332.

sented: the see was vacant since the death of bishop Muiredach Ó Dubthaig in 1150. That vacancy was filled at the synod itself where Aed Ó hOisín was appointed and consecrated archbishop of Tuam.

The *acta* of the synod have not survived, though John of Salisbury was aware that its decrees were once preserved in Ireland and in the papal archives, where evidently he inspected them.[7] However, some of them can be reconstructed, at least in part, from chronicles and other sources.

1. The synod 'extirpated and condemned all forms of simony and usury'. According to the annals this extended to centuries-old customary payments made for the sacraments: 'Seek no payment for unction or baptism'. The annalist adds: 'However, it is not good not to make such payments if one is able to'. An additional detail reported by the annalist is: *gan lógh do ghabháil ar domhan n-ecclastucdha* 'that payment is not to be taken for church property'. Here *domhan* can mean influence as well as property in the sense of real estate, and may refer to simoniacal payments for church property or for influence in church matters such as appointments and the grant of benefices. Here, then, simony and usury are used as catch-all terms for suspect payments and dealings in church.[8]

2. The synod 'ordered the payment of tithes by apostolic authority', expressed by the annalist as *deachmhadh do ghabhail go h-iondraic* 'that the tithe should be received according to law'.[9] This brief record may hide some complexity. The concern of the fathers is not merely that tithes should be paid (for there is a long history of tithe-paying in early medieval Ireland)[10] but that they should be paid to the right persons, that is, that they should support the new secular hierarchy and its vicars and rectors, and not the traditional coarbs and erenaghs. The payment of tithes was essential for funding the new territorial dioceses. It was difficult to prise their ecclesiastical estates from the coarbs and erenaghs – after all estates were their last card – and it was some time before the episcopal churches got an effective income from many of their assets. This made the proper payment of tithes all the more urgent. Besides, wrongful conversion of tithes was a long-established abuse, eloquently condemned in the 'Vision of Adomnán', which speaks of the doomed as fettered to fiery columns in a sea of fire, with fiery chains about their waists:

7 *Historia pontificalis*, §36 (Chibnall, 72). 8 Keating, *History*, iii 314, 356; AFM 1152. 9 Ibid. 10 'De decimis' (Cologne, Dombibl. 210, 46c–47v; Rome, Bib. Vallicelliana, t. XVIII, 75v; Oxford, Bodley, Hatton 42, 28r–v), a chapter of *Hibernensis*, book 19, recension B; inc. 'Decimas tuas et primitiuas tuas non tardabis offere Domino'. Bieler, *Irish penitentials*, 166–8 (Canones Hibernenses III); Kuno Meyer (ed. & tr.), 'Duties of a husbandman', *Ériu*, 2 (1905), 172 §3; D. Ó Corráin, L. Breatnach & A. Breen, 'The laws of the Irish', *Peritia* 3 (1984), 382–438: 395–9, 408, 410–12. *Coir ecalsa o tuaith: decmada & primite & primgene dliged ecalsa dia membraib* 'the right of the church from the lay community: tithes, first fruits, and firstlings are the entitlement of the church from its members' (CIH ii 530, lines 32–3).

Is iat iarom filet isin phéin sin pecdaig & fingalaig & áes aidmillte ecailse Dé & airchinnig etrócair bíte ós inchaib martra na náeb for danaib & dech-madaib na hecailsi & dogníat dona indmasaib selba sainrudcha sech aígedu & aidlicnechu in Comded

Those, then, who are in that torment are sinners and kin-slayers and the destroyers of God's church, the merciless superiors who, in the presence of the relics of the saints, have charge of the gifts and the tithes of the church, and they convert these possessions into private property and defraud the guests and the needy of the Lord.[11]

In addition, tithe-farming and the levying of tithes by secular lords (they of course took the levying share of one third) appear to have been long estab-lished.[12] The ancient practice was to divide church income into four parts: one for the bishop (*quarta episcopalis*), one for the clergy, one to support the poor, and one to maintain the fabric of the church. In medieval Ireland, the tithes were also divided in four: one for the bishop, one for the rector, one for the vicar, and one for the support of the poor. There is some evidence that this may have been the twelfth-century practice: the Register of Clogher relates that Malachy obtained from pope Innocent II a grant of a quarter of the tithes of his diocese for his brother, Gilla Críst Ó Morgair, bishop of Clogher (*sed.* 1135–8)[13] – a revenue enjoyed by the bishops of Clogher until the seventeenth century.

3. The synod condemned crimes of violence: 'robbery and rape, bad morals and evils of every kind besides'.[14]

4. The synod legislated on marriage. John of Hexham has a very general statement about Paparo's mission: 'and he corrected in many things a people not accustomed to the law of marriage'. The annals preserve more detail: *mna cuil & cairdeasa d'ionnarbhadh ó fheraibh* 'that incestuous wives and concubines be banished by men'.[15] Two types of relationships are envisaged here: marriages

11 CLH 169; 'Fís Adomnán' in R.I. Best & Osborn J. Bergin (ed.), *Lebor na hUidre* (Dublin, 1929), 67–76: 73, lines 2174–8; C.S. Boswell (tr.), *An Irish precursor of Dante: a study on the vision of heaven and hell ascribed to the eighth-century Irish saint Adamnán, with translation of the Irish text*, Grimm Library, 18 (London, 1908; repr. New York, 1972), 28–47: 40 §25. 12 CIH ii 525.1, 526.20–23 ('Córus bésgnai'); cf. Mac Murchada's grant of Baldoyle to Aed Ua Caellaide, bishop of Louth in a charter of c.1162, 'cum omni lib-ertate sine aliqua decimarum exactione' (Marie Therese Flanagan, *Irish royal charters: texts and contexts* (Oxford, 2005), 280–1); Richard Butler (ed.), *Registrum prioratus omnium sanctorum juxta Dublin* (Dublin, 1845), 50–1 (§49); Mac Murchada's charter of 1160–2 to St Mary's, Ferns, refers to 'omnes deci-mas et primitias de dominico meo per Hukenselich [Uí Chennselaig]' (Flanagan, *Irish royal charters*, 284–5); Herbert Hore, *History of the town and count of Wexford* (6 vols, London 1900–11), vi 180); *dominicum* means (amongst other things) 'demesne'. 13 K.W. Nicholls (ed. & tr.), 'The register of Clogher', *Clogher Rec*, 7/3 (1972), 361–431: 371–2; William Reeves (ed.), *Acts of archbishop Colton: visita-tion of … Derry* (Dublin, 1850), 112–19: 114. 14 Keating, *History*, iii 356. 15 John of Hexham, 326; AFM

within the degrees of kindred, by consanguinity or affinity, forbidden by current canon law; and concubinage. In turn, those here described as concubines
are not simply women who engage in informal non-marital relationships (will-
ingly or unwillingly) but the secondary wives of Irish law to whom *coibche*
'bridewealth' was paid and who bore their husbands children who were legitimate heirs in Irish law. This problem remained long after the twelfth century
and was legislated against again and again.

5. At the instance of Paparo, the synod made rules about the suppression of
small sees and of *chorepiscopi*. As pointed out above, there is a later medieval
record of this:

> he ordained that, as *chorepiscopi* and the bishops of the smaller sees in
> Ireland died off, archpriests, these being constituted by the diocesan
> bishops, should be elected in their place and should succeed them. These
> should have responsibility for the clergy and people within their bounds,
> and their sees should become so many seats of rural deaneries.[16]

This policy was put into effect, but results took time. Roscrea, which was recognised as a diocese at Kells, went that way (admittedly, pushed also by political
circumstances): when bishop Ó Cerbaill died in 1168 it became a rural deanery
in the diocese of Killaloe. Scattery also became part of Killaloe. This policy was
ostensibly the basis for the later amalgamation of the dioceses of Dublin and
Glendalough (where there had been a bishop and a *co-episcopus*), and the
policy was still working itself out in Meath in the early thirteenth century.[17]

6. John of Salisbury's eccentric clerical interests preserve another decree of
the council: 'That the abbesses of St Brigit should no longer take precedence
over bishops in public assemblies'.[18] The centuries-old status of the abbess of
Kildare had to yield to conventional notions of male clerical etiquette.

One of Paparo's major tasks, as later papal letters and documents record, was
'to form and delimit the dioceses of Ireland'.[19] The arrangements made were that

---

1152; Gwynn, 'Centenary', 164. **16** 'ordinaverit, ut decedentibus chorepiscopis, et exiliorum sedium episcopis in Hibernia, in eorum locum eligerenter et succederent, archipresbyteri a dioecesanis constituendi,
qui cleri et plebis solicitudinem gerant infra suos limites, et ut eorum sedes in totidem capita
decanatuum ruralium erigerentur', in David Wilkins (ed.), *Concilia Magnae Britanniae et Hiberniae* (4
vols, 1737, repr. Brussels 1964), i 547 (cited in the record of the diocesan synod of Kells, held by Simon de
Rochfort, bishop of Meath in 1216); William Reeves (ed.), *Ecclesiastical antiquities of Down, Connor and
Dromore* (Dublin, 1847), 127–8. **17** Aubrey Gwynn & D.F. Gleeson, *A history of the diocese of Killaloe*, 128–
30; Anne O'Sullivan, 'Limerick, Killaloe, and Kells 1194–1250', *Éigse*, 17 (1977–9), 451–5; NHI ix 305, 307–
8. Sheehy, *Pontificia*, i 171–2 (§93), 187–88 (§103); Charles McNeill (ed.), *Calendar of archbishop Alen's
Register c.1172–1534* (Dublin, 1950), 38–41; Lawlor, *Malachy*, pp xxvii–xxix, xlviii–lii; John Brady, 'The
archdeacons of Meath', *Ir Ecclesiast Rec*, 65 (1945), 89–100; idem, 'The origin and growth of the diocese
of Meath', ibid. 72 (1949), 1–13, 166–76. **18** *Historia pontificalis*, §36 (Chibnall, 72). **19** Sheehy, *Pontificia*,

there should be four metropolitans: Armagh with nine suffragans, viz. Connor, Down, Clogher-Louth, Clonard, Kells, Ardagh, Raphoe, Duleek, Derry; Cashel with twelve suffragans, viz. Killaloe, Limerick, Scattery, Kilfenora, Emly, Roscrea, Waterford, Lismore, Cloyne, Cork, Ross, Ardfert (and two others, Ardmore and Mungret, claimed they ought have bishops); Dublin with five suffragans, viz. Glendalough, Ferns, Kilkenny (= Ossory), Leighlin, Kildare; and Tuam with six suffragans, viz. Mayo, Killala, Roscommon, Clonfert, Achonry, Kilmacduagh.[20] Armagh and Down strongly resisted the creation of the two new archbishoprics, and they were not alone: 'For Ireland thought it enough to have a pallium in Armagh and a pallium in Cashel, and particularly it was in spite of the church of Armagh and the church of Down that other pallia were given …'.[21] However, the legates' diplomacy, backed by the authority of the papacy, won the day. This settlement, then, was a carefully wrought compromise between keenly competing political and ecclesiastical interests, and many conflicts and counter-claims remained to be resolved, at diocesan level and below. For two reasons not all of these dioceses and their boundaries were to survive: some were changed territorially after Kells in response to local pressures, especially in the province of Tuam; and, as we have seen, Paparo himself laid down at the synod the conditions under which some were to be absorbed into other dioceses.

Kells was very much a Cistercian affair, indeed the high point of Cistercian influence in the direction of the Irish church. Pope Eugenius III (*sed.* 1145–63) had been a Cistercian monk of Clairvaux and Gilla Críst Ó Con Áirge, his *legatus totius Hiberniae*, had been his fellow-monk, then founding abbot of Mellifont, and he may have been consecrated bishop of Lismore at Rome in 1151, before being despatched to Ireland with cardinal Paparo. In the background was Bernard, the most influential churchman in Europe, recruited to the cause of Irish reform by Malachy, and actively committed to the realisation of Malachy's plans for Ireland that had been cut short by his death in 1148. Bernard was probably a friend of Paparo's. Certainly, he followed his movements closely and in a letter of 1152 to the bishop of Ostia, intended to be read to the pope, he eulogised Paparo and his legatine acts in Ireland.[22] And lastly, some of the great public occasions of the synod, notably the grant of the pallia, may have taken place at Mellifont.

i 171–2 (§93), 187–8 (§103).   **20** H.J. Lawlor, 'A fresh authority for the synod of Kells, 1152', *Proc Roy Ir Acad (C)*, 36 (1922), 16–22.   **21** Keating, *History*, iii 314 (citing the Annals of Clonenagh); London, BL Additional 4782 (a collection by Sir James Ware) names 'the community of Colum Cille' as another objector (S.H. O'Grady & Robin Flower, *Catalogue of Irish manuscripts in the British Museum* (2 vols, London, 1926), ii 525).   **22** Mabillon, *Bernardi Opera*, i 576–57 (§290); James, *Letters of St Bernard*, 431–2 (§355).

CHAPTER VIII

Henry II and Ireland

LAUDABILITER SATIS

THE ACHIEVEMENTS OF THE SYNOD of Kells upset influential elements in the English church. Some believe that a disappointed and vengeful Canterbury, which had tried unsuccessfully to wreck Malachy's plans for an Irish primacy independent of itself, now embarked on an extraordinary diplomatic initiative, nothing less than a plan to bring about an invasion of Ireland by Henry II, with papal approval. This may be the case, but evidence either way is scarce.

There were two English missions to Rome in 1155/6. The first was Canterbury's. In seeking the pope's approbation, and preferably his blessing, the principal was archbishop Theobald of Canterbury (*sed.* 1138–61), nepotist, able dealer, keener perhaps on the income of his see than its privileges. His agent was the learned John of Salisbury, humanistic scholar and Theobald's secretary. We do not know when Canterbury's representations to Rome began, how hard they were pushed, or what actually transpired between Adrian IV and John of Salisbury. Canterbury had lost three suffragans at Kells in 1152 and, as if to taunt it, one suffragan, Dublin, was made an archbishop. If Canterbury had asked the pope to unpick the arrangement made at Kells, and this is likely, he refused, though he may not have admired it (too many dioceses, too many provinces, too much politics). Henry II's own high-powered delegation to Adrian IV was despatched in October 1155. It was led by the Benedictine abbot Robert of St Albans 'to promote certain difficult royal matters'[1] – the main one was to get the pope's authority for his proposed Irish venture, in which success eluded him. Hollister thinks it is unlikely that the one had no link to the other.[2] That link was rivalry and jealousy, and the pope played on it. He did not do what Canterbury probably wanted but, with a malevolent sense of humour, he granted to John of Salisbury a privilege rather less than what Robert of St Albans badly wanted for himself and his king.

John of Salisbury, writing morosely on the evil state of the world and his own burdens in October 1159 and recollecting his deep and intimate friendship

---

1 *Gesta abbatum S. Albani*, i 126.   2 C.W. Hollister, *Monarchy, magnates and institutions in the Anglo-Norman world* (London, 1986), 268–70.

with his fellow-countryman, pope Adrian IV (who had died 1 September 1159), and the now lost prospect of papal preferment, recounts how he got a papal privilege in favour of Henry II.

The papal letter *Laudabiliter satis* was addressed to the young king, and is still extant in the transcript of Giraldus Cambrensis.[3] As John of Salisbury states:

> It was in acquiescence to my petition that Adrian granted and entrusted Ireland to the illustrious king of England, Henry II, to be possessed by him and his heirs, as the papal letters still give evidence. This was by virtue of the fact that all islands are said to belong to the Roman Church, by an ancient right, based on the Donation of Constantine who established and conceded this privilege. By me he despatched a golden ring, set with a magnificent emerald, whereby he invested Henry II with the authority to rule Ireland. It was ordered that this ring be kept in the public treasury where it is still to be found.[4]

Self-satisfied and indeed boastful, John here greatly exaggerates what he got. He himself dates his mission: he was with the pope at Beneventum between November 1155 and July 1156, and within those dates he obtained the privilege.[5]

Already and without wasting time waiting for papal approval, a royal council was held at Winchester on 29 September 1155. The assembled magnates included the king's brother William, the archbishops of Canterbury and York, and the bishops of Chichester, Hereford, Lincoln, London and Norwich. They discussed the proposal that Henry II should invade Ireland: 'Henry the younger, king of England, had a large army with much military equipment which he proposed to lead against Ireland to subject it to his dominion and, in accordance with the counsels of the bishops and religious men, to constitute his brother king of that

---

3 Much of the bulky literature on *Laudabiliter satis* is cited in the following papers: M.P. Sheehy, 'The bull *Laudabiliter*: a problem in medieval *diplomatique* and history', *J Galway Archaeol Hist Soc*, 29 (1961), 53–70; Michael Haren, '*Laudabiliter*: text and context', in Marie Therese Flanagan & Judith A. Green (ed.), *Charters and charter scholarship in Britain and Ireland* (Basingstoke, 2005), 140–63; Anne J. Duggan, 'The making of a myth: Giraldus Cambrensis, *Laudabiliter*, and Henry II's lordship of Ireland', *Studies in Medieval & Renaissance History*, 3rd ser., 4 (2007) 107–58; idem, 'The power of documents: the curious case of *Laudabiliter*', in Brenda Bolton & Christine Meek (ed.), *Aspects of power and authority in the middle ages* (Turnhout, 2007), 251–72. Duggan's reconstruction of *Laudabiliter satis* is a step too far. **4** C.C.J. Webb (ed.), *Metalogicon* (Oxford, 1929), 217–18 (iv 42); Daniel D. McGarry (tr.), *The Metalogicon of John of Salisbury* (Berkeley CA, 1962), 274–5. **5** Text: M.P. Sheehy (ed.), *Pontificia hibernica*, i 15–6 §4; Michael Haren, '*Laudabiliter*: text and context', in M.T. Flanagan & J.A. Green, *Charters and charter scholarship in Britain and Ireland*, 140–63: 160–3; Adrian IV, *Epistolae et privilegia*, Pl, 188, 1441–2 §76; Translation: D.C. Douglas & G.W. Greenaway, *English historical documents*, ii 828–30.

island; but he turned it against the king of the French'.[6] Since large armies and provisions are not got together in a matter of weeks, the plan must have been afoot for a long time. Robert of Torigny, whose sympathies were strongly with Canterbury, states that 'because his mother, the empress, was opposed to it, that expedition was deferred for the time being'.[7] We cannot now be sure why the empress Matilda was averse to the undertaking (probably to avoid the inevitable conflict between her sons) or why Henry II was persuaded by her. In any case, prudence and other projects won the day, including a struggle with Louis VII, king of France (r. 1137–80), over Aquitaine, his wife's inheritance.

The papal letter *Laudabiliter satis* has been the object of lively controversy. Long alleged to be a forgery, it has the marks of authenticity: its wording, diction and style show it to be a product of the papal chancery in the pontificate of Adrian IV.[8] In fact, it bears a close resemblance to another letter of Adrian IV (*Satis laudabiliter*) issued in 1159 to king Louis VII of France, in response to a like request for papal approval. Louis VII proposed to invade Spain, with Henry II, 'to expand the bounds of the Christian people, to make war on the barbarism of pagans, and to subject to the yoke and rule of Christians apostate peoples and those who flee from or reject the truth of the Catholic faith',[9] at a time of dynastic crisis and fragile peace between and within the five Christian kingdoms of Spain, still threatened seriously by the Almohads. The pope refused Louis VII because he had not been invited by the Spanish lay and church leaders, but he had conceded a limited and ambivalent approval of an incursion into Ireland by Henry II when no Irish party, lay or clerical, as far as we know, sought or supported any English intervention in Ireland. However, despite wordy expressions of papal goodwill, the pope's approval is conditional. Drawing on the spurious Donation of Constantine, the pope writes

> *insulam illam ingrediaris et que ad honorem Dei et salutem illius terre*
> *spectaverint exequaris, et illius terre populus te recipiat et sicut dominum*
> *veneretur, iure nimirum ecclesiarum illibato et integro permanente …*

You may enter that island and do there what has to do with the honour of God and the salvation of the land. And may the people of that land

---

6 Sigebert de Gembloux, Auctarium Affligemense, MGH SS 6 (Hannover, 1844) 403 (s.a. 1156).   **7** Howlett, *Chronicle of Robert de Torigni*, 186 = MGH SS 6, 505 (s.a. 1155). Further evidence for the Winchester council of 1155 occurs in a charter of John of Eu dated 'at Winchester in the year in which the conquest of Ireland was discussed' (see Flanagan, *Irish society*, 305–7 for an edition; 38–53, for a valuable discussion of the historical background to the Winchester council).   **8** Kate Norgate, 'The bull *Laudabiliter*', *Engl Hist Rev*, 8 (1893), 18–52; J.F. O'Doherty, 'Rome and the Anglo-Norman invasion of Ireland', *Ir Ecclesiast Rec*, 42 (1933), 131–45; Sheehy, 'Bull *Laudabiliter*'.   **9** PL 188, 1615–17 §241.

receive you with honour and revere you as their lord, and that the rights of the churches remain whole and unimpaired.[10]

In law (if law be relevant to the pope's considerations), this is in no sense the grant of the lordship, or kingship, of Ireland to Henry II. While taking this opportunity to denounce vehemently the vices of the Irish, the pope is diplomatic, ambivalent, indeed deeply ambiguous: the decision to accept Henry II remains with the Irish. But a quick reading might lead to other conclusions. The issue of *Laudabiliter satis* cannot have been kept secret in the small and gossipy city that was Rome. There was an Irish community at Santa Trinità, and a constant stream of Irish pilgrims to fetch the news back to Ireland. Though it did not tamper with the settlement made at Kells, it had consequences of some moment. Its language is, to say the least, most immoderate about the religious practices of the Irish, despite the activities of Irish reformers. In the first place, it is likely to reflect Canterbury's continuing hostile and disparaging attitude to the Irish church, its usages, and its reformers, perhaps as represented by the astute John of Salisbury who, as we have seen, was well aware of what had been done at Kells. The terms of *Laudabiliter satis* are far from complimentary:

> … insofar as you plan, as a Catholic ruler, to extend the boundaries of the Church, to declare the truth of the Christian faith to untaught and barbarous peoples, to root out the weeds of vice from the field of the Lord. … You have expressed your desire to us, dearest son in Christ, that you want to enter the island of Ireland to subject its people to the laws and to root out from it the weeds of vice, and that you are willing to pay a yearly tribute to St Peter of one penny from every house, and to preserve the rights of the churches of that land whole and intact, we therefore duly favour your pious and praiseworthy desire, grant our generous assent to your petition, and are well pleased to agree that, in order to extend the boundaries of the Church, to restrain vice, to correct morals, to implant virtues, and to increase the Christian religion, you may enter that island … If therefore you should carry your plan into effect, take care to form that nation with good morals; and may you so act, yourself and those you choose for their faith, words, and their life to be well qualified for this task, that the Church may be adorned, the Christian religion planted and made to flourish, and what pertains to the honour of God and the salvation of souls be so ordered that you may deserve to get

10 Translation from Sheehy, *Pontifica hibernica*, i 16, lines 23–6.

from God the crown of everlasting reward; and, on earth, a name glorious throughout the ages.[11]

The only purpose, the pope makes clear, is explicitly the good of religion. Any other motive should invalidate the pope's approval.

Second, disparagement, even contempt, of the Irish church entered the thought and practices of the papal chancery and reappear as a matter of fact, not opinion, and in extreme form, in the letters of pope Alexander III (*sed.* 1159–81) who, as chancellor Rolando of Siena, was in charge of the papal chancery when *Laudabiliter satis* was issued. The charges of barbarism and of being outside the boundaries of the church are highlighted by being embedded in the pope's apparent warm approval of the king's professedly virtuous proposals. The explicit expression of royal dependence on the pope, fits snugly, as it was intended, with the high Gregorian programme of Adrian IV. And if the Donation of Constantine applied to Ireland, it applied also to the island of Britain – an uncomfortable matter.

In a way, this is crusade and conversion, but it is unlike Louis VII's specious plan for Spain where, however morally dubious the proposal, there were at least pagans and lands for Christian *reconquista*. The proposed enlargement of the boundaries of the church by Henry II's taking of Ireland and the revelation of Christianity to untaught barbarians had to be invented, just as the achievements of Irish Christianity had to be suppressed and the successes of the indigenous Irish reform movement had to be air-brushed out of history, in order to construct what now appeared as the Irish policy of a burgeoning, if not bumptious, papacy. This was ironic: Irish reform had been conducted independently and without any practical help from the papacy until the middle years of the twelfth century, when Malachy with the aid of Bernard briefly won its whole-hearted support, a success publicly marked by the cardinal legate's role at the synod of Kells in 1152.

Within a mere three or four years, however, papal endorsement was dramatically withdrawn from the Irish reformers, and Henry II appeared to be called upon to put the reform into effect and mend the morals of the Irish. No surviving documents indicate the effect of *Laudabiliter satis* on the Irish church. Evidently, it had serious negative effects on its leaders, men keenly and naively loyal to a papacy that seems, in a short time, to have lost confidence in them, their institutions, and their kings. On the surface and in the short term, *Laudabiliter satis* appeared to have had little effect: there was no crusade.

11 Translation from Sheehy, *Pontificia hibernica,* i 15–6; cf. Scott & Martin, *Expugnatio,* 144–7 (ii 5).

Ireland and its church remained undisturbed; and reforming synods continued to meet – Drogheda–Mellifont 1157; Breemount or Brí Meic Thaidc (Co. Meath) 1158, attended by Gilla Meic Liac, archbishop of Armagh, Gilla Críst Ó Con Áirge, papal legate and 25 bishops; Roscommon 1158; Dairbrech al. Dervor (Co. Meath) 1161; Clane al. Clóenad (Co. Kildare) 1162; Lismore 1166; Athboy (Co. Meath) 1167. Had Diarmait Mac Murchada not sought English help, had there been no English Invasion,[12] the matter might have been forgotten. However, given the English Invasion in 1169 and the subsequent and decisive involvement of Henry II in Irish affairs, papal policy as earlier evidenced in *Laudabiliter satis*[13] and Rome's policy on Henry II and Angevin ambitions became weighty and decisive matters – and not merely for the twelfth century but for the whole of the middle ages.[14]

HENRY II IN IRELAND

Henry II's expedition to Ireland, accompanied by his leading knights, was at the head of a well-equipped and well-supplied army of about, it is said, 4000. He had enormous stores, much military equipment and the resources for a major military campaign (perhaps in the spring of 1172).[15] He arrived at Waterford on 17 October 1171[16] and left Ireland on 17 April 1172. His expedition has the character not of a military conquest but of the royal progress of a great king through a dependent lordship. The Irish annalists betray no glimmer about the significance of the events. The earlier English invaders, who had been running out of control (1169–71), quickly came to heel and made their peace with Henry II, but the actions of the Irish kings are the most striking. Diarmait Mac Carthaig, king of Desmond, came of his own accord to Waterford, did homage, took an oath (whether of feudal fealty or simple loyalty is unclear), gave hostages and promised to hold his kingdom of Henry II, under royal tribute.

---

12 The term 'English' is here used as an umbrella term for Norman, Anglo-Norman, Cambro-Norman, Fleming, Welsh, Saxon, Breton, English &c. The Leinster king list in the Book of Leinster calls the new-comers *Saxain* (LL facs. p. 39d; BL i 184, line 5504). In any case, the involvement of any in Ireland was by consent of the king of England. **13** Alexander III' s expression 'in eo quod laudabiliter incepisti' in his letter *Celebri fama* to Henry II (20 September 1172) may be a deliberate echo of *Laudabiliter satis* (Sheehy, *Pontificia hibernica*, i 22, line 18). **14** J.A. Watt, 'Laudabiliter in medieval diplomacy and propaganda', *Ir Ecclesiast Rec*, 87 (1957), 420–32; idem, *Church*, esp. 35–84; idem, *The church in medieval Ireland* (Dublin 1972, rev. repr. 1998); Sheehy, *When the Normans came to Ireland*, 1–86, 103–28. **15** James Lydon, *The lordship of Ieland in the middle ages*, 2nd ed. (Dublin, 2003), 41–3. **16** AU report Henry's arrival in Latin: 'Venit in Hiberniam Henricus (*gloss* Mac na Perisi) potentissimus rex Angliae et idem dux Normannie et Aquitanie et comes Andegauue et aliarum multarum terrarum dominus cum ducentis quadraginta nauibus'.

Lesser lords did likewise. Domnall Mór Ó Briain, king of Thomond, met Henry on the Suir, not far from Cashel, and did the same. Both kings agreed to admit Henry's constables and royal officers into their cities of Cork and Limerick. Other southern kings did likewise. Henry marched unopposed to Dublin, 1–11 November 1171. On the way, or in Dublin, the Irish lords of Leinster submitted to him, even though Henry II had already granted Leinster (and their lands) to Richard de Clare, who did him homage for it. The other kings – Murchad Ó Cerbaill, king of Airgialla, Tigernán Ó Ruairc, king of Breifne, Donn Slébe, king of Ulaid, and Domnall Bregach Ó Maelechlainn, king of Meath – also submitted to Henry II, and gave hostages. As vassals, they took Henry as their lord of whom they held their lands, and swore an oath of loyalty. The *Annals of Ulster* state, in the Irish idiom of kingship, that 'he took the hostages of Munster ... Leinster, Meath, Breifne, Airgialla and Ulaid', the *Annals of Tigernach* that he 'took the kingship of Leinster, Meath, Breifne, Airgialla and Ulaid'.[17] Ruaidrí Ó Conchobair, king of Connacht, who still imagined himself king of Ireland, held aloof. The far northern kings – Niall Mac Lochlainn and Aed Ó Néill of Ailech, and the king of Cenél Conaill – were too busy with a local internecine war, reported by the annalists, to do or think of anything, and made no contact with Henry II. A great wooden palace was built for Henry in Dublin by the Irish. Here he entertained his Irish and English vassals splendidly, and held Christmas in great style. In 1171/2 he issued a charter granting Dublin to his men of Bristol and made arrangements for royal land-holding in Dublin, Leinster and Waterford. Some time after 1 March 1172, he granted his follower, Hugh de Lacy, the kingdom of Meath for the service of fifty knights[18] – land which its king, strictly speaking, held as a vassal of Henry II. This was apparently ignored by the Irish kings. Henry put constables and garrisons in strategic seaport towns. He appointed Hugh de Lacy royal governor of Ireland. The *Annals of Tigernach* state that Henry II 'took the southern half of Ireland and the eastern part of its northern half',[19] a fair summary of what had happened. He sailed from Waterford for England on Easter Monday, 17 April 1172, to do public penance and mend his fences with the papacy over the murder of Becket.

The Irish kings quite understood what their submissions meant and the obligations they had undertaken. Over a hundred years of trade, travel and

---

17 ATig 1171.12. 18 For the text of this grant, see Orpen, *Ireland under the Norman*, i 285–6 ('sicuti Murchardus Ha Mulachlyn melius eam tenuit vel aliquis alius ante illum vel postea'). The reference appears to be to Murchad Ua Maelechlainn, king of Meath (1106–53). Domnall Bregach (r. 1169–73), the contemporary king of Meath, had submitted to Henry II but, given the terms of Henry's grant, his title seems to have been regarded as defective in some way. The grant is dated Wexford, March 1172 (J.H. Round, *The commune of London* (London, 1899), 152). 19 ATig 1172.4.

political relations with Norman England ensured that they understood the English legal system. Irish clerical leaders were familiar with the nature of law and government in France and in the Empire, and Irish clerics were well able to work the patronage of the German Emperor to their advantage. One cannot plead ignorance of feudal law and custom as an excuse. Did the Irish kings conclude that they were quite unable to manage a defensive war against Henry II? Why did they choose to submit to Henry II? Did they, in fact, decide that Ireland should be part of the far-flung Angevin lands under the rule of the second most powerful king in the West?[20] One is moved to quote Yeats: 'Where are now the warring kings? An idle word is now their glory … the kings of the old time are dead'.

COUNCIL OF CASHEL

This is the remarkable political background to Henry II's startling dealings with the Irish church. His large army was meant to overawe. The bishops felt impressed, very likely cowed, by a great king who brooked no episcopal opposition, as they knew very well. There was menace in the air: one cannot rule out coercion. Henry spent two days with the papal legate, Gilla Críst Ó Con Áirge,[21] and then marked out the site of a castle at the legate's episcopal church of Lismore – a portent of things to come. Then he went to Cashel to meet its archbishop[22] and on 6 November sent his programme managers, Ralph archdeacon of Llandaff and Nicholas his chaplain, to summon the bishops to council. The leaders of the Irish hierarchy duly met in council at Cashel in winter 1171/2.[23] We know nothing of any discussions that preceded their consent to assemble, whether there was any dissent, whether any doubted the propriety of the proceeding, whether any objected to the unseemly haste, whether any considered a king under personal interdict for the killing of an archbishop unfit to summon a national council of the Irish church (or any other church), whether any weighed the political consequences of their actions. The bishops will cer-

---

20 Orpen *Ireland under the Normans*, i 247–84. 21 Gilla Críst Ó Con Áirge had been made papal legate by pope Eugenius III, twenty years before. Technically, his legation lapsed with the death of Eugenius in 1153. He may have been re-appointed by Adrian IV (†1159) since he is referred to as legate at the consecration of Mellifont (1157) and the synod of Brí Meic Thaidc (1158). A legate was present at the synod of Clane (1162). Thus, he must have been re-appointed by Alexander III not later than 1162 (Marie Therese Flanagan, private comm.). 22 CLH 1357; G.H. Orpen, *Song of Dermot and the earl* (Oxford, 1892), 194–5, lines 2660–9; idem, *Ireland under the Normans*, i 260–1. 23 For an excellent analysis of the council and its context, see Marie Therese Flanagan, 'Henry II, the council of Cashel and the Irish bishops', *Peritia*, 10 (1996), 184–211.

tainly have known about the privilege of Adrian IV – and they may have read it more closely than some modern historians. However, as papal loyalists, they will have accepted that Henry's activity in Ireland had some limited, if inexplicit and somewhat dated, papal approval.

Those assembled included Gilla Críst Ó Con Áirge, bishop of Lismore and papal legate; Donnchad Ó hUalacháin, archbishop of Cashel; Lorcán Ó Tuathail, archbishop of Dublin; Cadla Ó Dubthaig, archbishop of Tuam; and their suffragans.[24] None is noted as absent except the primate archbishop of Armagh, Gilla Meic Liac, who absented himself on grounds of advanced age but who later consented to the decisions of the council. Henry II did not himself attend (nor ought he as an excommunicate) but he had his managers present at the council: Ralph abbot of Buildwas; Ralph archdeacon of Llandaff, one of the king's intimates; Nicholas the king's chaplain, an important court cleric; and other officials.

Giraldus Cambrensis has a detailed and partial account of its proceedings.[25] He states that 'the enormities and filth of that land and people (*terre illius et gentis tam enormitatibus quam spurciciis*) were inquired into, recounted in a public hearing, and recorded under the seal of the bishop of Lismore, the papal legate', who presided[26] – a statement that may derive from his later reading of pope Alexander III's subsequent letters. He then states that the king issued 'many constitutions' – here he means the decrees of the council which he summarises. On this matter, Giraldus is no reliable witness. It is difficult to establish what precisely was the role of the king at the council: he convoked it, with the consent of the papal legate, but should not, as king, issue its decrees, which have much to do with church discipline. Besides, the crisis following the murder of archbishop Becket was at its height and no papal legate, not even the biddable Ó Con Áirge, should encourage direct royal intervention in a church council at this point.

Giraldus claims to give the decrees of the council verbatim. They have nothing to say about enormities of vice, even as preamble, and there is not a word about the king, his policy, or his powers. In fact, the legislation of the synod of Cashel is so pedestrian that it must be genuine. In itself it reflects no revolutionary programme: its commonplace decrees are concerned primarily with the perennial problems of church organisation and with ordinary administrative matters. Long ago, John Lanigan rightly observed that 'there is nothing relative

---

24 William Stubbs (ed.), *Gesta regis Henrici secundi Benedicti abbatis*, RS 49 (2 vols, London, 1867), i 26–7. **25** Scott & Martin, *Expugnatio*, 96–8 (cap. 34). The evidence for the holding of the council, its site, and date is analysed by Watt, *Church*, 38–9. **26** Scott & Martin, *Expugnatio*, 96 §34.

to religious dogmas, to matters of faith, or to points of essential discipline; and some of these decrees refer to matters rather of a political than of an ecclesiastical nature'[27] – by political Lanigan means its decree about lay exactions.

It may be worthwhile to quote the decrees.[28] The first is 'that all the faithful throughout Ireland repudiate cohabitation with their relations by consanguinity or affinity and contract and observe lawful marriages' – this is no more than a reiteration of the perennial injunction to obey the church's marriage laws and especially to observe the church's increasingly difficult contemporary rules about consanguinity and affinity. This is a decree applicable in Ireland and everywhere else in Europe, and could be found in the rulings of many synods throughout the West. Howden adds: 'Many of them had as many wives as they wished and even married their wives's sisters' – both well-founded charges if one took a rigorous canonical point of view. The second is 'that infants be catechised before the doors of the church, and baptised in the holy font in baptisteries', by priests,[29] as Howden adds. Though it is evident that there were baptismal fonts in at least some churches, John Comyn, archbishop of Dublin, ruled in 1186 that 'all baptismal churches have a fixed baptistery of wood or stone erected in the middle of the church'.[30] *Gesta Henrici* further states: 'In many parts of Ireland, the previous custom was that when a child was born the father, or somebody else, immersed him three times in water, and if he was the son of a rich man, he was immersed three times in milk'.[31] It is difficult to know what to make of this and one notes that no formal claim is made that this latter procedure was considered canonical baptism. It is likely that the decree was directed against private baptism in a non-baptismal church, and perhaps ones performed without chrism (a matter long ago condemned by Lanfranc in his letter to Tairdelbach ua Briain). Triple unction with chrism is prescribed in the Stowe Missal.[32] The third urges 'that all Christ's faithful pay tithes of animals, crops and all other produce to the church of which they are parishioners'. The

---

27 John Lanigan, *An ecclesiastical history of Ireland from the first introduction of christianity among the Irish to the beginning of the thirteenth century* (4 vols, Dublin, 1822), iv 210. **28** Scott & Martin, *Expugnatio*, 98–101 (the copy in ASMD 1172 is taken from Giraldus and has no independent value; *contra* Gwynn, *Irish church*, 306–7). Three decrees are recorded in English chronicles, with one or two additions: Stubbs, *Gesta regis Henrici secundi Benedicti abbatis*, i 28 (in reality, a first draft of *Chronica Rogeri de Hoveden*, hereafter Howden); Stubbs, *Chronica Rogeri de Hoveden*, ii 31. The translations of the decrees are mine but they have benefited greatly from those of Lanigan (*History*, iv 206–7), Scott, and Sheehy (*When the Normans came to Ireland*, 103–5). **29** Already prescribed by Gille of Limerick (Ussher, *Whole works*, iv 505). **30** Sheehy, *Pontificia*, i 48–52: 50 (§16); tr. Sheehy, *When the Normans came to Ireland*, 61. **31** Stubbs, *Gesta regis Henrici*, i 28. Immersion in milk has nothing to do with baptism (Flanagan *Transformation of the Irish church*, 207–8). **32** Clover & Gibson, *Letters of Lanfranc*, 70–1 (letter 10); Margaret W. Pepperdene, 'Baptism in the early British and Irish churches', *Ir Theol Q*, 22 (1955), 110–23: 120 F.E. Warren, *The liturgy and ritual of the Celtic church*, ed. Jane Stevenson (Woodbridge, 1987) 63–7.

fathers at Cashel had the same concerns about income as those of Kells. Evidently they believed there were parishes and parish churches in Ireland, though modern historians have thought otherwise.

The fourth deals with lay exactions made on church properties in the form of taxes, renders in kind and obligatory hospitality, itself a characteristic method of taxation:

> that all church lands and all property belonging to them be wholly free from all lay exactions; and in particular that neither petty kings nor lords nor any of the magnates of Ireland nor their sons together with their families should levy exactions of food and hospitality on church lands in accordance with their usual custom, nor should they dare extort them from this time forward; and that that detestable food-levy which neighbouring lords require from ecclesiastical estates four times a year should not be exacted at all any more.

The synod of Cashel (1101) had already legislated on this, but older practices die hard.

The fifth deals with the problem of composition for homicide and orders that clerics who are kindred of the offender should not, like other kinsmen, be obliged to contribute to the composition payment: 'when laymen who have committed homicide compound for it with their enemies, clerics who are kindred of these laymen should not pay any part of this payment in composition [i.e., *éraic*] for, just as they were not complicit in the crime, so too they are not liable for the payment'. This is, of course, a long-standing problem and one dealt with in the same way in the eighth century and earlier. Under the rubric 'Of the liberty of the catholic church which does not pay the liabilities of the wicked', the *Hibernensis* states that 'the church does not discharge under exaction the cost of the offences of others' and specifies, in particular, that the church is not liable for the offences of the lay kindred of its clergy.[33]

The fathers of the council were also preoccupied with wills and testamentary dispositions, and here there is a little more novelty:

> that all the faithful, when in their last illness, should in the presence of their confessor and their neighbours make their will with due solemnity;

---

33 Hib 42:29: 'De libertate ecclesiae catholicae non reddente debita malorum. [Synodus Hibernensis]: Non reddet ecclesia in tribulatione delicta aliorum ... mali fratris delictum non maculabit fratrem religiosum sive spiritualiter sive mundialiter in delicto ejus reddendo'; cf. CIH i 31.6–18 (= ALI v 234.20–236.9), CIH iii 1045.27–32, v 1841.33–7.

if a man have a wife and children, he should divide his movable property (excluding what is owed to others and the wages of servants) into three parts: he should bequeath one to his children, one to his lawful wife, and the final third [to the church] to cover the cost of his own funeral; should he happen to have no legitimate offspring, his property should be divided equally between himself and his wife; should his wife have predeceased him, it should be divided between himself and the children.

Division into three of *mobilia* has a long history and is well attested in the *Hibernensis* where different divisions, reflecting local usage, are proposed: in one passage, a third to the king, a third to the sons, a third to the church;[34] in another, a third to the testator's servants, a third to his heirs, a third to the church as the price of his burial.[35] In reality, all that is new here is the insistence that only the lawful wife and the legitimate children benefit (thus excluding, amongst others, priests' wives and their offspring), and this is in line with the preoccupations of the Gregorian reformers. The reversion of the dying testator's *mobilia* to himself, in the absence of a canonical wife or legitimate offspring, may strike one as strange but it is merely a way of saying that, in these circumstances, it becomes part of his ordinary estate, inheritable by his nearest kindred as is his real estate. In effect, this is a further provision against concubines and non-marital children. The final provision – 'that those who die, having made a good confession, should receive the degree of ceremony which is due to them in the matter of masses, vigils and mode of burial' – rounds off the provisions about obsequies: those who die a good death in the arms of the church, and endow her appropriately, should have all due institutional ceremonies, requiem masses and prayers.

If this is all the legislation passed at Cashel, and it may be, the council was a careful and conservative one, even banal. It paid close attention to local conditions and in its legislation it evidently reflects the preoccupations of the Irish bishops, and not those of Henry II nor his managers. Its novelty lies not in its legislation but in its political context and in the far-reaching political decisions taken by the bishops: here was a departure so radical that Irish church organisation was changed beyond recognition. Watt considers it 'the most important event in the history of the Irish Church between the fifth and the sixteenth centuries': he is not wrong.[36]

Giraldus states that the king's policy was to bring the usages of the Irish church into total conformity with those of the English church: 'Thus, in all

---

34 Hib 32:13 and note (b). **35** Hib 32:22. **36** Watt, *Church*, 40.

parts of the church, all religious matters are to be conducted henceforth after the fashion of holy Church, in accordance with the observances of the English church'.[37] Whatever about liturgy and local custom (and these may have been of some superficial moment),[38] this was a legal and administrative revolution: the bishops were now to be tenants-in-chief of the crown, part of the baronage, and their recruitment and election were to be matters for royal policy and patronage, as in England. The relationship of church and king – royal power in church, the competence of church courts, the privileges of clergy and the rights of church estates – were assimilated to the English model.

Having made these momentous decisions, on some occasion before, during, or immediately after the council, the bishops swore an oath to Henry II (whether of fealty or simple loyalty is uncertain). According to what is a semi-official English account of this proceeding, Henry II received from the four archbishops and from twenty-nine bishops, many listed by name, 'their letters in the form of a charter with seals attached confirming to him and his heirs the kingdom of Ireland, testifying that they had constituted him and his heirs kings and lords over them forever'[39] – they gave what was not theirs to give, and what Adrian IV had not given. So much for the prudence of the Irish bishops.

Gilla Críst, as papal legate, and the Irish bishops had their negative observations on the morality of their own people and the government of the Irish kings, and their own decisions, political and ecclesiastical, written up as a report. That report was conveyed to pope Alexander III not by the papal legate, nor by an Irish bishop charged with that mission, but by Henry II's manager, instructed by the king himself, Ralph archdeacon of Llandaff, a man well experienced in dealing with the papacy on Henry's behalf and his loyal servant (as Alexander pointedly remarks in his letter). Ralph also gave the pope a verbal account of what had transpired and what he thought he had himself observed of the Irish, evidently well slanted to the interests of his master.[40] To judge from the pope's reaction, the report of the Irish bishops and the manner of its delivery was a sorry piece of diplomatic naivety, if not gullibility.

---

37 Scott & Martin, *Expugnatio*, 98, 100 (i 34–5); cf. 142 (ii 5). This is the outcome Giraldus wished, and it is not one of the decrees of the synod. It does not occur as one of the decrees as listed in ASMD 372–3, though that source drew on *Expugnatio*. However, it appears that the bishops consented to Henry II's policy. **38** Gwynn imagines that Giraldus's statement is the eighth decree of the council and that it applies only to liturgy (*Irish church*, 307); see DACL ii 336 for the same view. **39** Stubbs, *Gesta regis Henrici secundi Benedicti abbatis*, i 26 (here *regnum* of the original may mean 'kingdom' or 'rule'); Orpen, *Normans*, i 277–8. **40** Alexander III to Henry II, September 1172, Sheehy, *Pontificia*, i 21–2 §6; Curtis & McDowell, *Historical documents*, 20–1.The written report of the bishops is lost but it can be reconstructed in part from Alexander's letter. See also, for the papal letters, J.H. Round, *The commune of London* (London, 1899), 181–92.

Cadla Ó Dubthaig, archbishop of Tuam, may have learned to repent his actions at Cashel on encountering the remonstrances, if not the wrath, of his king and fellow provincials:

> *Senudh Erenn la Cóicid Con<n>acht, laechaib cleirchib, ic Tuaimm Da Gualand, im Ruaidhri Ua Conc<h>obair im ri<g> nErenn & im Chadhla Ua nDubthaig airdespoc Con<n>acht, & tri tempuill do cosecradh léo and*[41]

The synod of Ireland was held by the province of Connacht, church and laity, at Tuam, led by Rúaidrí Ó Conchobair, king of Ireland, and by Cadla Ó Dubthaig, archbishop of Connacht, and three churches were consecrated by them at that synod.

The annalist's terminology makes it clear that this was Ó Conchobair's response to the Council of Cashel. He had made no submission to Henry II, and hardly expected his archbishop do so for him. But it was too little too late.

Alexander III, correspondent of Becket, was fully aware of the character, actions and policies of Henry II, long before and after the killing of Becket. On 2 September 1172, Alexander signed the bull that ratified his agreement with a publicly penitent Henry II, thus resolving, in the interest of a beleaguered papacy and for reasons of political expediency alone, the conflict between pope and king that resulted from the archbishop's murder. Less than three weeks later, on 20 September 1172, the pope despatched three separate and extraordinary letters to the Irish bishops (*Quantis vitiorum enormitatibus*), the Irish kings (*Ubi communi*), and Henry II (*Celebri fama*), and these were delivered, it appears, by the ever-diligent Ralph, archdeacon of Llandaff. So extreme is the pope's flattery of the king that one cannot at all recognise the persona of Henry II in his letters. In fact, his description of the king is false, and meant to mislead. He orders his papal legate and the bishops to support Henry II in ruling Ireland. His instructions are embedded in an arresting denunciation of the Irish. Basing himself on their own letters, he writes to the bishops, describing Henry II as 'this Catholic and most Christian king who has heard us in respect of tithes and other rights of the church, and in restoring to you … those things which pertain to the liberty of the church':

> With what shocking abuses the Irish people are infected and how, lapsed from the fear of God and reverence for the Christian faith, and what

41 ATig 1172.

leads to the peril of their souls, has been made known to Us in your series of letters, and also it has often come to the notice of the Apostolic See by the truthful accounts of others.[42] Hence – understanding from your letters that our most dear son in Christ, the illustrious king of England, moved by divine inspiration, with all his forces, has subjected to his rule that barbarous and uncivilised people, ignorant of the divine law, and that the wicked things practised in your land, with God's help, have now already started to diminish – We are overjoyed and have offered our grateful prayers to Him who has granted that king so great a victory and triumph, humbly beseeching that by his vigilance and care that most undisciplined and untamed nation may in all things persevere in devotion to the practice of the Christian faith and that you and your ecclesiastical brethren may rejoice in all due honour and tranquillity. Since, therefore, it is fitting that you should afford all due care and support to carry on what has had so pious and happy a beginning, We command and enjoin upon you by these our apostolic letters that you will diligently and manfully and as far as you are able, saving your order and office, help the king, a great man and a devout son of the church, to maintain and preserve that land and to wipe out the filth of such an abomination (*tante abominationis spurcitiam*).[43]

Can the pope have believed what he wrote of Henry II or his own statement to the effect that the vices of the Irish 'have now already started to diminish' as a result of king's actions? Can he have expected the bishops to credit this quite implausible claim? After all, they had some pastoral experience and they well knew that changes in social practice are inevitably slow.

In his letter to the Irish kings, clearly no reply to any of theirs, the pope pointedly ignores king Ruaidrí Ó Conchobair's claim to the kingship of Ireland and his refusal to submit to Henry. Neither had the kings of the north submitted nor taken any oath whatever that could have put them under any obligation to Henry II. In fact, they had not met him nor had they had any communication with him. Was the pope deliberately mis-informed by Henry and his agents? He orders the Irish kings to preserve their fealty to Henry II, described

---

42 The pope's charge *frater uxorem fratris eo vivente abutitur, unus duabus se sororibus concubinis inmiscet...* 'a brother abuses the wife of his brother in his brother's lifetime, one has concubinary intercourse with two sisters' appears to echo the heinous offences of Magnus Mac Duinn Shlébe, king of Ulaid (r. 1166–71), who was killed in Downpatrick by his brother in 1171. Magnus's abominable deeds, described above, shocked Irish opinion and gossip about these may have added piquancy to Ralph's oral communication to the pope.   43 Sheehy, i 19–20 §5; Curtis & McDowell, op. cit. 19–20.

by the pope as 'that powerful and majestic king who is a devout son of the church', and from this will flow benefits:

> by God's aid and the power of this king in your land, there will be greater peace and tranquillity and the Irish people in proportion as, through the enormity and filth of their vices they have fallen away from the divine law, so they shall be all the more readily moulded in it and receive all the more fully the discipline of the Christian faith.[44]

The most extreme statement of Irish vice was kept for Henry II, perhaps to spur him on to greater efforts at reform. If so, it notably and predictably failed. But did the pope honestly expect any royal reforms or is this more silver-tongued flattery of the second-most powerful king in Western Europe by a needy pope menaced until 1177 by Emperor Frederick Barbarossa's string of antipopes? He writes:

> By frequent report and trustworthy evidence and with much joy, we have been assured that, like a pious king and magnificent prince, you have wonderfully and gloriously triumphed over that people of Ireland, who, ignoring the fear of God, in unbridled fashion wander at random through the depths of vice and have renounced all reverence for the Christian faith and virtue, and destroy themselves in mutual slaughter, and over a kingdom that the Roman emperors, the conquerors of the world, so we read, left untouched in their time, and, by the will of God (as we firmly believe), have extended the power of Your Majesty over that same people, a race uncivilised and indisciplined.

He goes on to say that he 'omits for the present other monstrous abuses which the same race, neglecting the observance of the Christian faith, irreverently practises'; he describes and condemns what he sees as the sexual perversity of the Irish (discussed above); and ends with a few more random denunciations: 'all of them eat meat indiscriminately in Lent; and they do not pay tithes nor, as they ought, respect God's churches or the clergy'.[45]

Those Irish bishops whose views carried the day at Cashel – like their reforming predecessors who prated indiscriminately into any ear prepared to listen to their ingenuous complaints about the morals of their countrymen –

---

44 Sheehy, op. cit. i 22–23 §7; Curtis & McDowell, op. cit. 22 (with minor changes).   45 Sheehy, op. cit. i 21–2 §6; Curtis & McDowell, op. cit. 20–1 (with minor changes).

displayed all too much holy simplicity in their support of Henry II as a rod of correction, if that was their expectation in reality. Morally lax publicly and privately, subject to violent rages, bellicose and aggressive, Henry II was no church reformer. He was married to Eleanor of Aquitaine, the divorced wife of Louis VII of France. Among his illegitimate issue, whom he placed in good church livings, were Geoffrey (born c.1153), first his father's chancellor, then bishop of Lincoln on his father's nomination, and subsequently archbishop of York (†1212); and Maud fitz Roy, appointed abbess of Barking by her father. His relationship with the church, in his own dominions, in law and practice, was difficult beyond measure, and more than menacing. He would have seen church reform only within the narrowest political framework, if it mattered to him at all. His policy of controlling the church could not be reconciled with its freedom and was repugnant to contemporary canon law.

Besides, his business in Ireland was not church reform but the consolidation of a new dominion won by an overwhelming show of force that cowed the Irish kings, and the legitimisation of its seizure by putting pressure on a weak and needy pope – and thus an unprincipled one. Howden says he could have easily conquered the king of Connacht next summer had he the chance[46] and in his early negotiations with the papal legates he is said to have stormed out of a meeting saying he would return to Ireland 'where he had much to do'.[47] He and his successors were sure to anglicise the Irish church as his predecessor, William I, had so thoroughly and so quickly normanised the English church, and reward his own followers with its best benefices. His baronage in Ireland would soon seize more church estates than his council of Cashel ever liberated, and plunder venerable churches.[48]

Neither did the bishops learn any of the obvious lessons from the bitter and protracted conflicts between the English kings and the church – between William Rufus and St Anselm, king Stephen and his bishops, and in particular between Henry II and Becket, which ended in the archbishop's murder.[49] The king had yet to meet the pope's legates and do public penance for the murder of the archbishop when the council of Cashel met by the royal order of a king under interdict; that king had yet to purge himself when the bishops reached their final decisions at Cashel; and still the bishops sailed on. They and their advisors cannot have been unaware of the Constitutions of Clarendon (1164) by which the king controlled communication between the English church and the

46 Stubbs, *Gesta regis Henrici secundi*, i 29–30. 47 Flanagan, 'Council of Cashel', 185. 48 D. Ó Corráin, 'What happened Ireland's medieval manuscripts?', *Peritia*, 22–3 (2001/2), 191–223: 208–9. 49 Warren, *Henry II*, 399–555; John Guy, *Thomas Becket* (London, 2012), 313–34.

papacy, limited church censure, and governed the exercise of ecclesiastical juris-dictions.[50] Nor can they have been ignorant of the nature of Henry II's church appointments and the subsequent violent conflicts in the English church.

If Giraldus's statements are at all close to the truth and if the bishops accepted the ecclesiastical usages of the English church (at least according to Giraldus, who was not disinterested), it is difficult to understand their purpose. Perhaps they let themselves be led on by the papal legate Ó Con Áirge, an uncritical and over-zealous reformer who may have seen Henry II as a source of political stability as well as improvement in the church;[51] perhaps they felt threatened, even bullied, by Henry's reputation and menacing presence; perhaps some of them felt that his intervention and the English attack would come to nothing, and they could tem-porise until the storm had blown over; perhaps some, or more likely the many, using reform as a flag of convenience, desired to be powerful and rich feudal bishops with a role in royal government, as ministers, chancellors, diplomats and royal judges, like their contemporaries elsewhere in England and continental Europe, and seized their opportunity with alacrity when they thought it had come. If so, they were fatuous beyond measure. Whatever their motivations, they consented to the most radical departure in the history of the Irish church since the rise of monasticism in the sixth century.

They took the dramatic decision to turn their backs on their own church, on its traditional usages and inherited pieties, on its long and distinguished his-tory, on its newly reformed structure put in place, with great public ceremony and papal approval, at the synod of Kells as recently as 1152. They abandoned rights of property and election that they had long enjoyed. These rights are later set out in the protest made at the ecumenical council of Vienne (1311–12) by the Irish church against the violation of clerical rights and privileges by the king:

> The Irish church states that before the coming of the English into Ireland it was thus free: that it knew no superior in regard to *temporalia*, that it had and exercised jurisdiction in all ways, spiritual and temporal. A cer-tain king of England obtained by request a licence from the lord pope to enter the said land and subjugate it to himself, saving the right of the Roman and Irish church. On the pretext of that licence that king entered

---

50 Warren, *Henry II*, 473–85. **51** Flanagan, 'Council of Cashel', 209–11; Gwynn, *Irish church*, 302–6. **52** F. Ehrle, 'Ein Bruckstück der Acten des Konzils von Vienne', *Archiv für Literatur u. Kirchengeschichte*, 4 (1888), 361–470: 370–1; J.A. Watt, 'Laudabiliter in medieval diplomacy and propaganda', *Ir Ecclesiast Rec*, 87 (1957), 420–32: 426–27; Sheehy, 'Laudabiliter', 51n; see, too, August Theiner, *Vetera monumenta* (Rome, 1864), 37 §94 = Sheehy, *Pontificia*, ii 74–5 §235; Maurice P. Sheehy, 'English law in medieval Ireland: two illustrative documents', *Archivium Hibernicum*, 23 (1960), 167–75.

that land and subjected a certain part of it to himself; and in the subju-
gated part he and his successors, little by little and successively, usurped
the estates, effects, rights, and jurisdictions of the church …[52]

This document is an *ex parte* statement but it contains a clear assertion of what
we know from elsewhere: the pre-Conquest Irish church, whatever its other
problems, did not hold of kings and lay investiture, as such, did not exist. Now
the Irish bishops agreed to hold the temporalities of the Irish church of the
king, as royal tenants-in-chief, and be as the English bishops in everything – all
for a very doubtful prospect of Angevin-led reform that was nothing more than
a pious and forlorn hope.

The precise effect, in the later twelfth century and subsequently, of their
actions and of the claim of the king of England to authority over the Irish
church is not quite clear, though the intent is, namely, that the Irish church
should occupy the same position in regard to the king as the English church –
and this is implicit in the assertion of the king's rights to Ireland, backed up by
the threat of excommunication, proclaimed by the papal legate, cardinal Vivian,
at the synod of Dublin in 1177.[53] However, the papacy remained ambiguous
about the parts of Ireland that remained under Irish rule: in 1190 pope Clement
III explicitly appointed a legate to England, Wales and that part of Ireland
under the dominion of John, count of Mortain (later king John), thus dividing
the Irish church; in 1200/1 Innocent III confirmed to Cathal Crobderg Ó
Conchobair, king of Connacht (r. 1189–1224), the rights in episcopal elections
claimed by the king of England; and in 1237 the chapter of Cashel stated to the
papacy that it was bound 'neither by right nor indeed by custom' to seek a *congé
d'élire*[54] from the king.[55]

ACHIEVEMENTS AND AIMS OF THE REFORMERS

A thorough-going administrative reform, in which the Irish kings were leaders
as well as collaborators, had been completed; new monastic organisations had
been put in place by Malachy and his fellows, aided by royal patronage that was
not disinterested; but the bishops apparently despaired of the Irish kings as the

---

53 AU 1177; Scott & Martin, *Expugnatio*, 180–82 (ii 19); Watt, *Church*, 43; Marie Therese Flanagan,
'Hiberno-papal relations in the late twelfth century', *Analecta Hibernica*, 34 (1976–7), 55–70; Orpen,
Ireland under the Normans, ii 25.   54 The licence from the king of England issued to the cathedral dean
and chapter to elect a bishop when the see was vacant. Royal assent, after the election, was required.
55 Sheehy, *Pontificia*, i 67–68 (§22); 113 (§§46–48), ii 74–75 (§235); Theiner, *Vetera monumenta*, 1 §1.

agents of moral reform. They also appear to have despaired of them as political rulers: Alexander III's description of Ireland as 'torn by internecine slaughter' and his expectation that 'greater peace and tranquillity will be made to prevail in your land' as a result of Henry II's intervention[56] seems to reflect unrealistic views expressed by the bishops in their correspondence with the pope. If so, they were ruthless enough to sacrifice their kings in pursuit of their objectives; and ingenuous enough to believe that papally approved Angevin rule would deliver their programme. They cannot have been unaware that the socio-sexual reform they required, which in any case was hardly the end-all of Christian life (in Ireland or elsewhere), was impossible without a root-and-branch transformation of royal and aristocratic society, as difficult in Ireland as in any other part of Christian Europe. Is it possible that they saw conquest as the only means of bringing about that change and deliberately chose it, at the urgings of the reformed papacy? They may have been so impressed by the prospect of integration into the culture that had emerged in Western Europe, that had absorbed England from the late eleventh century, and in which some of them were formed, that they thought conquest and, in the process, the destruction of the aristocracy from which most of them sprang, a reasonable price to pay. And they cannot have been quite unaware how thoroughly William I (the Conqueror) uprooted the native English aristocracy nor could they have expected less from Henry II and his heirs. If this is true, they were prepared to envisage a social revolution that entailed the overthrow of their own ruling cadre and the rise of a foreign land-holding class loyal (at least in theory) to an absent king – all in the interest of an international mother church and an unrealistic programme of perceived moral betterment. Ironically, Irish kings, whatever their faults and they were many, did not have, nor did they yet seek, the extensive powers over the church enjoyed by continental rulers and by English kings, though they were quick to learn. Here the bishops lost out badly. The Angevins had no peculiar interest in moral reform, their episcopal appointees in Ireland were king's men before they were the pope's or the church's,[57] and the English invasion brought chronic warfare, racial conflict in church and the wider society, legal inequity and severe social disruption that gravely affected the church. Here the bishops lost again. Naively, they put their trust in princes, and quite misread the political landscape.

---

56 Sheehy, *Pontificia*, i 21, 23.   **57** A. Gwynn, 'Henry of London, archbishop of Dublin', *Studies*, 38 (Dublin, 1949), 295–306, 389–402; idem, 'Archbishop John Cumin', *Reportorium Novum*, 1 (1956), 285–310; Sheehy, *When the Normans came to Ireland*, 57–86; Watt, *Church*, 52–84, 226–30.

CHAPTER IX

The harvest of reform

T HE COUNCIL OF KELLS had completed the territorial and administrative structure of the Irish church but, from the point of view of reformers, much was still to be done. They thought that pastoral care and parishes had yet to be re-organised in accordance with the new arrangements. Significant lay control of church offices and estates, lay exactions and clerical marriage still remained to be dealt with. In the second half of 1179, Lorcán Ó Tuathail, archbishop of Dublin and papal legate, presided over 'a great convocation of the clergy of Ireland' at Clonfert to implement the decrees of the Third Lateran Council, from which he had just returned. According to the annalistic account, it ruled 'that no layman should have the rule of any church or church matters from thenceforth … that holy orders should not be given to bishops' nor priests' sons and, for example of these constitutions, they took the livings of seven bishops that had bishoprics and were laymen'.[1] Evidence from the diocese of Killaloe confirms that many older practices still remained unchecked and the older hereditary clergy remained influential. Domnall Ó Lonngargáin, bishop of Killaloe (*sed.* c.1131–1137/8), was translated to Cashel which he ruled until his death in 1158. His brother, Tadc, succeeded him in Killaloe and ruled until 1164. These brother bishops belonged to a hereditary ecclesiastical family that was an offshoot of the royal dynasty: their father, grandfather and great-grand-uncle had been abbots of Terryglass. In Killaloe, for example, no canonical bishop ruled the see from the time of the early reformer Domnall Ó hÉnna (†1098) until 1355 who was not either a member of the dynasty or a member of an old ecclesiastical family. From 1161 to 1164 the diocese was ruled by Diarmait Ó Briain, brother of the kings Conchobar (r. 1118–42), Tairdelbach (r. 1142–1152, 1153–67) and Tadc Glae (r. 1152–3). He left a family known to the genealogists as Clann in Espaig 'the bishop's family'.[2] He was directly succeeded as bishop by his nephew, Consaidín (*sed.* 1164–94), who was bishop when his father Tairdelbach (†1167) and his

---

1 AC pp 213–4 i.e. 1179 (1170); Gwynn, *Church*, 135–8; cf. Hefele-Leclerq, *Conciles*, v/2 1086–1108: 1097–9; N.P. Tanner (ed.), *Decrees of the ecumenical councils* i (London & Washington DC, 1990), 217–19 (§§11, 14). Presumably these were men who held the income of the diocese but failed to take orders. 2 Lec. facs. 229vb40–41; his descendants were a landowning family in the barony of Inchiquin; further details in Ó Donnchadha, *Leabhar Muimhneach*, 342 note 93.

brothers Muirchertach (†1168) and Domnall Mór (r. 1168–94) were kings. He, too, left a family, Clann Chonsaidín, now Considine.³ Rule of the diocese then passed to hereditary aristocratic clergy, Uí Chonaing and Uí Énna, more distant members of the royal lineage. Things were little different elsewhere in Ireland and outside it. To take an English example, Nigel bishop of Ely (*sed.* 1133–69) lived openly with his concubine Maud of Ramsbury, to whom he entrusted his castle of Devizes; his son Richard was bishop of London (*sed.* 1189–98) and treasurer of Henry II. There were many like him.

It is hardly surprising that the Connacht clerical family Uí Dubthaig clung to episcopal office. When Cadla Ó Dubthaig, archbishop of Tuam, died in 1201, a papal legate, John cardinal priest of St Stephen, was detailed to preside over the election of his successor in 1202. Pope Innocent III wrote to the legate about 'that detestable abuse that you have found to be flourishing, especially in the church of Tuam and in other parts, that not only in the case of minor ecclesiastical dignities but even in archbishoprics and bishoprics, sons succeed their fathers directly'. While it is impossible to demonstrate genealogically, Cadla may have been a son of Muiredach, archbishop of Tuam, who died at Cong in 1150, and grandson of Domnall (†1136), bishop of Elphin and coarb of Clonmacnoise. He, in turn, is likely to have been a son of Flannacán Ó Dubthaig (†1097), erenagh of Roscommon and lector of Tuam.⁴ Mael Coluim Ó Brolcháin (†1122), a member of a prominent learned and clerical family, was consecrated bishop in 1107, probably by Cellach and other reforming bishops, and seems to have been bishop of Derry. His son Flaithbertach (†1175) was abbot of Derry and of Iona and one of the most eminent Irish clerics of his generation.⁵ Hereditary succession and clerical marriage receded, but were not rooted out, in the twelfth and early thirteenth centuries when the reformers were riding high; but they re-established themselves in full vigour in the later middle ages, in Ireland and in much of Europe.

The church lands of the early middle ages, in origin mostly monastic though some were episcopal, belonged as hereditary property to the ecclesiastical lineages, great and small, that had ruled and served the churches. The new diocesan bishops had little and the incoming continental orders that were to be endowed by Irish kings and lords, often with old ecclesiastical lands, had nothing. In order to fund themselves, the bishops asset-stripped the traditional churches in two ways: first, they demanded that the tithes paid to the older

---

3 Lec. facs. 229vb44–45; Ó Donnchadha, *Leabhar Muimhneach*, 342; Ó Corráin, 'Dál Cais – church and dynasty', 51–63.   4 Sheehy *Pontificia*, i 121 §53; Etchingham, 'Episcopal hierarchy in Connacht', 13–29.
5 AU 1107, 1122, 1158, 1163, 1164, 1175.

churches be paid wholly to them; and, second, they tried to transfer the owner-ship of the lands of the older churches to themselves. As we have seen, these were the resources that supported the scholarship and art of the monastic schools of literature, history, law, scripture and theology, and when they lost their property the schools and workshops rapidly declined. In reaction to the appropriation of their property, older houses turned for an income more to the cult of their saints, to pilgrimage and relics, and some at least of the hagiogra-phy and hagiology of the period was written to win support for these cults and earn the necessary investment in them.[6]

Unlike their continental peers, the new bishops did not set up and endow cathedral schools though one or two attempts were made. The synod of Clane, held in 1162 and presided over by Gilla Meic Liac, archbishop of Armagh, ordered that nobody should be a head of school (*fer léigind*) in any church school in Ireland unless he was a graduate of Armagh. In 1169, doubtless at the urgings of the clergy, Ruaidrí Ó Conchobair, king of Ireland, permanently endowed a lectorship at Armagh to educate scholars from Ireland and Scotland.[7] These entries suggest that a cathedral school was set up at Armagh, but there is little evidence for any others.

When territorial dioceses were established, the resources of the older churches – their lands, their churches, and their community of worshippers – were transferred to the bishops, at least in theory. During and after the reform, the indigenous monastic forms came under great pressure and seemed to dis-appear, or at least fall below the horizon: usually, the houses were either taken over by Augustinian canons (Irish clergy in new habits), became parish churches (and most parish churches were on old monastic land), or were secu-larised, but the land-owning lineages, now mostly displaced from their previ-ous ecclesiastical functions, remained in possession. There were attempts to dislodge them, and most were unsuccessful. A notable effort to take over their assets was made in Connacht at the provincial synod of 1210: there was a major convocation of the clergy, presided over by the archbishop of Tuam, Felix Ó Ruanada, 'to make constitutions for taking away the termon lands or the coarb lands and annexing them to the bishoprics of the dioceses where they lay'.[8] In reality, this was more a formal change in legal title than a practical land-hold-ing one. The resolution of the problem was a compromise, varying with place and time: the hereditary lineages remained in possession, retained a certain

6 Peter Harbison, 'Church reform and Irish monastic culture in the twelfth century', *J Galway Hist Archaeol Soc*, 52 (2000), 1–12; idem, *Pilgrimage in Ireland: the monuments and the people* (London, 1991); MartO 70. **7** AU, AFM 1162; AU, AFM 1169. **8** AC 1210.

clerical status, and paid rent and services to the bishop. The lineage heads, later
known collectively as termoners (*termonnaig*), were appointed or confirmed by
the bishop after election by the kindred and bore the title erenagh (*airchinnech*;
Latin *herenacius*), or coarb (*comarba*; Latin *converbius, comorbanus*) if they
were thought to be the heirs of the founder, and this was a higher dignity. In
fact, these were quasi-clerics, usually in minor orders and married, occasionally
in priestly orders, often learned in Latin and Irish, sometimes with a stall in the
choir, the rector's portion of tithes, and a voice in the chapter in matters tem-
poral. The termoner was the head of a lineage who had the bishop for his lord
and the members of his lineage farmed their ecclesiastical estate as a partible
inheritance, each being the quasi-proprietor of his portion. Their dependants
and tenants corresponded to the earlier *manaig*. All claimed the privilege of
clergy in canon law and thus exemption from lay control and secular taxation.
Where such lineages died out, their places were taken by the descendants of
bishops or by clericalised lineages of the aristocracy, but the institutions
remained. Very many of the clergy of the later middle ages belonged to termoner families who, despite wars, religious changes and expropriation, preserved their churchly identity, a spiritual aura, and often the relics and insignia
of the founding saint, far beyond the end of the middle ages.[9] Termoners were
few within the English-ruled area of the country, where much church land was
seized very violently by the barons who used it as castle sites, as secular estates,
or as endowments for foreign religious orders.[10]

Very quickly, the tide of reform turned, many of the old church lineages
made it back to high church office, and by the fourteenth century, hereditary
clergy again dominated much of the church, and subverted the Augustinians
and Cistercians. In an important sense, the Gregorian reform imposed a relatively shallow superstructure on the pre-reform church, and beneath that cara-
pace much of the early medieval indigenous church survived – its personnel,
land-holding, religious practices and traditional pieties.

The Gregorian reform was a re-ordering of priestcraft and property, and
thus of power. It imposed a costly episcopal superstructure that increased the
burden on the community. By weakening the hereditary church lineages, it

9 Ussher, *Whole works*, xi 421–45; John Begley, 'The termons of St Patrick in the county of Limerick', *Ir
Ecclesiast Rec*, 6 (1915), 236–47; St John D. Seymour, 'The coarb in the medieval Irish church', *Proc Roy Ir
Acad (C)*, 41 (1932–4), 219–31; D.F. Gleeson, 'The coarbs of Killaloe diocese', *J Roy Soc Antiq Ire*, 79 (1949),
160–9; K.W. Nicholls, 'Gaelic society and economy in the high middle ages', NHI ii 397–438: 433–35;
Katharine Simms, 'Frontiers in the Irish church: regional and cultural', in R. Frame, T.B. Barry & K.
Simms (ed.), *Colony and frontier in medieval Ireland* (Dublin, 1995), 177–200; Henry A. Jefferies,
'Erenaghs in pre-plantation Ulster', *Archivium Hibernicum*, 53 (1999), 16–9. **10** MacCarthy's Book, 1173
(1174), 1178, 1179, 1180; ALC 1184, 1186; Simms, 'Frontiers', 177–200.

opened the way for increasing royal influence on ecclesiastical appointments, whether English or Irish. In effect, kings had much more power over the new dioceses than over the ancient churches that had centuries of privilege and protection behind them, and they saw to it that members of the dynasty and its servitors were promoted in church. It is ironic that the reformers, with their eyes open, should create in Ireland a church like the feudalised church of continental Europe and England and bring the doubtful benefit of the conditions of the Concordat of Worms (1122), or worse ones, to a church where lay investiture was absent, though not lay influence.

The papal legate Ó Con Áirge was taught a smart lesson in 1173 by Henry II's chief governor in Ireland, Richard de Clare, earl of Striguil: 'The same earl came into Munster to Lismore and plundered it completely, and levied a thousand marks on the legate as an amercement from the cathedral'.[11] Evidently, this huge fine was levied with violence on the papal legate because he had failed to condemn or excommunicate the Irish kings and lords who resisted the invaders, as he was required by Alexander III's letter. Some historians have thought it unfortunate that the English invasion should have taken place before the Irish hierarchy had time to consolidate itself and develop a strong corporate identity; and before the administrative re-organisation of the reformers had been completed. This cannot hold: there was no lack of collegiality among the Irish bishops at the Council of Cashel and, apart from tidying up, the establishment of bishops and dioceses had gone as far as it could by 1152. What do we hear of reform after the English invasion?

Some of the leaders of the reform were men of great piety who led exemplary lives and, in the convention of the times, they were regarded as saints, notably Cellach (S. Celsus), Malachy, Gilla Meic Liac (S. Gelasius), Lorcán Ó Tuathail (S. Laurence). They were unworldly in a worldly enterprise. Where other bishops stood is far from clear.

Reform did little for the generality. It does not seem that the clergy became more virtuous, more learned, or more dutiful. There is no good evidence for an improvement in pastoral care: the reverse is more likely. It is doubtful whether the reform had any real effect on the mores of the laity, sexual or otherwise. The elective mix of married clergy and the austerely chaste (with, of course, the usual complement of sinners) in the older church was replaced by a clergy that was very often publicly celibate and privately incontinent.[12] The incidence of the

---

11 MacCarthy's Book, 1173 (1174); cf. AI 1173.4; ATig 1173. I owe this interpretation to Prof Marie Therese Flanagan.   12 Sheehy, *Pontificia*, i 48–52: 51, lines 15–27; 52, lines 13–9 (§16), dated Lent 1186; A. Gwynn, 'Provincial and diocesan decrees of the diocese of Dublin during the Anglo-Norman period', *Archivium*

besetting vices of a would-be celibate and chaste caste inevitably rose with the increasing success of the reformers. Concubines took the place of clerical wives who, however, reappeared after some time.

Neither was the great increase in the numbers of regular clergy the unmixed blessing that some naively think. Unlike their continental peers, there were, in their own estimation, no saints among them in the later middle ages. Were they right? Their cultural contribution to Irish life never equalled their endowment, nor that of the older houses whose property they were granted. Parishes impropriate to them were often served by ill-paid vicars whilst they drew the profits. And the rigour of their rules was soon relaxed to the point of corruption, and, in the case of the Cistercians, violence.

Without, the Irish church now had the appearance of the contemporary European model, and that satisfied many; within, the business of souls (and the properties attached to it) was put on a better business footing, and that was enough for others. The English invasion brought the evil of racism to Ireland and the Irish church, and divided the population into those who had the benefit of English law (the colonists and those who could pretend to be such) and those who did not (the Irish, unless granted English law by royal charter). The impact on the Irish church was disastrous.[13]

One suspects that the lower clergy, in Gaelic Ireland and far outside it, lived their lives and went about their business much as they did before the reform, but with the necessary nod to the new order. And the laity kept their saints, sites, cults and devotional practices as they had been long before Hildebrand.

Hibernicum, 11 (1944), 39–127: 45–6 §§3–4; cf. *Giraldi Cambrensis opera*, v 172 §27 = O'Meara, *Topography*, 112 §104 (extracted from a sermon preached by Giraldus in Lent 1186, being a retort to a previous Irish sermon accusing the English and Welsh of bringing their own abuses to Ireland). **13** Watt, *Church and the two nations*, 108–216; Philip Wilson, *The beginnings of modern Ireland* (Dublin & Baltimore MD, 1913), 126–34; Jocelyn Otway-Ruthven, 'The native Irish and English law in mediaeval Ireland', *Ir Hist Stud*, 7 (1950/1), 1–16; Maurice P. Sheehy, 'English law in medieval Ireland', *Archivium Hibernicum*, 23 (1960), 166–75; Geoffrey J. Hand, *English law in Ireland, 1290–1324* (Cambridge, 1967), 172–218; Seymour Phillips, 'David MacCarwell and the proposal to purchase English law, *c.*1273–*c.*1280', *Peritia*, 10 (1996), 253–73.

Bibliography

Anderson, A.O. & M.O. Anderson (ed. & tr.), *Adomnán's Life of Columba* (Edinburgh, 1961, 2nd ed. Oxford, 1991)

Arnold, T. (ed.), *Symeon of Durham: historical works*, RS 75 (2 vols, London, 1882–5)

Barrow, G.W.S., 'Scottish rulers and the religious orders, 1070–1153', *Trans Roy Hist Soc*, 5th ser., 3 (1953), 77–100

Bartlett, Robert, 'Cults of Irish, Scottish and Welsh saints in twelfth-century England', in Brendan Smith (ed.), *Britain and Ireland, 900–1300: Insular responses to medieval European change* (Cambridge, 1999), 67–86

Begley, John, 'The termons of St Patrick in the county of Limerick', *Ir Ecclesiast Rec* 6 (1915), 236–47

Bellesheim, Alphons, *Geschichte der katholischen Kirche in Irland* (3 vols, Mainz, 1890)

Best, R.I. & Osborn J. Bergin (ed.), *Lebor na hUidre* (Dublin, 1929) [diplomatic edition]

Bethell, Denis, 'English monks and Irish reform in the eleventh and twelfth centuries', in T.D. Williams (ed.), *Hist Stud*, 8 (1971), 111–35

Betzig, Laura, 'Medieval monogamy', *J Family Hist*, 20/2 (1995), 181–286

Bieler, Ludwig (ed. & tr.), *The Irish penitentials*, SLH 5 (Dublin, 1963)

Bieler, Ludwig (ed. & tr.), *Patrician texts in the Book of Armagh*, SLH 10 (Dublin, 1979)

Binchy, D.A. (ed. & tr.), 'Bretha crólige', *Ériu*, 12 (1938), 1–77

Binchy, D.A., 'The legal capacity of women in regard to contracts', in D.A. Binchy & Myles Dillon (ed.), *Studies in early Irish law* (Dublin, 1936), 207–34

Binchy, D.A. (ed.), *Críth gablach*, MMI 11 (Dublin, 1941)

Binchy, D.A. (tr.), 'The Old-Irish penitential', in Ludwig Bieler (ed.), *Irish penitentials* (Dublin, 1963), 248–77

Binchy, D.A. (ed. & tr.), 'Distraint in Irish law', *Celtica*, 10 (1973), 21–71

Blair, John & Richard Sharpe (ed.), *Pastoral care before the parish* (Leicester, 1992)

Boswell, C.S. (tr.), *An Irish precursor of Dante: a study on the vision of heaven and hell ascribed to the eighth-century Irish saint Adamnán, with translation of the Irish text*, Grimm Library, 18 (London, 1908; repr. New York, 1972)

Boswell, John, *The kindness of strangers: the abandonment of children in Western Europe from late antiquity to the middle ages* (New York, 1988)

Bouchard, Constance B., 'Consanguinity and noble marriage in the tenth and eleventh centuries', *Speculum*, 52 (1981), 268–87

Boyle, Alexander, 'St Cadroe in Scotland', *Innes Rev*, 31 (1980), 3–6

Boyle, Elizabeth, 'The authorship and transmission of *De tribus habitaculis animae*', *J Mediev Latin*, 22 (2012), 49–65

Boyle, Elizabeth, 'On the wonders of Ireland: translation and adaptation', in Elizabeth Boyle & Deborah Hayden (ed.), *Authorities and adaptations: the reworking and transmission of textual sources in medieval Ireland* (Dublin, 2014), 233–61

Bracken, Damian & Dagmar Ó Riain-Raedel (ed.), *Ireland and Europe in the twelfth century: reform and renewal* (Dublin, 2006)

Brady, John, 'The archdeacons of Meath', *Ir Ecclesiast Rec*, 65 (1945), 89–100

Brady, John, 'The origin and growth of the diocese of Meath', *Ir Ecclesiast Rec*, 72 (1949), 1–13, 166–76

Breatnach, Liam (ed. & tr.), 'The first third of *Bretha nemed*', *Ériu*, 40 (1989), 1–40

Breatnach, Liam, *Companion to the Corpus iuris hibernici*, EILS 5 (Dublin, 2005)

Breatnach, P.A., *Die Regenburger Schottenlegende – Libellus de fundacione ecclesie consecrati Petri* (Munich, 1977)

Breatnach, P.A., 'The origins of the Irish monastic tradition at Ratisbon', *Celtica*, 13 (1980), 58–77

Brett, Martin, 'Canterbury's perspective on church reform and Ireland, 1070–1115', in Damian Bracken & Dagmar Ó Riain-Raedel (ed.), *Ireland and Europe in the twelfth century: reform and renewal* (Dublin, 2006), 13–35

Brewer, J.S., J.F. Dimock & G.F. Warner (ed.), *Giraldi Cambrensis Opera*: v. *Topographia hibernica et Expugnatio hibernica* (London, 1867)

Brundage, James A., *Law, sex and christian society in medieval Europe* (Chicago, 1987)

Brundage, James A., 'Sex and canon law', in Vern L. Bullough & James A. Brundage, *A handbook of medieval sexuality* (New York & London, 1996)

Bulst, N., 'Irisches Mönchtum und cluniazensische Klosterreform', in Heinz Löwe (ed.), *Die Iren und Europa im früheren Mittelalter* (Stuttgart, 1982), 958–69

Butler, Richard (ed.), *Registrum prioratus omnium sanctorum juxta Dublin* (Dublin, 1845)

Byrne, Paul, 'The community of Clonard, sixth to twelfth centuries', *Peritia*, 4 (1985), 157–73

Candon, Anthony, 'Barefaced effrontery; secular and ecclesiastical politics in twelfth century Ireland', *Seanchas Ardmhacha*, 14 (1990–1), 1–25

Canny, N.P., *The Elizabethan conquest of Ireland: a pattern established* (Hassocks & New York, 1976)

Carey, John (tr.), *King of mysteries: early Irish religious writings* (Dublin, 1998)

Charles-Edwards, T.M., 'Honour and status in some Irish and Welsh tales', *Ériu*, 29 (1978), 123–41

Charles-Edwards, T.M., 'The church and settlement', in Próinséas Ní Chatháin & Michael Richter (ed.), *Ireland and Europe: the early church* (Stuttgart, 1984), 167–75

Charles-Edwards, T.M., *Early Irish and Welsh kinship* (Oxford, 1993)

Charles-Edwards, T.M., '*Érlam*: the patron saint of an Irish church', in Alan Thacker &

Richard Sharpe (ed.), *Local saints and local churches in the early medieval West* (Oxford, 2002), 267–90

Chibnall, Marjorie (ed.), *The ecclesiastical history of Orderic Vitalis*, Oxford Medieval Texts, 6 vols (Oxford, 1968–80)

Chibnall, Marjorie (ed. & tr.), *The Historia pontificalis of John of Salisbury* (Oxford, 1986)

Clancy, Thomas Owen & Gilbert Márkus (tr.), 'The alphabet of devotion', in idem (ed.), *Iona: the earliest poetry of a Celtic monastery* (Edinburgh, 1995)

Clarke, Howard B., 'Conversion, church and cathedral: the diocese of Dublin to 1152', in James Kelly & Dáire Keogh (ed.), *History of the catholic diocese of Dublin* (Dublin, 2000), 19–50

Clover, Helen & Margaret Gibson (ed. & tr.), *The letters of Lanfranc archbishop of Canterbury* (Oxford, 1979)

Colgrave, Bertram & R.A.B. Mynors (ed. & tr.), *Bede's Ecclesiastical history of the English people* (Oxford, 1969)

Comyn, David & P.S. Dinneen (ed. & tr.), *Forus feasa ar Éirinn: History of Ireland by Geoffrey Keating*, ITS 4, 8, 9, 15 (4 vols, London 1908–14; repr. Dublin 1987)

Connolly, Seán & Jean-Michel Picard (tr.), 'Cogitosus's Life of St Brigit: content and value', *J Roy Soc Antiq Ire*, 117 (1987), 5–27

Conway, C., *The story of Mellifont* (Dublin, 1958)

Cowdrey, H.E.J., 'The peace and the truce of God in the eleventh century', *Past & Present*, 46 (1970), 42–67

Crosthwaite, John Clarke (ed.), *Martyrology and book of obits of Christ Church* (Dublin, 1846)

Curtis, Edmund, 'Murchertach O'Brien, high king of Ireland, and his Norman son-in-law, Arnulf de Mongomery, circa 1100', *J Roy Soc Antiq Ire*, 20 (1921), 116–24

Curtis, Edmund & R.B. McDowell (ed.), *Irish historical documents, 1172–1922* (Dublin, 1943)

d'Alès, A. (ed.), *Dictionnaire apologétique de la foi catholique* (4th ed., 5 vols, Paris, 1925–31)

Dilworth, Mark, 'Marianus Scotus – scribe and monastic founder', *Scott Gael Stud* 10 (1965, 125–48)

Dobbs, Margaret E. (ed. & tr.), 'The Ban-Shenchus', *Revue Celtique*, 48 (1931), 189–200

Doherty, Charles, 'Some aspects of hagiography as a source for Irish economic history', *Peritia*, 1 (1982), 300–28

Doherty, Charles, 'Cluain Dolcáin: a brief note', in Alfred P. Smyth (ed.), *Seanchas: studies in early and medieval Irish archaeology, history and literature in honour of Francis J. Byrne* (Dublin, 2000), 182–8

Dold, Alban, 'Wessobrunner Kalendarblätter irischen Ursprungs', *Archivalische Z*, 58 (1962), 11–33

Douglas, D.C. & G.W. Greenaway (ed.), *English historical documents* ii (2nd ed. London, 1981)

Duby, Georges, *Mâle moyen âge: de l'amour et autres essais* (Paris, 1988)

Duby, Georges, *Medieval marriage: two models from twelfth-century France* (Baltimore MD, 1978)

Duby, Georges, *The knight, the lady and the priest: the making of modern marriage in medieval France* (London, 1985)

Duggan, Anne J., 'The making of a myth: Giraldus Cambrensis, *Laudabiliter*, and Henry II's lordship of Ireland', *Studies in Medieval & Renaissance History*, 3rd ser., 4 (2007) 107–58

Duggan, Anne J., 'The power of documents: the curious case of *Laudabiliter*', in Brenda Bolton & Christine Meek (ed.), *Aspects of power and authority in the middle ages* (Turnhout, 2007), 251–72

Dumville, D.N., *Councils and synods of the Gaelic early and central middle ages*, Quiggin Pamphlets on the Sources of Mediaeval Gaelic History, 3 (Cambridge, 1988)

Dumville, D.N., 'Saint Cathróe of Metz and the hagiography of exoticism', in John Carey, Máire Herbert & Pádraig Ó Riain (ed.), *Studies in Irish hagiography: saints and scholars* (Dublin, 2001), 172–88

Dunning, P.J., 'The Arroasian order in medieval Ireland', *Ir Hist Stud*, 4 (1944–5), 297–315

Ehrle, F., 'Ein Bruckstück der Acten des Konzils von Vienne', *Archiv für Literatur u. Kirchengesch*, 4 (1888), 361–470

Elrington, C.R. & J.H. Todd (ed.), *The whole works of the Most Rev. James Ussher, D.D.* (17 vols, Dublin, 1847–64)

Etchingham, Colmán, 'The early Irish church: some observations on pastoral care and dues', *Ériu*, 42 (1991), 99–118

Etchingham, Colmán, 'Bishops in the early Irish church: a reassessment', *Studia Hibernica*, 28 (1994), 35–62

Etchingham, Colmán, *Church organisation in Ireland AD 650 to 1000* (Maynooth 1999)

Etchingham, Colmán, 'Episcopal hierarchy in Connacht and Tairdelbach Ua Conchobair', *J Galway Archaeol Hist Soc*, 52 (2000), 13–29

Etchingham, Colmán, 'The battle of Cenn Fúait, in 917: location and military significance', *Peritia*, 21 (2010), 208–32

Flachenecker, Helmut, *Schottenklöster: irische Benediktinerkonvente im hochmittelalterlichen Deutschland*, Quellen und Forschungen aus dem Gebiet der Geschichte, NF 18 (Paderborn, 1995)

Flanagan, Marie Therese, 'St Mary's Abbey, Louth, and the introduction of the Arrouaisian observance in Ireland', *Clogher Rec*, 10 (1980), 223–34

Flanagan, Marie Therese, 'Hiberno-papal relations in the late twelfth century', *Archivium Hibernicum*, 34 (1976–7), 55–70

Flanagan, Marie Therese, *Irish society, Anglo-Norman settlers, Angevin kingship: interactions in Ireland in the late twelfth century* (Oxford, 1989)

Flanagan, Marie Therese, 'Henry II, the council of Cashel and the Irish bishops', *Peritia* 10 (1996), 184–211

Flanagan, Marie Therese, 'Irish and Anglo-Norman warfare in twelfth-century Ireland', in T. Bartlett & K. Jeffrey (ed), *A military history of Ireland* (Cambridge, 1996), 52–75

Flanagan, Marie Therese, *Irish royal charters: texts and contexts* (Oxford, 2005)

Flanagan, Marie Therese, *The transformation of the Irish church in the twelfth and thirteenth centuries*, SCH 29 (Woodbridge, 2010)

Fleming, John, *Gille of Limerick (c.1070–1145), architect of a medieval church* (Dublin, 2001)

Fournier, Paul, *Mélanges de droit canonique*, ed. Theo Kölzer (2 vols, Aalen, 1983)

Frank, K.S., 'Grimlaicus, Regula solitariorum', in Franz J. Felten & Nikolas Jaspert (ed.), *Vita religiosa im Mittelalter: Festschrift für Kaspar Elm zum 70. Geburtsta*g, Berliner Historische Studien, 31 (Berlin, 1999), 21–35

Freisen, Joseph, *Geschichte des kanonischen Eherechts* (Paderborn, 1963)

Fröhlich, W. (tr.), *The letters of St Anselm of Canterbury*, Cistercian Studies, 96, 97, 142, 3 vols (Kalamazoo, MI, 1990–94)

Fuhrmann, Horst, *Einfluss und Verbreitung der pseudoisidorischen Fälschungen*, MGH Schriften 24 (3 vols, Stuttgart, 1972–4)

Fuhrmann, Horst, 'Provincia constat duodecim episcopatibus: zum Patriarchsplan Erzbischof Adalberts von Hamburg-Bremen', *Studia Gratiana*, 11 (1967), 391–404

Gillingham, John, *The English in the 12th century: imperialism, national identity and political values* (Woodbridge, 2000)

Gillingham, John, 'Civilizing the English? The English histories of William of Malemesbury and David Hume', *Hist Res*, 74 (2001), 17–43

Gleeson, Dermot F., 'The coarbs of Killaloe diocese', *J Roy Soc Antiq Ire*, 79 (1949), 160–9

Goody, Jack, *The development of the family and marriage in Europe* (Cambridge, 1983)

Gougaud, Louis, 'Les saints irlandais dans les traditions populaires des pays continentaux', *Revue Celtique*, 39 (1922), 199–226, 355–8

Gougaud, Louis, *Christianity in the Celtic lands* (London, 1932, repr. Dublin, 1993)

Greene, David (ed.), *Fingal Rónáin and other stories* (Dublin, 1955)

Guy, John, *Thomas Becket* (London, 2012)

Gwynn, Aubrey, 'Irish monks and the Cluniac reform', *Studies* (Dublin) 29 (1940), 409–29

Gwynn, Aubrey, 'Pope Gregory VII and the Irish church', *Ir Ecclesiast Rec*, 58 (1941), 97–109

Gwynn, Aubrey, 'Lanfranc and the Irish church', *Ir Ecclesiast Rec*, 57 (1941), 481–500

Gwynn, Aubrey, 'St Anselm and the Irish church', *Ir Ecclesiast Rec*, 59 (1942), 1–14

Gwynn, Aubrey, 'Bishop Samuel of Dublin', *Ir Ecclesiast Rec*, 60 (1942), 81–8

Gwynn, Aubrey, 'The origins of the diocese of Waterford', *Ir Ecclesiast Rec*, 59 (1942), 289–96

Gwynn, Aubrey, 'Papal legates in Ireland during the twelfth century', *Ir Ecclesiast Rec*, 63 (1944), 361–70

Gwynn, Aubrey, 'Provincial and diocesan decrees of the diocese of Dublin during the Anglo-Norman period', *Archivium Hibernicum*, 11 (1944), 39–127

Gwynn, Aubrey, 'The first synod of Cashel', *Ir Ecclesiast Rec*, 66 (1945), 81–92; 67 (1946), 109–22

Gwynn, Aubrey, 'The diocese of Limerick in the twelfth century', *N Munster Antiq J*, 5 (1946), 35–48

Gwynn, Aubrey, 'Henry of London, archbishop of Dublin', *Studies* (Dublin) 38 (1949), 295–306, 389–402

Gwynn, Aubrey, 'St Malachy of Armagh', *Ir Ecclesiast Rec*, 70 (1948), 961–78; 71 (1949), 134–48, 317–31

Gwynn, Aubrey, 'The bishops of Cork in the twelfth century', *Ir Ecclesiast Rec*, 74 (1950), 17–29, 97–109

Gwynn, Aubrey, 'The centenary of the synod of Kells', *Ir Ecclesiast Rec*, 77 (1952), 161–76, 250–64

Gwynn, Aubrey, 'The continuity of the Irish tradition at Würzburg', Vorstand d. Würzburger Diözesangeschichtsvereins (ed.), *Herbipolis jubilans: 1200 Jahre Bistum Würzburg: Festschrift zur Sakularfeier der Erhebung der Kiliansreliquien* (Würzburg, 1952), 57–81

Gwynn, Aubrey, 'Ireland and the Continent in the eleventh century', *Ir Hist Stud*, 8 (1953), 193–216

Gwynn, Aubrey 'The first bishops of Dublin', *Reportorium Novum*, 1 (1955), 1–26

Gwynn, Aubrey (ed. & tr.), *The writings of bishop Patrick, 1074–84*, SLH 1 (Dublin, 1955)

Gwynn, Aubrey, 'Archbishop John Cumin', *Reportorium Novum*, 1 (1956), 285–310

Gwynn, Aubrey, *The Irish church in the eleventh and twelfth centuries*, ed. Gerard O'Brien (Dublin, 1992)

Gwynn, Aubrey & Dermot F. Gleeson, *A history of the diocese of Killaloe* (Dublin, 1962)

Gwynn, Aubrey & Neville Hadcock, *Medieval religious houses: Ireland* (London, 1970; repr. Dublin, 1988)

Gwynn, E.J. (ed. & tr.), 'An Irish penitential', *Ériu*, 7 (1914), 121–95

Gwynn, E.J. (ed. & tr.), 'The rule of Tallaght', *Hermathena*, 44 (1927), second supplemental volume

Gwynn, E.J. & W.J. Purton (ed. & tr.), 'The monastery of Tallaght', *Proc Roy Ir Acad (C)*, 29 (1911), 115–79

Haddan, A.W. & W. Stubbs (ed.), *Councils and ecclesiastical documents* (3 vols, Oxford, 1869–78; repr. Oxford, 1964)

Hammermayer, Ludwig, 'Die irischen Benediktiner "Schottenklöster" in Deutschland und ihr institutioneller Zusammenschluss vom 12. bis 16. Jahrhundert', *Studien und Mitteilungen zur Geschichte des Benediktinerordens und seiner Zweige*, 87 (1976), 249–338

Hand, Geoffrey J., *English law in Ireland, 1290–1324* (Cambridge, 1967)

Harbison, Peter, *Pilgrimage in Ireland: the monuments and the people* (London, 1991)

Harbison, Peter, 'Church reform and Irish monastic culture in the twelfth century', *J Galway Hist Archaeol Soc*, 52 (2000), 1–12

Haren, Michael, '*Laudabiliter*: text and context', in Marie Therese Flanagan & Judith A. Green (ed.), *Charters and charter scholarship in Britain and Ireland* (Basingstoke, 2005), 140–63

Head, Thomas F., 'The development of the peace of God in Aquitaine (970–1005)', *Speculum*, 74 (1999), 656–86

Head, Thomas F. & R.A. Landes, *The peace of God: social violence and religious response in France around the year 1000* (Ithaca NY, 1992)

Hefele, C.J. & J. Hergenröther, *Histoire des conciles*, tr. & corr. Henri Leclercq & Charles de Clercq (11 vols, Paris, 1907–52)

Henry, Françoise & Geneviève Marsh-Micheli, 'A century of Irish illumination (1070–1170)', *Proc Roy Ir Acad (C)*, 62 (1962), 101–64

Herbert, Máire, *Iona, Kells and Derry: the history and hagiography of the monastic* familia *of Columba* (Oxford 1988, repr. Dublin, 1996), 82–3

Herbert, Máire (tr.), 'The vision of Adomnán' in Máire Herbert & Martin McNamara (ed.), *Irish biblical apocrypha: selected texts in translation* (Edinburgh, 1989), 137–48

Herbert, Máire (tr.), 'Letter of Jesus on Sunday observance' in Máire Herbert & Martin McNamara (ed.), *Irish biblical apocrypha: selected texts in translation* (Edinburgh, 1989), 50–4

Hochholzer, Ernst, 'Bemerkungen und Ergänzungen zu ein missglückten Edition', *Studien und Mitteilungen zur Geschichte des Benediktinerordens und seiner Zweige*, 106 (1995), 333–76

Hogan, Edmund, *Onomasticon Goedelicum* (Dublin, 1910)

Holland, Martin, 'Dublin and the reform of the Irish church in the eleventh and twelfth centuries', *Peritia*, 14 (2000), 111–60

Holland, Martin, 'The synod of Kells in MS BL, Add. 4783', *Peritia*, 19 (2005), 164–72

Hollister, C.W., *Monarchy, magnates and institutions in the Anglo-Norman world* (London, 1986)

Hore, Herbert, *History of the town and county of Wexford* (6 vols, London, 1900–11)

Howlett, R. (ed.), *Chronicle of Robert de Torigni*, RS 82 (London, 1890)

Hudson, Benjamin T., 'Gaelic princes and Gregorian reform', in Benjamin T. Hudson & Vickie Ziegler (ed.), *Crossed paths: methodological approaches to the Celtic aspect of the European middle ages* (Lanham MD & London, 1991), 61–82

Hughes, Kathleen, 'The Celtic church and the papacy', in C.H. Lawrence (ed.), *The English church and the papacy in the middle ages* (London, 1965), 3–28

Hughes, Kathleen, *The church in early Irish society* (London, 1966)

Hughes, Kathleen, 'Some aspects of Irish influence on early English private prayer', *Studia Celtica*, 5 (1970), 48–61

Hull, Vernam E., 'The date of *Aipgitir crábaid*', *Z Celt Philol*, 25 (1956) 88–90

Hull, Vernam E. (ed. & tr.), 'Cáin domnaig', *Ériu*, 20 (1966), 151–77

Hull, Vernam E. (ed. & tr.), 'Apgitir chrábaid: the alphabet of piety', Celtica, 8 (1968), 44–
    89
Immenkötter, Herbert, 'Ecclesia Hibernicana: die Synode von Inis Pádraig im Jahre 1148',
    Annuarium Archivum Historiae Conciliorum, 17 (1985), 19–69
Jaffé, Philip (ed.), Monumenta gregoriana (Berlin, 1865)
James, Bruno Scott (tr.), The letters of St Bernard of Clairvaux (London, 1953; repr.
    Stroud, 1998)
Jefferies, Henry A., 'Erenaghs in pre-plantation Ulster', Archivium Hibernicum, 53 (1999),
    16–9
Jochens, Jenny, M., 'The politics of reproduction: medieval Norwegian kingship', Am
    Hist Rev, 92 (1987), 27–49
Kehnel, Annette, Clonmacnois – the church and lands of St Ciarán: change and continu-
    ity in an Irish monastic foundation (Münster, 1999)
Lalor, Brian, The Irish round tower: origins and architecture explored (Cork, 1999)
Lanigan, John, An ecclesiastical history of Ireland from the first introduction of christian-
    ity among the Irish to the beginning of the thirteenth century (4 vols, Dublin, 1822; 2nd
    ed. Dublin, 1829)
Lappenberg, I.M. (ed.), Adami Gesta Hammaburgensis ecclesiae pontificum, MGH SS 7
    (1845), 267–389
Lawlor, H.J., 'The reformation of the Irish church in the twelfth century', Ir Church Q, 4
    (1911), 216–28
Lawlor, H.J., 'Notes on St Bernard's Life of St Malachy, and his two sermons on the pass-
    ing of St Malachy', Proc Roy Ir Acad (C), 35 (1919), 230–64
Lawlor, H.J. (tr.), St Bernard of Clairvaux's Life of St Malachy of Armagh (London & New
    York, 1920)
Lawlor, H.J., 'A fresh authority for the synod of Kells, 1152', Proc Roy Ir Acad (C), 36
    (1922), 16–22
Lawlor, H.J., 'Notes on the church of St Michan's, Dublin', J Roy Soc Antiq Ire, 56 (1927),
    11–21
Lawlor, H.J., 'The foundation of St Mary's Abbey, Dublin', J Roy Soc Antiq Ire, 56 (1927),
    22–8
Lawlor, H.J. & R.I. Best (ed.), 'Ancient list of the coarbs of Patrick', Proc Roy Ir Acad (C),
    25 (1919–20), 316–62
le Prévost, Augustus & Léopold Delisle (ed.), Historia ecclesiastica (Paris, 1840–5)
Lea, Henry C., A history of sacerdotal celibacy in the christian church (2 vols, 3rd ed. rev.
    London, 1907)
Leclercq, Jean, Recueil d'études sur saint Bernard et ses écrits (3 vols, Rome 1962–9)
Leclercq, Jean, C.H. Talbot & H.M. Rochais (ed.), Sancti Bernardi opera (8 vols, Rome,
    1957–77)
Lefèvre, Yves, R.B.C. Huygens & Brian Dalton (ed. & tr.), Giraldus Cambrensis: Speculum
    duorum (Cardiff, 1974)

Lucas, A.T.,'The plundering and burning of churches in Ireland, 7th to 16th century', in Etienne Rynne (ed.), *North Munster studies* (Limerick, 1967), 172–229

Lydon, James, *The lordship of Ireland in the middle ages* (2nd ed. Dublin, 2003)

Mabillon, Jean (ed.), *Sancti Bernardi abbatis Claræ-Vallensis Opera omnia* (4th ed. rev. Paris, 1839), ii 1465–1524; repr. PL 182, 1073–1118

Mac Carthy, Bartholomew (ed.), *The Codex Palatino-Vaticanus No. 830*, TLS 3 (Dublin, 1892)

Mac Erlean, John, 'Synod of Ráith Bresail: boundaries of the dioceses of Ireland', *Archivium Hibernicum*, 3 (1914), 1–33

McGarry, Daniel D. (tr.), *The Metalogicon of John of Salisbury* (Berkeley CA, 1962)

McNeill, Charles (ed.), *Calendar of archbishop Alen's Register, c.1172–1534* (Dublin, 1950)

MacNeill, Eoin (tr.), 'Ancient Irish law: the law of status or franchise', *Proc Roy Ir Acad (C)*, 36 (1923), 265–316

Mac Niocaill, Gearóid, *Na manaigh liatha in Éirinn* (Dublin, 1959)

Mac Niocaill, Gearóid (ed.), *Notitiæ as Leabhar Cheanannais, 1033–1161* (Dublin, 1961)

Mac Niocaill, Gearóid, 'The Irish "charters"', in Felicity O'Mahoney (ed.), *The Book of Kells* (Aldershot, 1994), 253–65

Mac Shamhráin, Ailbhe S., *Church and polity in pre-Norman Ireland: the case of Glendalough* (Maynooth, 1996)

Mac Shamhráin, Ailbhe S., 'The emergence of the metropolitan see: Dublin, 1111–26', in James Kelly & Dáire Keogh (ed.), *History of the catholic diocese of Dublin* (Dublin, 2000), 51–7

Marshall, Jenny White & Grellan D. Rourke, *High Island: an Irish monastery in the Atlantic* (Dublin, 2000)

Meersseman, G.-G., 'Two unknown confraternity letters of St Bernard', *Cîteaux in de Nederlanden*, 6 (1955), 173–8

Meyer, Kuno (ed. & tr.), 'Fingal Rónáin: how Rónán slew his son', *Revue Celtique*, 13 (1892), 368–97

Meyer, Kuno (ed. & tr.), 'Duties of a husbandman', *Ériu*, 2 (1905), 172

Meyer, Kuno (ed. & tr.), *Cáin Adamnáin: an Old-Irish treatise on the Law of Adamnan*, Anecdota Oxoniensia, Mediaeval & Modern Series, 12 (Oxford, 1905)

Meyer, Kuno (ed. & tr.), *The triads of Ireland*, TLS 13 (Dublin, 1906)

Meyer, Kuno (ed.), 'Mitteilungen aus irischen Handschriften', *Z Celt Philol*, 10 (1915), 338–48

Meyer, Kuno (ed. & tr.), 'Bruchstücke der älteren Lyrik Irlands', *Abh Preuss Akad Wiss*, phil-hist Kl. Jhrg 1919, Nr 7 (Berlin, 1919)

Mitrofanov, Andrey, *L'ecclésiologie d'Anselme de Lucques (1036–1086) au service de Grégoire VII: Genèse, contenu et impact de sa "Collection canonique"*, Instrumenta Patristica et Mediaevalia 69 (Turnhout, 2015)

Morgan, Hiram, 'Giraldus Cambrensis and the Tudor conquest of Ireland', in idem (ed.), *Political ideology in Ireland, 1541–1641* (Dublin, 1999), 22–44

Mulchrone, Kathleen (ed.), *Bethu Phátraic: the Tripartite Life of Patrick* (Dublin, 1939)

Murphy, Gerard (ed. & tr.), *Early Irish lyrics* (Oxford, 1956)

Ní Bhrolcháin, Muireann, 'The manuscript tradition of the Banshenchas', *Ériu*, 33 (1982), 109–35

Ní Bhrolcháin, Muireann, 'The *Banshenchas* revisited', in Mary O'Dowd & Sabine Wichert (ed.), *Chattel, servant or citizen: women's status in church, state and society*, Historical Studies 19 (Belfast, 1995), 70–81

Nicholls, K.W. (ed.), 'The register of Clogher', *Clogher Rec*, 7/3 (1972), 361–431

Nicholls, K.W., 'Gaelic society and economy in the high middle ages', in Art Cosgrove (ed.), *New history of Ireland, ii. Medieval Ireland, 1169–1534*, 397–438

Norgate, Kate, 'The bull *Laudabiliter*', *Engl Hist Rev*, 8 (1893), 18–52

Ó Briain, Felim, 'Irish missionaries and medieval church reform', *Miscellanea historica Alberti de Meyer* (Louvain, 1946), 228–54

Ó Cathasaigh, Tomás, 'The rhetoric of *Fingal Rónáin*', *Celtica*, 17 (1985), 123–44

Ó Corráin, Donnchadh, 'Dál Cais – church and dynasty', *Ériu*, 24 (1973), 51–63

Ó Corráin, Donnchadh, 'Mael Muire Ua Dúnáin (1040–1117), reformer', in Pádraig de Brún, Pádraig Ó Riain & Seán Ó Coileáin (ed.), *Folia gadelica: essays presented to R. A. Breatnach* (Cork, 1983), 47–53

Ó Corráin, Donnchadh, 'Irish vernacular law and the Old Testament', in Próinséas Ní Chatháin & Michael Richter (ed.), *Ireland and christendom: the bible and the missions* (Stuttgart, 1987), 284–310

Ó Corráin, Donnchadh, 'Ireland c.800: aspects of society', in Dáibhí Ó Cróinín (ed.), *A new history of Ireland, i. Prehistoric and early medieval Ireland* (Oxford, 2005), 549–608

Ó Corráin, Donnchadh, 'What happened Ireland's medieval manuscripts?', *Peritia*, 22–23 (2011/12), 191–223

Ó Corráin, Donnchadh, 'Mael Muire the scribe: family and background', in Ruairí Ó hUiginn (ed.), *Lebor na hUidre*, Codices Hibernenses Eximii, 1 (Dublin, 2015), 1–28

Ó Corráin, Donnchadh, 'Vikings in Ireland: the catastrophe', in Howard B. Clarke & Ruth Johnson (ed.), *The Vikings in Ireland and beyond: before and after the battle of Clontarf* (Dublin, 2015), 485–98

Ó Corráin, Donnchadh, Liam Breatnach & Aidan Breen, 'The laws of the Irish', *Peritia*, 3 (1984), 382–438

O'Doherty, J.F., 'Rome and the Anglo-Norman invasion of Ireland', *Ir Ecclesiast Rec*, 42 (1933), 131–45

Ó Donnchadha, Tadhg (ed. & tr.), 'Cert cech ríg co réil', in Osborn J. Bergin & Carl Marstrander (ed.), *Miscellany presented Kuno Meyer* (Halle a. S., 1912), 258–72

Ó Donnchadha, Tadhg (ed. & tr.), 'Advice to a prince', *Ériu*, 9 (1921–3), 43–54

Ó Donnchadha, Tadhg (ed.), *An Leabhar Muimhneach* (Dublin, 1940)

Ó Fiaich, Tomás, 'The church of Armagh under lay control', *Seanchas Ardmhacha*, 5 (1969), 75–127

O'Grady, Standish H., 'The last kings of Ireland', *Engl Hist Rev*, 4 (1889), 286–303

O'Grady, Standish H. (ed. & tr.), *Silva gadelica* (2 vols, London, 1892)

O'Grady, Standish H. (ed. & tr.), *Caithréim Thoirdhealbhaigh*, ITS 26–7 (2 vols, London, 1929, repr. Dublin, 1988)

O'Grady, Standish H., Robin Flower & Myles Dillon, *Catalogue of Irish manuscripts in the British Museum* (3 vols, London, 1925–53, repr. (2 vols only) Dublin, 1992)

O'Keeffe, J.G. (ed. & tr.), 'The rule of Patrick', *Ériu*, 1 (1904), 216–24

O'Keeffe, J.G. (ed. & tr.), 'Cain domnaig, 1. The epistle concerning Sunday', *Ériu*, 2 (1905), 189–214

O'Keeffe, J.G. (ed. & tr.), 'A poem on the day of judgment', *Ériu*, 3 (1907), 29–33

O'Loughlin, Thomas, 'Giraldus Cambrensis and the sexual agenda of the twelfth-century reformers', *J Welsh Relig Hist*, 8 (2000), 1–15

O'Meara, J.J. (tr.), *The history and topography of Ireland* (London, 1982)

Ó Murchadha, Diarmuid, 'Gill Abbey and the "rental of Cong"', *J Cork Hist Archaeol Soc*, 90 (1985), 31–45

Ó Murchadha, Diarmuid, 'Where was Ráith Breasail?', *Tipperary Hist J* (1999), 151–61

Ó Murchadha, Diarmuid, 'The Cork decretal letter of 1199 AD', *J Cork Hist Archaeol Soc*, 106 (2001), 79–100

O'Neill, Joseph (ed. & tr.), 'The rule of Ailbe of Emly', *Ériu*, 3 (1907), 92–115

Ó Néill, Pádraig P., 'The date and authorship of *Apgitir chrábaid*: some internal evidence', in Próinséas Ní Chatháin & Michael Richter (ed.), *Ireland and christendom: the bible and the missions* (Stuttgart, 1987), 203–15

O'Rahilly, Cecile (ed. & tr.), *Táin bó Cúalgne from the Book of Leinster* (Dublin, 1967)

Ó Riain, Pádraig, 'Boundary associations in early Irish society', *Studia Celtica*, 7 (1972), 12–29

Ó Riain, Pádraig (ed.), *Corpus genealogiarum sanctorum Hiberniae* (Dublin, 1985)

Ó Riain, Pádraig (ed. & tr.), *Beatha Bharra: St Finbarr of Cork: the complete Life* (London, 1993)

Ó Riain, Pádraig, 'Dublin's oldest book? A list of saints "made in Germany"', in Seán Duffy (ed.), *Medieval Dublin*, 5 (Dublin, 2004), 52–72

Ó Riain-Raedel, Dagmar, 'Aspects of the promotion of Irish saints' cults in medieval Germany', *Z Celt Philol*, 29 (1982), 220–34

Ó Riain-Raedel, Dagmar, 'Twelfth- and thirteenth-century Irish annals in Vienna', *Peritia*, 2 (1983), 127–35

Ó Riain-Raedel, Dagmar (ed.), 'Das Nekrolog der irischen Schottenklöster: Edition der Handschrift Vat. lat. 10100 mit einer Untersuchung der hagiographischen und liturgischen Handschriften der Schottenklöster', *Beitr Gesch Bistums Regensburg*, 25 (1992), 7–119

Ó Riain-Raedel, Dagmar, 'The travels of Irish manuscripts: from the Continent to Ireland', in Toby Barnard, Dáibhí Ó Cróinín & Katharine Simms (ed.), *'A miracle of learning': studies in manuscripts and Irish learning: essays in honour of William O'Sullivan* (Aldershot, 1998), 52–67

O'Sullivan, Anne, 'Limerick, Killaloe, and Kells 1194–1250', *Éigse*, 17 (1977–9), 451–5

Orpen, Goddard H., *Ireland under the Normans* (4 vols, Oxford 1911–20, repr. Oxford, 1968; repr. Dublin, 2005 [one vol., with intro. by Seán Duffy])

Orpen, Goddard H. (ed. & tr.), *The song of Dermot and the earl* (Oxford, 1892)

Otway-Ruthven, Jocelyn, 'The native Irish and English law in mediaeval Ireland', *Ir Hist Stud*, 7 (1950/1), 1–16

Pender, Séamus (ed.), *The O Clery Book of genealogies = Analecta Hibernica*, 18 (Dublin, 1951)

Pepperdene, Margaret W., 'Baptism in the early British and Irish churches', *Ir Theol Q*, 22 (1955), 110–23

Petrie, George, *The ecclesiastical architecture of Ireland* (2nd ed. Dublin, 1845)

Pfeil, Brigitte, *Die 'Vision des Tnugdalus' Albers von Windberg: Literatur- und Frömmigkeitgeschichte im ausgehenden 12. Jahrhundert mit einer Edition der lateinischen 'Visio Tnugdali' aus Clm 22254*, Mikrokosmos: Beiträge zur Literaturwissenschaft und Bedeutungsforschung 54 (Frankfurt-am-Main etc., 1999)

Phillips, Seymour, 'David MacCarwell and the proposal to purchase English law, c.1273–c.1280', *Peritia*, 10 (1996), 253–73.

Picard, Jean-Michel, '*Princeps* and *principatus* in the early Irish church: a reassessment', in Alfred P. Smyth (ed.), *Seanchas: studies in early and medieval Irish archaeology, history and literature in honour of Francis J. Byrne* (Dublin, 2000), 146–60

Picard, Jean-Michel, 'The cult of Columba in Lotharingia (9th–11th centuries): the manuscript evidence', in John Carey, Máire Herbert & Pádraig Ó Riain (ed.), *Studies in Irish hagiography: saints and scholars* (Dublin, 2001), 221–36

Picard, Jean-Michel & Yolande de Pontfarcy (tr.), *The vision of Tnugdal* (Dublin, 1989)

Plummer, Charles (ed.), 'Vie et miracles de S. Laurent, archévêque de Dublin', *Analecta Bollandiana*, 33 (1914), 121–86

Plummer, Charles (ed. & tr.), *Bethada náem nÉrenn: Lives of Irish saints* (2 vols, Oxford, 1922)

Plummer, Charles (ed. & tr.), *Irish litanies*, HBS 62 (London, 1925), 78–85

Poole, R. Lane, *Studies in chronology and history* (Oxford, 1934)

Raine, James (ed.), *The historians of the church of York and its archbishops*, RS 71 (3 vols, London, 1879–94)

Reeves, William (ed.), *Ecclesiastical antiquities of Down, Connor and Dromore* (Dublin, 1847)

Reeves, William (ed.), *Acts of archbishop Colton: visitation of … Derry* (Dublin, 1850)

Reeves, William (ed.), *The Life of St Columba, founder of Hy. Written by Adamnan* (Dublin, 1857)

Reeves, William, *The Culdees of the British Isles as they appear in history with an appendix of evidences* (Dublin, 1864; repr. Feilinfach, 1994)

Reiche, Rainer, 'Iren in Trier', *Rheinische Vierteljahrblätter*, 40 (1976), 1–17

Reynolds, P.L., *Marriage in the western church: the christianization of marriage during the patristic and early medieval period* (Leiden, 1994)

Richardson, H.G., 'Some Norman monastic foundations in Ireland', in J.A. Watt, J.B. Morrall & F.X. Martin (ed.), *Medieval studies presented to Aubrey Gwynn SJ* (Dublin, 1961), 29–43

Richter, Michael (ed.), *Canterbury Professions*, Canterbury & York Society, 67 (Torquay, 1973)

Ross, Margaret Clunies, 'Concubinage in Anglo-Saxon England', *Past & Present*, 108 (1985), 3–34

Round, J.H., *The commune of London* (London, 1899)

Rule Martin (ed.), *Eadmeri Historia novorum in Anglia*, RS 81 (London, 1884)

Ryan, John, 'Early Irish-German associations', *Capuchin Ann* (Dublin), 36 (1969), 148–59

Saltman, Avrom, *Theobald, archbishop of Canterbury* (London 1956, repr. New York, 1969)

Scammell, Jean, 'Freedom and marriage in medieval England', *Econ Hist Rev*, 27 (1974), 523–7

Schiaparelli, Luigi, *Influenze straniere nella scrittura italiana dei secoli VIII e IX*, Studi e Testi 47 (Rome, 1927)

Schmeidler, B. (ed.), *Adami Gesta Hammaburgensis ecclesiae pontificum*, MGH SRG us (Hannover & Leipzig, 1917)

Scott, A.B. & F.X. Martin (ed. & tr.), *Expugnatio hibernica: the conquest of Ireland by Giraldus Cambrensis* (Dublin, 1978)

Scully, Diarmuid, 'The portrayal of Ireland and the Irish in Bernard's Life of St Malachy', in Damian Bracken & Dagmar Ó Riain-Raedel (ed.), *Ireland and Europe in the twelfth century: reform and renewal* (Dublin, 2006), 239–56

Sellar, W.D.H., 'Marriage, divorce and concubinage in Gaelic Scotland', *Trans Gaelic Soc Inverness*, 51 (1978), 464–93

Selmer, Carl, 'The beginnings of the St Brendan legend on the Continent', *Cath Hist Rev*, 29 (1943–4), 169–76

Selmer, Carl (ed.), *Navigatio Sancti Brendani* (Notre Dame IN, 1956, repr. Dublin, 1989)

Semmler, Josef, 'Iren in der Lothringischen Klosterreform', in Heinz Löwe (ed.), *Die Iren und Europa im früheren Mittelalter* (Stuttgart, 1982), 941–57

Seymour, St John D., 'The coarb in the medieval Irish church', *Proc Roy Ir Acad (C)*, 41 (1932–4), 219–31

Sharpe, Richard, 'Churches and communities in early medieval Ireland', in John Blair & Richard Sharpe (ed.), *Pastoral care before the parish* (Leicester, 1992), 81–109

Sharpe, Richard (tr.), *Adomnán of Iona: Life of St Columba* (London, 1995)

Shaw, Frank, 'Karl der Grosse und die schottischen Heiligen', *Medium Ævum*, 45 (1976), 164–86

Sheehy, M.P., 'English law in medieval Ireland: two illustrative documents', *Archivium Hibernicum* 23 (1960), 167–75 [London, BL Cotton Augustus II f.104a; London, Lambeth Palace, 619, f. 206a]

Sheehy, M.P., 'The bull *Laudabiliter*: a problem in medieval *diplomatique* and history', *J Galway Hist Archaeol Soc*, 29 (1961), 45–70

Sheehy, M.P (ed.), *Pontificia Hibernica: medieval papal chancery documents concerning Ireland, 640–1261* (2 vols, Dublin, 1962–5)

Sheehy, M.P. *When the Normans came to Ireland* (Cork, 1998)

Simms, Katharine, 'Frontiers in the Irish church: regional and cultural', in Robin Frame, T.B. Barry & Katharine Simms (ed.), *Colony and frontier in medieval Ireland* (Dublin, 1995), 177–200

Smith, William & Samuel Cheetham, *Dictionary of christian antiquities* (2 vols, London, 1875–80)

Stacey, Robin Chapman (tr.), '*Berrad airechta*: an Old Irish tract on suretyship', in T.M. Charles-Edwards & D.B. Walters (ed.), *Lawyers and laymen: studies in the history of law presented to Professor Dafydd Jenkins* (Cardiff, 1986), 210–33

Stafford, Pauline, 'Sons and mothers: family politics in the early middle ages', in D. Barker (ed.), *Medieval women* (Oxford, 1978), 79–100

Stalley, Roger, *The Cistercian monasteries of Ireland: an account of the history, art and architecture of the White Monks in Ireland from 1142 to 1540* (London, 1987)

Stern, Ludwig Christian (ed.), *Epistolae beati Pauli glosatae glosa interlineali* (Halle, 1910)

Stokes, Whitley (ed. & tr.), *The Tripartite Life of Patrick* (2 vols, London, 1887)

Stokes, Whitley (ed. & tr.), *Lives of the saints from the Book of Lismore* (Oxford, 1890)

Stokes, Whitley (ed. & tr.), 'Adamnan's Second Vision', *Revue Celtique*, 12 (1891), 420–43

Stokes, Whitley (ed. & tr.), 'The Boroma', *Revue Celtique*, 13 (1892), 32–124

Stokes, Whitley (ed. & tr.), *Martyrology of Gorman*, HBS 9 (London, 1895)

Stubbs, William (ed.), *Gesta regis Henrici secundi Benedicti abbatis*, RS 49 (2 vols, London, 1867)

Stubbs, William (ed.), *Chronica magistri Rogeri de Houedene*, RS 51 (4 vols, London 1868–71)

Stubbs William (ed.), *Willemi Malemesbiriensis De gestis regum*, RS 90 (2 vols, 1887–90)

Tanner, N.P. (ed.), *Decrees of the ecumenical councils* i (London & Washington DC, 1990)

Thacker, Alan & Richard Sharpe (ed.), *Local saints and local churches in the early medieval West* (Oxford, 2002)

Theiner, August, *Vetera monumenta* (Rome, 1864)

Thomas, Charles, 'Cellular meanings, monastic beginnings', *Emania*, 13 (1995), 51–67

Thornton, Andrew (tr.), *Grimlaicus, Rule for solitaries* (Collegeville MN, 2011)

Thurneysen, Rudolf (ed. & tr.), 'Aus dem irischen Recht II', *Z Celt Philol*, 15 (1925), 238–76

Thurneysen, Rudolf (ed. & tr.), 'Die Bürgschaft im irischen Recht', *Abh Preuss Akad Wiss*, phil-hist Kl, Jahrg 1928, Nr. 2 (Berlin, 1928)

Thurneysen, Rudolf (ed. & tr.), 'Irisches Recht', *Abh Preuss Akad Wiss*, phil-hist Kl, Jhrg 1931, Nr. 2 (Berlin, 1931)

Thurneysen, Rudolf (ed. & tr.), 'Cáin lánamna', in D.A. Binchy & Myles Dillon (ed.), *Studies in early Irish law* (Dublin, 1936), 1–80

Thurneysen, Rudolf, 'Heirat', in D.A. Binchy & Myles Dillon (ed.), *Studies in early Irish law* (Dublin, 1936), 108–28

Tock, B.-M. (ed.), *Monumenta Arroasiensia*, CCCM 175 (Turnhout, 2000)

Todd, J.H., *St Patrick, apostle of Ireland: a memoir of his life and mission* (Dublin, 1864)

Tommasini, Anselmo M., *Irish saints in Italy*, tr. J.F. Scanlan (London, 1937)

Ussher, James, 'Of the original and first institution of corbes, herenaches and termon lands', in C.R. Elrington (ed.), *The whole works of James Ussher* xi (Dublin, 1864), 421–45

van Hamel, A.G. (ed.), 'A poem on Crimthann', *Revue Celtique*, 37 (1917/9), 325–44

Volmering, Nicole (ed. & tr.), 'The Second Vision of Adomnán', in John Carey, Emma Nic Cárthaigh & Caitríona Ó Dochartaigh (ed.), *The end and beyond: medieval Irish eschatology*, Celtic Studies Publications 17, (2 vols, Aberystwyth, 2014), ii 647–84

Waddell, Helen, *The wandering scholars* (6th ed., London, 1954)

Waitz, Georg (ed.), *Mariani Scotti Chronicon*, MGH SS 5 (Hannover, 1844)

Walsh, T.J. & Denis O'Sullivan, 'St Malachy, the Gill Abbey of Cork, and the rule of Arrouaise', *J Cork Hist Archaeol Soc*, 54 (1949), 41–60

Warren, F.E., *The liturgy and ritual of the Celtic church*, ed. Jane Stevenson (Woodbridge, 1987)

Warren, W.L., *Henry II* (London, 1973; 2nd ed. New Haven and London, 2000)

Wasserschleben, Herrmann (ed.), *Die Bussordnungen der abendländischen Kirche* (Halle, 1851; repr. Graz, 1958)

Wasserschleben, Herrmann (ed.), *Die irische Kanonensammlung* (Leipzig 1885; repr. Aalen, 1966)

Watt, J.A.,'Laudabiliter in medieval diplomacy and propaganda', *Ir Ecclesiast Rec*, 87 (1957), 420–32

Watt, J.A., *The church and the two nations in medieval Ireland* (Cambridge, 1970)

Watt, J.A., *The church in medieval Ireland* (Dublin 1972)

Watt, J.A., J.B. Morrall & F.X. Martin (ed.), *Medieval studies presented to Aubrey Gwynn SJ* (Dublin, 1961)

Webb, C.C.J. (ed.), *Metalogicon* (Oxford, 1929)

Weber, Stefan (ed. & tr.), *Iren auf dem Kontinent. Das Leben des Marianus Scottus von Regensburg und die Anfänge der irischen Schottenklöster* (Heidelberg, 2010)

Wiley, Dan M. (ed. & tr.), An edition of *Aided Diarmata meic Cerbaill* from the Book of Uí Maine (PhD, Harvard University, 2000)

Wiley, Dan M., 'Stories about Diarmait mac Cerbaill from the Book of Lismore', *Emania*, 19 (2002), 53–9

Wilkins, David (ed.), *Concilia Magnae Britanniae et Hiberniae* (4 vols, London, 1737; repr. Brussels, 1964)

Wilmart, André, 'La Trinité des Scots à Rome', *Revue Bénédictine*, 41 (1929), 218–30; 44 (1932) 359–61

Wilson, Philip, *The beginnings of modern Ireland* (Dublin & Baltimore MD, 1913)

Windisch, Ernst (ed.), 'Die Vision des Adamnán: Fís Adamnáin', in idem (ed.), *Irische Texte*, i (Leipzig, 1880), 165–96

Young, Simon, 'Donatus, bishop of Fiesole 829–76, and the cult of St Brigit in Italy', *Cambr Mediev Celt Stud*, 35 (1998), 13–26

Young, Simon, 'Brigid of Kildare in early medieval Tuscany', *Studia Hibernica*, 30 (1998–9), 251–5

Zimmerman, Harald (ed.), *Papsturkunden, 896–1046* (Vienna, 1984–5)

Index

(ab = abbot; abp = archbishop; *air* = *airchinnech*; bp = bishop;
cb = coarb/*comarba*)